Managing Firms and Families
Work and Values in a Russian City

Since the 1990s, when Russia initiated its breakthrough to the market, Russian capitalism has been commonly portrayed as a failure, based on its far-reaching divergence from the core principles and values of the market economy. This aberration has puzzled mainstream economists and demands an explanation. To solve the puzzle, social scientists have paid close attention to Russia's long-term historical trajectories, cultural norms and social arrangements, seeing in them the key to grasping the Russian experience of market transformations. Such explanations vary greatly in their understanding of the role that social and cultural factors have played in the transition to the market. While some analysts see them as an obstacle to marketization, others tend to hail them as a means of resistance to the ravages of capitalism. This book strives to move away from this either/ or perspective by exploring the complexities of Russian private businesses on the ground. Drawing on an ethnographic enquiry into the small-scale private sector in the city of Smolensk, the book addresses the moral dimensions of Russian petty capitalism.

Theoretically the book is anchored in approaches to the moral economy elaborated by E. P. Thompson and James Scott. It situates the moral frameworks of petty entrepreneurs within the broader dynamics of local and global politico-economic restructurings by examining how changing ideas of personhood, understandings of moral responsibilities and obligations, and conceptions of work and labour are entangled in circuits of production and struggles for reproduction in present-day Russia. Given that many small businesses are family-based enterprises, the book examines the role of family ties and kinship morality in the operations of small firms. By doing so, it discusses how obligations of kinship, social reproduction and structures of provisioning overlap with capital accumulation.

The research in this book is grounded in debates about postsocialism. It discusses the relevance of the Soviet experience of work and labour to the social reproduction of capital in post-reform Russia. It argues that the moral frameworks of Russian entrepreneurs incorporate multiple discrete and conflicting values, such that egalitarian ideals, reciprocity, family obligations and a nostalgia for socialism overlap with values associated with the new order, such as self-interest, competition and commodification. The multiplicity and at the same time the incongruity of value-making practices complicates their assessment when it comes to resistance to or compliance with capitalist norms and mores. The book views such complexities in actual economic behaviour as responses to the local and global pressures that are generated by capitalism, thereby helping us to incorporate postsocialist developments into the larger processes of global expansion and the accumulation of capital.

Halle Studies in the Anthropology of Eurasia

General Editors:

Christoph Brumann, Kirsten W. Endres, Chris Hann, Burkhard Schnepel, Lale Yalçın-Heckmann

Volume 45

LIT

Daria Tereshina

Managing Firms and Families

Work and Values in a Russian City

LIT

Cover Photo: An employee making signboards at a small firm in Smolensk (Photo: Daria Tereshina, 2015).

This book is a revised version of a dissertation manuscript, submitted to the Faculty of Philosophy I at Martin Luther University Halle-Wittenberg in 2019.

This book is printed on acid-free paper.

Bibliographic information published by the Deutsche Nationalbibliothek
The Deutsche Nationalbibliothek lists this publication in the Deutsche Nationalbibliografie; detailed bibliographic data are available in the Internet at http://dnb.dnb.de.

ISBN 978-3-643-91408-8 (pb)
ISBN 978-3-643-96408-3 (PDF)

A catalogue record for this book is available from the British Library.

©**L**IT **V**ERLAG Dr. W. Hopf
Berlin 2021
Fresnostr. 2
D-48159 Münster
Tel. +49 (0) 2 51-62 03 20
Fax +49 (0) 2 51-23 19 72
E-Mail: lit@lit-verlag.de
https://www.lit-verlag.de

LIT **V**ERLAG GmbH & Co. KG Wien,
Zweigniederlassung Zürich 2021
Flössergasse 10
CH-8001 Zürich
Tel. +41 (0) 76-632 84 35
Fax
E-Mail: zuerich@lit-verlag.ch
https://www.lit-verlag.ch

Distribution:

In the UK: Global Book Marketing, e-mail: mo@centralbooks.com
In North America: Independent Publishers Group, e-mail: orders@ipgbook.com
In Germany: **L**IT Verlag Fresnostr. 2, D-48159 Münster
Tel. +49 (0) 2 51-620 32 22, Fax +49 (0) 2 51-922 60 99, e-mail: vertrieb@lit-verlag.de

Contents

	List of Illustrations	ix
	Acknowledgements	xi
	Note on Transliteration	xiii
1	**Introduction**	**1**
	Anthropological Theories of Value, Moral Economy and Flexible Capitalism	5
	Postsocialism(s) and Transformations of Value	10
	Fieldwork and Methods	15
	Chapter Outlines	20
2	**The Political Economy of Russia: Historical Overview**	**23**
	Early Capitalist Developments in Tsarist Russia	23
	State Socialism (1917-1991): Social Identities, Work and Labour in a 'Classless Society'	24
	Theorizing Socialism: The Economy of Shortage and its 'Dead Ends'	28
	Russian Capitalism in the Macro-Perspective	31
	Postsocialism 'From Below': The Social Consequences of Neoliberal Policy-Making	36
	Conclusion	41
3	**Russia's Moral Background: Orthodoxy, Soviet Values and Multiple Moralities of Postsocialism**	**43**
	The Study of Morality in Anthropology: Social Norms, Freedom and Conflicts over Values	43
	Russian Orthodoxy: Otherworldly and Ascetic?	44
	Soviet Morality: Between Private Aspirations and Collective Values	48
	Soviet Secularism and the post-Soviet 'Religious Revival'	53
	Building a Class-Based Society: Multiple Moralities after Socialism	56
	Conclusion	59

4	**Smolensk and the Regional Economy: Mapping the Business Landscape**	**61**
	Pre-Revolutionary Years and the Soviet History of Smolensk	62
	The 'Wild' 1990s: Petty Trading, Criminal Gangs and Quick Fortunes	64
	State Practices and Policies in Relation to Small Businesses	68
	Wages and Employment in the Private Sector	73
	Conclusion	79
5	**Family-Based Firms: Reconfiguring the Value of Family Ties**	**81**
	The 'Family Trap': Family Business as a Dilemma	84
	The Family as a Pool of Flexible Labour	88
	Other Family Resources: Trust and Loyalty	93
	Fictive Kinship and the Authority of the Collective	102
	Conclusion	106
6	**Small Garment Manufacturing: Between Precarity, Creative Work and Developmental Hopes**	**109**
	Soviet-Era Developmental Hopes and Market Promises	112
	Not Market but *Bazaar*	117
	The Space of Creative Work and Market Value Suspended	124
	Creativity for Workers: Flexible Skills and Arbitrary Control	130
	Conclusion	136
7	**'I Will Never Let You Down': Personal Dependencies and Informal Assistance at Work**	**139**
	Oksana's Work Biography: Trying to Become her Own 'Master'	142
	Paternal Care, Reciprocity and Control	149
	Contested Values and a Disunited Collective	157
	Conclusion	164

8	**Conclusion: Neoliberalism and Flexible Capitalism in Postsocialist Conditions**	**167**
	Bibliography	173
	Index	191

List of Illustrations

Map

    The location of Smolensk   15

Plates

1	The shopping mall 'Galaktika'	63
2	Kolkhoz market	65
3	The cutter fulfilling individual orders in Alpha	132
4	Part of industrial workshop in Alpha	134
5	The signboards produced by the stamp firm	150
6	Working two jobs	152
7	The production process in the signboard workshop	158

Table

    Number of small businesses in the Smolensk region   68

(all photographs were taken by author [2015-2016])

Acknowledgements

This book would not have been possible without the collaboration and support of many people. First of all, I would like to thank my interlocutors in Smolensk, who kindly shared their stories and time with me, despite their busy and often unpredictable schedules. I am also grateful for the support and advice I received from the Smolensk Business Club and for their genuine interest in my project.

I am very grateful to the Max Planck Institute for Social Anthropology for its financial support. This book is a part of a research project, 'Realising Eurasia: Civilisation and Moral Economy in the 21st Century (REALEURASIA)', funded by the European Research Council. I would like to thank the project leader and my supervisor Chris Hann for his patience, time and guidance. I am also grateful to my colleagues at the Max Planck Institute and in the REALEURASIA group for their stimulating discussions and collegiality. Special thanks go to Sudeshna Chaki, Ceren Deniz, Lale Yalçın-Heckmann, Dimitra Kofti, Sylvia Terpe and Kristina Jonutyte for their insightful comments, criticism and support. The departmental seminars at the Max Planck Institute were a source of continuous inspiration at every step of working on the project.

I owe special gratitude and appreciation to Alexandra Kasatkina, Zina Vasileva, Julia Andreeva and Katerina Pasichnyk for intellectual exchange, inspiration and encouragement. My work benefited a great deal from comments and suggestions made by Detelina Tocheva, Jeremy Morris, and Nikolay Ssorin-Chaikov. I am grateful to the members of the Laboratory for Studies in Economic Sociology, HSE, for their helpful comments. Last but not least, I express deep gratitude to my family and friends, whose unwavering support, patience and encouragement kept me going.

Note on Transliteration

The Russian transliterations used in this book follow the Library of Congress system.

To my grandmother

Chapter 1
Introduction

It was late evening when Oksana[1], a receptionist at the hostel and the only member of staff on duty at this time, heard her boss's loud voice shouting her name. His late visit did not bode well, as she was well aware what would happen next. After making light-hearted conversation, Vadim, the owner of the hostel, made his way into the kitchen area. At this late hour he found there just one guest sitting alone at the kitchen table, staring at the huge TV screen on the wall. Vadim struck up a conversation with the stranger and learned that Muhammed, as he was called, had just recently arrived in Smolensk on business from the Caucasus in southern Russia. Instantly Vadim took a bottle of vodka out of the fridge together with some snacks and generously asked his new friend to join him. While they were drinking, their voices were increasing in volume, openly irritating Oksana, since it was her duty to maintain order in the hostel. On this occasion she felt helpless, not daring to order her boss to go home. After her timid attempts to calm Vadim down went unnoticed, Oksana called her boss's wife and asked her to take her husband away from the hostel before the guests started complaining. But Vadim's wife was reluctant to cooperate, instead asking Oksana to call a taxi and somehow sent her drunken husband home. Oksana became extremely nervous when she heard Vadim and the guest start arguing, turning pale in anticipation of a drunken brawl.

Luckily, Vadim soon retired from the kitchen and disappeared from the hostel. A minute later Muhammed showed up in front of the reception desk and loudly asked Oksana to give him his money back, determined to check out immediately. He explained that he did not want to stay any longer at a place that belonged to 'that greedy person' (*alchnyi chelovek*), as he described Vadim. It transpired that his calm chatting with Vadim at the kitchen table had unexpectedly turned into an argument over corruption, which caused a break between them. Muhammed, a young public official, had praised the state's measures against corruption. He was very optimistic

---
[1] All names are pseudonyms.

about the anti-corruption campaign in his home district and believed it would bring about real change to the point that his 'children will already be living in a new Russia'. Vadim had snorted with laughter at this. He could not believe that anyone could take the state's propaganda so seriously and tried to dispel his interlocutor's naïve attitudes. Vadim had then gone into the complexities of his own business, illustrating how state officials profiteered from controlling local businesses. However, this first-hand account did not have the desired effect, simply convincing Muhammed that he was dealing with an excessively cynical person who lacked morals and only craved to make money. Moreover, he was furious that Vadim had paid no respect to religion whatsoever but instead had flaunted his deep-seated atheism in front of Muhammed, a devoted Muslim. Vadim's cynicism filled Muhammed with indignation because it encroached upon his own ideals about justice and morality. In a state of intense agitation exacerbated by the alcohol, he asked to check out immediately and pleaded with Oksana to change her own job as soon as possible so as not to be contaminated by her boss's deadly cynicism. For her part, Oksana tried to calm her over-excited guest down and convince him to stay for at least one night so he could decide what to do in the morning, when he had a fresh mind. It took her an hour to talk him into going to bed. Having done so, Oksana breathed more easily: finally she could lock the hostel's entry door and have some rest in the hope that no other incident would occur until the end of her shift.

I have started this work with this late-night episode at the hostel because it encapsulates the range of topics and preoccupations that feed into the central theme of this book – the moral economy of small-scale, kinship-based private firms. In embarking on a study of capitalist morality in post-Soviet Russia, I will examine how local entrepreneurs in a Russian province negotiate their understandings of social justice, entitlements and obligations by resolving the everyday practical dilemmas they are faced with in their firms. In doing so, I will situate the moral frameworks of Russian businesses within the broader dynamics of marketization and the liberal economic restructuring that came to be known as 'flexible accumulation' (Harvey 1989).

There is a certain lack of ethnographically grounded research on capitalist morality in Russia. Recent decades have seen a surge of interest in studying how neoliberal subjectivities and values have reshaped and transformed earlier experiences of work and labour in postsocialist Russia. However, many such accounts are grounded in the realms of ideas and representations, being divorced from the concrete work of individuals and the modes of production. Yurchak (2002), Matza (2009), Cohen (2013), Ratilainen (2012) and Salmenniemi (2012a) have all investigated the ways in which neoliberal rationality is being domesticated and culturally appropriated through various media, whether TV shows, glossy magazines, female literature, self-help works or business courses. These analyses have yielded interesting results pointing at certain affinities between the logic of capitalism and Soviet technologies of self-cultivation, such as self-monitoring, self-evaluation and the management of one's emotions. The question nevertheless remains how these representations of ideal selves translate into real action and shape the particular forms that relationships of production and patterns of capital accumulation assume in post-reform Russia.

A fine-grained ethnography of capitalist morality will not only enrich our understanding of actual business behaviour in Russia, it also has the potential to challenge a range of underlying assumptions informing conceptualizations of Russian (or more broadly east European) capitalism in the mainstream economic and sociological literature. Since the 1990s, the study of 'transitology' has depicted the Russian economy as diverging from the core principles of a market economy based on contractual rights and the concept of private property. Russian economic actors have persistently been blamed for their failure to embrace market principles and engage in proper market exchanges. Linda Randall (2001) conveys this sense of refusal by calling Russian entrepreneurs 'reluctant capitalists' (cf. Buchowski 1997). Their blatant unwillingness to comply with capitalist norms and practices manifests itself in a number of ways: Russian business people are reluctant to use formal contracts and largely rely on informal agreements and social networks, they routinely violate tax codes and pay their workers off the books, they participate in mixed forms of ownership and blur the organizational boundaries of enterprises, and they neglect the profit principle while expecting the state to manage their liabilities (Stark 1996; Gaddy and Ickes 2002; Ledeneva 2006; Szelenyi 2016). Thelen (2011) and Tlostanova (2015) point out that mainstream analyses generally interpret this pronounced reluctance to embrace the logic of the market as a sign of a deficiency in and a malfunctioning of postsocialist institutions, thereby feeding the grand narrative of Russian backwardness and the country's persistent failure to catch up with modernity. To explain such divergence from 'normality', social scientists not uncommonly resort to historical explanations, taking into account long-term trajectories of institutional developments and the process of subjectivization in Russia. While some scholars explain Russia's path-dependence with reference to the persistence of patrimonialism as a dominant type of political authority (Hedlund 2005; Vasileva 2014; Szelenyi 2016), others appeal to the mysterious concept of 'Soviet mentality' and the deep-seated collectivist values of *Homo Soveticus*, which stand in the way of developing more individual conceptions of personhood (Levada 2003).

In this context, it is hardly surprising that alternative readings of Russian capitalism have gone to the other extreme by defining local forms of entrepreneurship in terms of resistance, for example, of 'passive resistance' to the state (Paneyakh 2008) or resistance to capitalism by preserving old structures, norms and forms of behaviour (Randall 2001). While this sort of analysis accomplishes the worthy task of challenging common-sense assumptions about the Russian economy and business in Russia, I find the trope of resistance to be equally problematic, since it quite commonly allows examples of compliance and agreement with market ideologies or state policies to be obscured by the analysts' own presuppositions and social ideals.

This book avoids positing morality as necessarily opposed to economic interest; rather, values are approached as forces that may well justify and strengthen the principles of economic rationality and endow them with 'a greater degree of moral legitimacy' (Cohen 2013: 727). Ultimately, the book argues that the moral frameworks of Russian entrepreneurs incorporate multiple, discrete and conflicting values, such that egalitarian ideals, reciprocity, family obligations and nostalgia for socialism overlap with values associated with the new order (though they were by no means unknown in the past), such as self-interest, competition and commodification. David Stark, an economic sociologist, argues that this coexistence of multiple values and logics of worth – what he calls 'the polyphonic discourse of worth' – constitutes a distinctive feature of east European capitalism (1996: 1015). In other words, he contends that postsocialist actors engage with multiple regimes of evaluations, rather than relying on considerations of profitability and efficiency alone. This sort of conclusion is premised on a highly abstract and universalist vision of the market economy as operating solely in accordance with the principle of profit maximization. Taking inspiration from the Polanyian oeuvre, economic anthropology suggests another theoretical framework for studying the 'polyphonic discourse of worth'. The multiplicity of value-making practices noted by Stark suggests the embeddedness of the economy in broader social and institutional arrangements whereby different standards of worth operate beyond the principle of exchange value, pure calculation and self-serving materialism (Narotzky and Besnier 2014). The major theme of this book echoes Stark's preoccupation with multiple regimes of evaluation but reformulates it in the language of economic anthropology and its expanded understanding of the economy. In doing so, the book aims to move away from the tendency to reduce the economy to market principles and attends to the multiple regimes of value that are entangled in the everyday workings of private firms. The methods of ethnography, rooted in the long-term observation of everyday practices, enable the researcher to grasp a more nuanced picture of the values that shape the behaviour of Russian firm owners and enable them to realize their agency in the face of structural constraints.

Small businesses provide a vantage point for the interrogation of different standards of value and the study of enmeshed values (Narotzky 2015). Family-based economies are particularly suitable for examining how obligations of kinship, social reproduction and structures of provisioning overlap with capital accumulation. In addition to the dimensions of kinship and the household, I will touch upon the role of religious forms of virtue. As a part of the MPI team researching 'Realising Eurasia', this study represents the Eastern Christian (Orthodox) component of a series of comparisons extending from Lutheran Denmark to Confucian China. As the project progressed, I discovered that the role of Eastern Christianity in shaping economic behaviour was quite insignificant even among those business people who identified themselves as Orthodox adherents. Nevertheless, religion was a starting point for my research, as it explains my persistent interest in and investigation of the realm of religious morality. In the next two sections, I will outline two strands of literature and the major theoretical debates I engage with in the book.

Anthropological Theories of Value, Moral Economy and Flexible Capitalism

My engagement with the spheres of morality and the economy mainly draws upon the rich anthropological tradition of studying values and exchange in their close interconnection with social life and the making of social relations. I follow the practice-oriented approach to values that sees them as being produced through people's actions, rather than being static evaluations of what is good and desirable (Munn 1992; Graeber 2001). I also draw on anthropological studies of exchange that ponder the conceptual distinction between gift and commodity, examining how different types of exchange are intertwined with certain kinds of social relations and moralities (Parry and Bloch 1989; Gregory 2015 [1989]). The distinctions between gift and commodity, between long-term and short-term morality, are useful for understanding the more ambiguous and complex exchanges that proliferate in the contexts of contemporary capitalist economies in which gift relations and exchanges of favours coexist with monetary transactions and commoditization.

The key theoretical concept guiding my enquiry into the realm of values is the moral economy. The concept of a moral economy was explored in the works of E.P. Thompson and James Scott. In his analysis of eighteenth-century food riots, Thompson (1971) argues that the 'English crowd' was driven not only by famine and poverty, but also by a moral economy of provision that clashed with the logic of price regulation by the market. In a similar fashion, in *'The Moral Economy of the Peasant'* (1976) James Scott points to the deeply antagonistic relationships between the peasant's conceptions of justice and the new market logic espoused by the state and elite groups. As a new conceptual tool, therefore, the moral economy made it possible to bridge the gap between studies of the value sphere and more rigorous economic analysis (Hann 2018). However, critics of the concept have argued that its holistic potential has not been explored in the subsequent decades that saw a rapid increase in the term's use (Palomera and Vetta 2016; Carrier 2018; Hann 2018). Opposition has been expressed to the danger of trivializing the concept and turning it into a catchy slogan to be applied to almost everything. As many critics point out – including E.P. Thompson himself in his late contribution in 1991 – the concept of the moral economy lost its analytical novelty as soon as the focus on values superseded the analysis of the material economy. Accordingly the 'moral economy has quickly become a strange guest in the bourgeoning field of "moral anthropology"' (Palomera and Vetta 2016: 414). In its narrow meaning as a realm of value, the term has usually been applied to the study of 'alternative' or 'informal' practices thriving 'outside' or 'in the cracks of' the market. In such studies the concept of a moral economy was equated with Polanyi's notion of embeddedness (Palomera and Vetta 2016; Carrier 2018). Such applications of the term significantly reduced its initial potential to account for economic behaviour in a holistic manner and instead entrenched the old binary between morality and the economy as opposed realms of value.

Some attempts have been made recently to rethink the concept and revive its analytical worth. This book draws inspiration from the approach proposed by Palomera and Vetta and their suggestion that we 'reclaim the radical foundations of the term by bringing capital and class back into the equation' (2016: 414). The authors remind us that E.P. Thompson not only captured the breakdown of the paternalist moral economy, he also described a shift from one moral economy towards another, newer one. Accordingly, all economies are moral economies in the sense that they are always embedded in institutions and social norms, even though many economic theories describe the sphere of the economy as being impersonal and dislodged from any social reality (see also Carrier 2018). The scope of the notion of the moral economy rests on the idea that the process of capital accumulation is not only driven by profit maximization and self-interest, it is also imbued with ambiguous logics and regimes of value that guide and sustain livelihood practices (Narotzky 2015). The moral economy comprises ambiguous and often contradictory values that 'can reproduce or strengthen patterns of capital accumulation [although] they can also alter and even short-circuit them' (Palomera and Vetta 2016: 414). Therefore, the dynamics of value works in different directions, either providing moral energy and the drive for resistance, or alternatively enforcing compliance with inequalities through the practices of ideological manipulation and cultural domination exerted by elite groups.

Looking through the prism of the moral economy approach, Dimitra Kofti (2016) examines how moral values create compliance with and reproduce inequalities in industrial work settings. In her ethnography of a postsocialist factory in Bulgaria, she inquires why industrial workers comply with conditions of employment that they unanimously found extremely exploitative and unfair. To answer this question, Kofti supplements her study of the social relationships of production by investigating social reproduction and the role of the household. She concludes that household values and family relationships are key to understanding the lack of solidarity on the shop floor, for workers' familial and gender relations affect their behaviour at work and intensify their compliance with inequalities. Her ethnography illuminates the ways in which the intertwining of diverse and antagonistic values fosters compliance with inequalities and increases the precarity of flexible capitalism.

The lack of resistance that Kofti addresses at this specific temporal and spatial conjuncture corresponds to the broader dynamics of capitalist development, especially the shift towards flexible forms of accumulation (Harvey 1989). The transition to a more flexible regime stemmed from the crisis of over-accumulation in the late 1960s. The new regime of accumulation has been marked by the increased flexibility and mobility of capital flows that facilitated geographical relocations of production to 'peripheral' countries and regions. This was accompanied by the increasingly global role of financial markets while the power of nation states to control flows of capital declined. Flexible capitalism has significantly reshaped the nature and composition of the global working class over the last half century. Economist Guy Standing (2011) introduced the term 'precariat' to designate a growing number of people for whom the increased flexibility of labour markets has resulted in precarious jobs and insecurities of income.

Anthropologists have made substantial contributions to these debates by demonstrating the devastating effects of flexibilization on ordinary working lives and experiences of labour across different settings, whether historical centres of capitalism (Ho 2009; Mollona 2009) or on its margins (Ong 2010; Kjaerulff 2015; Hann and Parry 2018). In contrast to the optimistic estimates of mainstream economists, job flexibility has generated growing insecurity and unpredictability in working lives to the extent that 'the only predictable things are uncertainty and change' (Ikonen 2013: 470; see also Sennet 1998). The global expansion of financial capitalism facilitated the spread of entrepreneurial ideals and values that legitimized and naturalized the dominance of capital by promoting certain types of self-regulation and personhood (Rose 1992). There is now a rapidly growing body of literature on neoliberal governmentality and the specific modes of subjectivation that are intrinsic to the era of late capitalism. In his critical engagement with this strand of literature, Kalb (2014) argues against the widespread understanding of neoliberalism as a form of all-encompassing culture that is reshaping the conceptions of action and self according to its own imperatives. Instead he introduces a more dynamic conception of neoliberalism as a form of hegemony 'that exerts specific pressures and sets certain limits on the possible paths of personal becoming' (ibid.: 198). In this sense, neoliberalism is inextricable from processes of class formation and its outcomes, such as the dispossession, precariatization and informalization of working lives.

Hanna-Mari Ikonen (2013) takes a similar path in her discussion of how the ideology of entrepreneurialism increasingly informs working lives by reorienting individuals to assume entrepreneurial attitudes and take care of their employability themselves as old institutions lose their ability to provide stability, reliability and predictability. In her study of self-employment in Finland, she suggests deconstructing entrepreneurialism as a concept that automatically implies middle-class and white-collar identity. She shows that increasing numbers of working poor end up in self-employment not because they have capital or are exercising a free choice but because of the lack of other possibilities to secure their livelihoods.

In response to Ikonen's paper, Jeremy Morris (2013) suggests entrepreneurialism be treated as an alternative 'tactic of labour'. He reflects on the growing tendency of many people to alternate between self-employment and wage work during their working lives. Ikonen and Morris both touch upon the gender dimension, since their ethnographies demonstrate that the precariatization of work affects women to a greater extent than men. Moreover, Morris captures 'the double-bind of precarious entrepreneurialism': entrepreneurial status gives 'a feeling of control and achievement' while simultaneously requiring 'ruthless self-exploitation that is for many women (and men) not sustainable' (ibid.: 3). Revealing the diverse class backgrounds and experiences beneath the generic notion of entrepreneurialism is important for my book, given that some of the small businesses in my sample would be better described as precarious entrepreneurs struggling to survive. Such businesses face uncertainties and insecurities associated with discontinuous and low incomes, indebtedness and self-exploitation, which situate them closer to the insecurities of the working poor rather than the stability of the middle class.

The paradox of 'the double-bind of precarious entrepreneurialism' reflects the growing ambiguities regarding the production, circulation and accumulation of value in flexible capitalism, which enables exploitation through the blurring of contradictions and shifting locations of conflict (Narotzky 2015). Weber's famous conceptualization of the spheres of life is helpful for understanding social relationships in industrial capitalism, but it fails to grasp the complexities of moral economies in times of global accumulation. In his writings, Weber identifies these spheres of life as the economy, politics, the law, religion, the family, friends and work (Terpe 2016). Each of these domains is guided by the particular logic of a moral judgment according to which people orient their actions in their everyday lives. Weber insists on the irreconcilable conflicts and moral dilemmas that arise from the inherent contradictions between the various value spheres. As modernization promotes the increasing differentiation of spheres, social actors are subjugated to more than one sphere of life. When the logics of different spheres clash, people strive to resolve the mismatches between contradictory and conflicting values. To this end, they develop different responses, ranging from 'moral closure' (subordinating the whole of life to the value orientations of just one value sphere) to 'moral relativization' (experiencing fundamental moral doubts and scepticism) (Terpe 2016: 17). Unlike more apparent segregations of spheres of life in the age of industrial capitalism, the dynamics of global capitalism work through multiple principles and blur the boundaries between different domains of value, thereby creating complex, often contradictory motivations for human action. Narotzky contends that 'present-day capitalism rests on a new moral hegemony based on the blurring of value regimes' (2015: 194). She points to the pervasive ambiguity between different domains of value, which makes it nearly impossible to distinguish between gift and commodity, market-oriented goals and reciprocity, affective and contractual moral obligations, commensurable and incommensurable kinds of value. In a similar way, Mollona (2009: 177) argues that the new capitalist regime 'reproduces itself through the whole of people's lives so that coercion and consent – dependency and entrepreneurship, freedom and self-discipline and working-class poverty and middle-class aspirations – are hardly distinguishable'. It is this overlapping and convergence of antagonistic values that enables particular forms of exploitation and that produces the precarity of working lives (cf. Kofti's ethnography, already mentioned, and her understanding of consent as resulting from the coexistence of different moral frameworks pertaining to the spheres of work and home). Accordingly, the study of values under global capitalism cannot ignore the interconnections between different moral frameworks that attest to the complexities of people's motivations and explain their difficulties in generating social change. This book aims to contribute to the discussions outlined above by sharing their general preoccupations and assumptions about the nature of morality and the economy in the present-day world.

Postsocialism(s) and Transformations of Value

The countries of the former Soviet Union and Eastern Europe are commonly analysed under the rubric of postsocialism. Critical questions asking whether it still makes sense to apply this concept in theorizing the aftermath of socialism have repeatedly been raised by scholars of postsocialism (Hann, Humphrey and Verdery 2002; Boyer and Yurchak 2008; Rogers 2010; Müller 2019). Anthropologists have reasonably criticized the concept for a number of reasons, pointing to the analytical weakness of geographically bounded approaches and arguing that the continued focus on postsocialism would miss developments and transformations in the region. On the one hand, the concept seeks to create a comparative framework for juxtaposing historical and ethnographic trends within the former Soviet bloc countries and beyond. Yet there is a certain lack of comparative endeavours in studies of postsocialism, which can partly be explained with reference to the contextualized nature of ethnographic knowledge, which is not easily suited to making comparisons across diverse historical and cultural backgrounds. More importantly, however, a great deal of the scholarship on postsocialism has been narrowly concerned with collecting detailed ethnographies in particular localities in Eastern Europe and the former Soviet Union. Due to this lack of theoretical ambition, studies of postsocialism have unavoidably become 'a branch of area studies with no particular theoretical aspirations' (Thelen 2011: 45). In the early years of the 'transition' and market reforms, ethnographies of postsocialism won prominence by famously criticizing the inadequacy of Western models such as 'civil society' or 'democracy' and their claims of universal applicability (Hann and Dunn 1996; Hann, Humphrey and Verdery 2002). But apart from this critique of the universalizing ambitions of Western knowledge and power, the level of theoretical engagement has been rather low. The attempt to wed postsocialism to colonial theories was one of the first promising endeavours to 'unbind postsocialism' and plug it into global theoretical discussions and conversations (Chari and Verdery 2009).

Critical reflections on global asymmetries of knowledge and power generated further insights about postsocialism as an operational concept. Tatjana Thelen (2011) opened up this pivotal debate by arguing that studies of postsocialism uncritically adopted the normative assumptions of the neo-institutional framework that crippled the analysis of socialism and injected it with colonial undertones: socialism and its 'post-' as the 'other' of capitalism (see also Hann 2002). Petrovici (2015: 96) traces the role of local scholars in appropriating hegemonic discourses of the Western academic core and co-producing the metropolitan narrative about 'actually existing socialism' as 'the evil "other" of capitalism'. Much like Thelen, he argues that this narrative implicitly equates the dynamics of Western capitalism with modernity and 'normal history', while the trajectories of socialism and postsocialism are treated as failures and a kind of 'partial' or 'mock modernity'. Both authors regard anthropology as the right discipline for producing counter-hegemonic discourses, as it is analytically well-equipped to capture voices from below. Both authors call for a search for new critical agendas and alternative readings of socialism and postsocialism that would allow us to move beyond the West-East dichotomy and its conceptual baggage. Thelen suggests going beyond economism in order to re-examine (post)socialist experiences as comprised of multifarious relationships that are not reducible to their opposition to capitalism.

A move away from the dichotomous perspective Thelen and others complain about is apparent in those studies that focus on the commonalities between actually existing capitalism and socialism. Such alternative readings open up new interpretive possibilities and broaden our gaze on both systems. Two works that benefit from such comparison and that have produced rather unexpected insights about capitalism (Visser and Kalb 2010) and socialism (Nikula and Tchalakov 2013) illustrate my point here.

Visser and Kalb propose to go beyond the oppositions between capitalism and socialism, or market versus hierarchy, in comparing the workings of financial capitalism with the planned economy of the Soviet Union in its late years. They argue that the two systems are strikingly similar in how they operate and produce similar 'distortions and perversions' that are exemplified by state capture by large enterprises, the existence of a 'virtual economy' and shadow systems that obscure the actual state of affairs and encourage the 'mystification of risk', actors' short-term orientations, and the silencing of civil society and institutions. Visser and Kalb suggest that a focus on the similarities between the two systems would improve understanding of the crisis of financial capitalism and its fundamental problems. The authors push back against the popular vision of capitalism as a neutral mechanism of regulation and demonstrate how the oligopolistic financial sector has captured both the state and society, that is, the media, politics and academia. They push the parallel with socialism even further by suggesting that the collapse of global financial capitalism and its aftermath might be analogous to the demise of the Soviet system.

Nikula and Tchalakov (2013) propose a similar agenda but pursue it from a different angle. They argue against reading socialism as a 'non-modern control society' and challenge the commonly held belief that there were no entrepreneurs under socialism (cf. Szelenyi 1988). They differentiate the group of actors they term 'socialist entrepreneurs', that is, Soviet citizens seeking economic opportunities within the constraints of administrative economies and acting in entrepreneurial ways. Many of these 'proto-entrepreneurs' were heavily implicated in the workings of the second economy, participating in petty trade, doing unofficial jobs or engaging in intra-firm barter, while others operated more in the realm of the official economy and belonged to the ranks of the Soviet *nomenklatura*. The authors pay special attention to this last group of 'socialist entrepreneurs', arguing that the economic *nomenklatura* fulfilled entrepreneurial functions by introducing technological innovations in socialist industries that were crucial in driving the further development of socialist economies and catching up technologically with the West. By situating entrepreneurial activities at the heart of socialist enterprise, Nikula and Tchalakov trace how 'socialist entrepreneurs' utilized their experiences and extensive networks to manage capitalist enterprises after the demise of the administrative economies. Although their historical sociology is firmly grounded within a capitalist discourse, it nevertheless offers a more complex and dynamic understanding of 'actually existing socialism' than the narrative of the all-powerful state and the rigid state bureaucracy.

I follow those voices that find in postsocialism a useful concept for describing societies and communities in which the socialist past remains a reference point for making judgments and decisions about the present. Russian entrepreneurs evoke socialism on numerous occasions, and the memories and mythologies of the past continue to animate the present. This applies even to the younger generations of business people and aspiring entrepreneurs. Even though some of them do not have any direct experience of living under socialism or have very vague personal experiences going back to their early childhood, they nevertheless express some nostalgia for socialism as an epoch that is seen as having been safer, more predictable and morally superior compared to what came next (on the 'nostalgic turn' in postsocialist contexts, see Todorova and Gille 2010; Angé and Berliner

2014). These nostalgic feelings and discourses convey a sense of social degradation and enable moral critiques of those conditions at the present day that cause anxiety and discomfort, ranging from bumpy roads and another failure of the national football team to win the world championship to the crisis of the welfare state and the loss of trust and respect in interpersonal relationships. Following Burawoy and Verdery (1999), I conceive such positive recollections of socialism and their persistence in everyday life not as 'legacies' inherited from the past, but as 'a response to exigencies of the present'. In their introduction, Burawoy and Verdery unpack how metaphors of 'Soviet legacies' or 'culture' have turned into convenient 'explanatory variables' that social scientists evoke in explaining the failure of the Russian transition to produce its intended results and 'incubate' new institutional arrangements that are conducive to the emergence of a market economy. In contrast to the analytically misleading cultural explanations, Burawoy and Verdery reformulate old values as a resource that allows people to interpret, respond to, or reject new institutions and policies. Such reformulations make the picture of ongoing transformations more complex and less predetermined by the linear configurations of narratives of the transition. In Chapter 6, I show how the owner of a failing enterprise that produces garments mobilizes the ideals of Soviet modernity, with its promises of endless development and progress, in order to address the stiff conditions of global competition that threaten to swallow the petty local producers and turn them into subcontractors working for low wages in global companies. This case study illustrates how commitments to socialist modernity and its moral imperatives help the firm's owner navigate the ongoing demise of her garment business and make sense of its incorporation into global circuits of capital.

At the same time, the deployment of moral sensibilities of the socialist past does not automatically mean the rejection of economic and political change. Anthropologists who criticize the concept of the transition for its simplicity and inscribed teleology have tended to concentrate more on the moments of resistance to market transformations by showing how postsocialist actors mobilized the moral resources and institutions of the socialist past in order to challenge the new policies and market institutions that threatened their lifestyles and collective identities (Burawoy and Verdery 1999; Verdery 2003; Dunn 2004). Cohen (2013) points out that this focus on the resistance to the 'transition' set the tone for studies of postsocialist moralities in general. She suggests that work on moral resistance be balanced with investigations into how 'people mobilize morality to endow capitalist practices with a greater degree of moral legitimacy' (ibid.: 727). Soviet morality is not being detached from the expansion of capitalism, for it is not necessarily antithetical to capitalist values and practices. Soviet-era idioms and symbols can be employed by actors in appropriating new ideologies and inequalities.

In her study of secretarial courses in St. Petersburg, Cohen brings out the link between on the one hand efforts to improve the image of the business environment and endow Russian capitalism 'with a much desired sense of moral grounding' and on the other the idea of 'culturedness' or *kulturnost'*, which is deeply grounded in the Soviet moral canon (ibid.: 749). Under Soviet rule, the idiom of 'culturedness' figured prominently as a central feature of the ideal Soviet person (Kelly and Volkov 1998) and guaranteed the Soviet intelligentsia their privileged positions (Fitzpatrick 1992). Since socialism, the ideology of 'culturedness' has continued to inform class-making processes and practices of consumption in the new Russia (Patico 2008). These findings recognize that memories and practices rooted in the Soviet past may unfold in an ambiguous manner, their intended and unintended consequences not being limited to the point of resistance only. Given my particular focus on the field of work and labour, I trace how Soviet values play themselves out within a capitalist enterprise and how they relate to modes of flexible accumulation and social inequalities. In Chapter 5, I discuss to what extent the kinship-like morality deployed in the workplace in relations with unrelated employees resembles the patterns of familiarity and relatedness that typified the Soviet organization of work. Attempts to foster kinship solidarity and transform a work team into a community of *svoi* people[2] do not defy the principles of market value or overcome inequalities in the workplace, but in fact seek to endow capitalist relations of production with a greater degree of moral legitimacy through references to familiar patterns of work and symbols of solidarity.

The case of the garment manufacturing firm I mentioned earlier is another example of how Soviet values interact with market rationalities. The head of this firm seems to be openly critical of capitalist modernity and its value orientations, but her rejection of the values of the market coexist with her compliance with its imperatives, since the way she extracts surplus value is very much in accord with the moral economy of flexible production (see Chapter 6). This example shows how 'everyday compliance and resistance' (Kofti 2016) are not easily distinguishable in real life and that the moments of resistance to the neoliberal order may well coexist with trying to be a part of it (see also Kesküla 2015). Close-up ethnographic examination allows the dynamics of the accumulation and circulation of value to be grasped by tracing how petty entrepreneurs negotiate the ambiguities of value in their daily lives.

---

[2] The term *svoi chelovek* (plural: *svoi ludi*) refers to a circle of related people, as opposed to outsiders and strangers.

Map. The location of Smolensk.

Fieldwork and Methods

In connection with this study, I conducted eleven months of ethnographic fieldwork in Smolensk between October 2015 and September 2016. I made extended ethnographic observations in four small-scale private businesses that relied on the assistance of family members and other relatives. Two of the firms I discuss belong to the garment manufacturing sector and are headed by women. I chose these two cases because they provided a good opportunity to compare and contrast 'old' Soviet-type entrepreneurs with the 'new' generation. The first firm arose out of the context of Soviet production, its start-up capital being acquired during the struggles over property of the early years of privatization. The second business was set up independently at the turn of the millennium with capital reinvested from earnings from trade.

Doing participant observation in the garment industry required that I had a good command of the professional jargon in order to understand the technology and production processes. First I joined Alpha, the inheritor of the Soviet garment industry, which became the starting point of my immersion into the world of garment manufacturing. I started coming to the factory every day for several hours and took up manual tasks like sorting through the pile of wares in the warehouse or counting the number of accessories and other supplies. After that I assisted the technical designer, relieving her from doing tedious manual tasks that she rightly saw as deskilling and was happy to hand over to someone else, if only temporarily. The designer, a worker with solid experience of working in the garment industry, introduced me to the basics of garment manufacturing, and we spent much time together, chatting and drinking tea in between carrying out our work tasks. For several months, I assisted her in performing tasks that required some basic skills, such as cutting out new paper layouts or mending the old ones. The next several months I spent on the shop floor, where the garments were assembled, ironed and packed. Here I had to learn how to operate different types of sewing machines, although my speed was nowhere close to those of the professional seamstresses, and it usually took me more time to redo things than to assemble the pieces together. Working with seamstresses and chatting to them during breaks extended my observations and allowed me to grasp more insights into the relations of production. All in all I worked in Alpha for six months, and I will present the results of these observations in Chapter 6.

I spent much less time, around two months all together, working in Little Bunny, the second garment firm. Due to my previous experience in Alpha and basic knowledge of technology, it was much easier to enter the new setting and get through the work there. Unlike Alpha, which mainly did subcontracting jobs, Little Bunny produced its own brand of clothes and had developed a regional chain of shops to market its wares. At this firm, I mainly performed manual unskilled tasks, working in the two production units located on the outskirts of the city. My observations at the production site were supplemented by a day spent with the firm's owner, Dina, who invited me to accompany her on a trip to one of their retail shops in the region.

In addition to garment manufacturing, I carried out two months of fieldwork working at two firms that belonged to the service sector. Both businesses, a mini-hotel and a printing firm, had a single owner, Vadim. This case was particularly interesting because of the semi-informal arrangements and the intricate story of the firm's ownership, which I will bring out in Chapters 5 and 7. I stayed at Vadim's hostel when I had just arrived in Smolensk in October 2015, my initial one-month stay there gradually turning into one more month of fieldwork as a receptionist. Like any other receptionist, I did round-the-clock shifts every three days and was in charge of various tasks mainly pertaining to bookings, receiving calls, accommodating clients, cleaning, doing the laundry and ironing never-ending piles of bedclothes. During that period I continued to stay at the hostel, occupying one of the beds in a dormitory room. After a month performing the duties of a receptionist, I was allowed to make regular visits to another of Vadim's businesses, the printing firm, which I frequented over the next month on a daily basis. I did not have any particular tasks at this firm, mainly just hanging out with workers and occasionally assisting them with work tasks. Since the firm employed only five people and did not have many orders at that time of the year, I could socialize more with the employees, inquire about their work trajectories, families and household situations, and get a better understanding of their relations in the workplace. I will describe these relationships in Chapter 7, drawing upon the life histories and work trajectories of two co-workers, Oksana and Sveta. Despite the resentment they felt for each other, they both became good friends of mine, and I continued to drop by Vadim's firms for a friendly chat long after I had moved on to other places to do fieldwork.

I conducted 49 semi-formal interviews with the owners of small businesses and the self-employed. I met my interview partners through contacts with their friends and acquaintances, as well as through business associations and professional organizations, namely the Smolensk Business Club, the Chamber of Commerce and Industry, the Association of Young Entrepreneurs and the Association of Entrepreneurs.

Among the last category of organizations, the Business Club was the most vibrant institution, one that offered a variety of events and gatherings for would-be and real entrepreneurs.[3] It put on lectures about marketing and management, coaching sessions, meetings with local administrators and policy-makers, and a large range of leisure and cultural activities, like games and quizzes. The Business Club, as a non-governmental agency, could be an interesting subject on its own due to its efforts to civilize the Russian business sphere by popularizing the image of the educated and enlightened entrepreneur (see Cohen 2013 on the similar efforts to 'bring culturedness and market together' made by secretarial schools in St Petersburg).

---

[3] But broadly, for all those interested in its agenda and events. The majority of events were charged for, with an entrance price around two euros.

I frequented the Business Club on numerous occasions that bore on business and economy-related topics; there I met some of my partners for interviews. Business people who attended such events were either interested in particular topics and came for one-off events[4] or were regular visitors. For the last category, the commitments to self-development and education did play a role, but networking opportunities were equally important. Some of the Business Club's regular visitors showed great enthusiasm for my research and were eager to participate. Even so, I tried not to limit my sample to this peculiar category of business owners (or aspiring entrepreneurs), who were cultivating entrepreneurial mindsets and neoliberal methods of self-regulation. There were very many more business people who never showed up in the Business Club and who were detached from any entrepreneurial discourses whatever, like older generations of business people. As a rule, the older generation was less enthusiastic about participating in the research but felt rather obliged to their friends or relatives who had kindly directed them to me. I also conducted interviews with the staff of the local business associations and attended their occasional events targeting business people.

In 2013 the government established the office of business ombudsmen to addresses issues of rights violations on behalf of the business owners. The office aimed to eliminate notorious administrative obstacles by mediating the conflicts between public bodies and businesses. As in other Russian regions, Smolensk has its own business ombudsmen. While I heard that some business people had sought his support, the majority of my informants were overtly sceptical and did not believe that a new state agency would bring about change. My attempts to talk with the officers from this newly established public body were not particularly successful, as my interlocutors were reluctant to talk. However, in visiting the office I came across an applicant who was eager to share her experience of engagement with the ombudsmen. Her detailed account provided more insights into state-business relationships and their political implications.

My fieldwork took place in the aftermath of the Ukraine crisis, with its sharp elevation of political and economic tensions between Russia and the West, Russia's unexpected annexation of Crimea and the military conflict in eastern Ukraine. These events became a hot topic in mainstream Russian media and were vividly discussed by local people, many of whom had friends and relatives in the Ukraine. Anti-Ukrainian attitudes popped up in my field site, although some people said they felt extremely tired of such debates and would prefer not to raise political topics at all because it might

---

[4] The talk about managing a firm in times of economic crisis attracted a large crowd of visitors, as did the meetings with local policy-makers.

strain their social ties. The tensions and conflicts surrounding the Ukraine complicated business relations as well. For instance, the Ukrainian crisis threatened to sever relations between two business associates because they held diametrically opposed views on political matters: one of the partners originated from Lvov, western Ukraine, and supported the discourse of Ukrainian nationalism, while the other was a local resident who sympathized with the pro-Russian nationalists. They were not just good partners but also close friends and spiritual kin, as one of them was a godfather to the other. Their fierce debates about politics posed a serious challenge to their relations at work, and they decided to drop any further discussions on the matter for fear that such divisive debates would escalate into a physical fight and ruin their twenty-year-long friendship. Neither partner changed his political allegiances, but they agreed to turn the topic into a taboo, explaining away each other's 'misconceptions' and 'fallacies' with reference to the pervasiveness of state propaganda on the both sides of barricades. In Chapter 7, I touch upon this issue by showing how anti-Ukrainian attitudes played themselves out in the workplace, thus aggravating conflicts between Russian and Ukrainian colleagues in the private firm.

Being a native Russian researcher, I did not experience any particular problems in acquiring access to the field, although my affiliation with a German institution, the MPI, sometimes raised suspicions with regard to the ultimate goals and political implications of my inquiry (the nickname of 'German spy' that stuck to me at one of the garment manufacturing enterprises is telling, yet it was always used with a pinch of irony). What raised more tangible concerns among my interlocutors was my interest in the issues of informality and taxation. For many small businesses, manipulations of the tax system function as a kind of 'open secret' – everyone knows how pervasive the practice is, yet this is still secret, unarticulated knowledge 'that no one discusses in a direct way' (Ledeneva 2011: 725). Being an insider was more of a disadvantage for me, as I was expected to share this tacit knowledge and to understand the ambiguities surrounding informality. Therefore, I strove to be more diplomatic and not to ask questions in a blatant and straightforward manner, but rather just hint at the subject. At moments like these, I was sometimes asked to put my recorder on pause. Without a recorder and beyond the formal settings of the interview, many entrepreneurs were keen to discuss taxation in more detail, and it was not uncommon that the most interesting and less formal discussions happened after the interview was technically over, at the point of saying goodbye.

Last but not least, I collected materials on local history, politics and the economy by reading the works of local historians, sociologists and economists, and by examining the local press and social media. To learn more about urban living in Smolensk, I went to the large city festivities, took city excursions, visited museums and memorials, made trips to the countryside and embarked on occasional visits to the Orthodox church, the synagogue and the chapel of one of the Pentecostal denominations.

Chapter Outlines

Chapters 2 and 3 provide an overview of the literature on topics related to the realms of the economy and morality respectively. Chapter 2 describes Russia's politico-economic background by tracing the major trajectories of Russian capitalism and the Soviet planned economy. The chapter looks critically at the dominant approaches to the study of (post)socialism as the Other of capitalism and indicates alternative readings that go beyond the market–hierarchy dichotomy. In addition to the economic background, Chapter 3 provides an introduction to the diverse field of morality, both religious and secular, and traces its historical transformations in Russia. The chapter questions the Weberian categorization of Orthodoxy as other-worldly and ascetic, drawing upon a body of literature that shows the multiplicity of religious identities, practices and interpretations in Eastern Christianity. Beyond the religious forms of virtue, the chapter outlines different dimensions of the Soviet moral framework by discussing Soviet official teachings and ideology, conceptions of public and private life, practices of consumption and Soviet secularism.

Chapter 4 opens the empirical part of the book. Here I introduce the locality and outline the business landscape of the city, which has been shaped by diverse economic activities, state policies, social norms, laws and regulations. This is intended to orient the reader within the broader landscape of the political, economic and social life of the city, in which entrepreneurial activities are deeply embedded. In this chapter, I provide an overview of the major economic transformations in Smolensk, namely the experiences of the first cohorts of entrepreneurs, who were mainly engaged in petty trade, government programmes for the small private sector, informal networks and negotiations between the state and business actors, and employment opportunities in the local labour market.

Chapter 5 interrogates the role of kinship morality and family obligations in small firms. It shows why the idea of a family-run enterprise takes on contradictory associations and meanings in contemporary Russia. I argue that this ambiguity stems from the entanglement of different values in the workings of family-based enterprises and discuss how different social actors experience their entanglement in diverse realms of value and how this structures capital accumulation within the small-scale sector. Chapter 6 details the moral framework of the owner of Alpha, a small-scale garment-manufacturing firm. This firm provides a good example of how resistance to and compliance with capitalism coexist so that commitments to socialism and critical engagement with market modernity, as articulated by the firm's owner, do not override the conditions of the further flexibilization and precaritization of labour that characterize flexible accumulation. Chapter 7 delves into relations between capital and labour by discussing the role of personal dependencies in the workplace. I ask why a worker would strive to forge a patron–client type of relationship with his or her employer and how this affects relations between co-workers. Finally, the conclusion summarizes the main findings and links them to broader discussions of how the symbolic hegemony of capitalism is sustained and reproduced in postsocialism.

Chapter 2
The Political Economy of Russia: Historical Overview

Early Capitalist Developments in Tsarist Russia

On the eve of the First World War, Russia was primarily an agrarian peasant country. Agriculture was responsible for over half the national income and three-quarters of all employment. Over 90 percent of the sown area was cultivated by some 20 million peasant households, the remainder consisting of landowners' estates (Davies 1998: 10). The distribution of property was under the control of the tsar and nobility. The peasants received a small amount of land after their emancipation in 1861, but they did not own land individually. The land was collective property, administered and distributed by the peasant commune (*mir, obshchina*) according to the strip method. The peasant commune was a self-governing territorial community and the main legal owner of the land held by its households. It granted its households strips of arable land (*nadel*), which were regularly redistributed according to egalitarian principles. The communal system of land redivision remained the dominant form of land use in tsarist Russia. The commune assured some collective security and welfare, such as caring for orphans and the aged, and it also served the state in its capacity as an administrative device for tax collection and local policing (Shanin 1985).

Peasant emancipation in 1861 paved the way for the rapid development of Russian capitalism. An economic boom in the 1880s was driven by an extensive programme of state-supported railway construction, harshly protectionist state policies and increases in exports of Russia's grain (Gatrell 1982; Shanin 1985; Davies 1998; Gregory 2014). At the beginning of the twentieth century, a number of economic structures co-existed in Russia: foreign-owned oligopolies in big industries, freely competing firms producing consumer goods, landowners' estates, small-scale artisan units and individual peasant micro-economies. The market was strongly influenced by the state, but most economic actors still produced many of the goods they consumed themselves (Davies 1998).

There is a debate among economic historians regarding the extent to which Russia could still be considered a 'backward' economy on the eve of the Revolution. While Alexander Gerschenkron (1962) famously argued that late tsarist Russia was on a path to becoming a modern capitalist economy and parliamentary democracy, other scholars have been more reluctant to see Russia's delayed industrialization as economic success, stressing instead its uneven character, oligopolistic tendencies and low technological base, as well as the Empire's growing political and social instability (McKay 1970; Crisp 1976; Shanin 1985; Haimson 1988). Discontent was widespread among the new classes that emerged with the growth of industry and the towns: factory workers were dissatisfied with their economic and social conditions, while the urban middle classes were demanding political rights. The discontent spread to large sections of the peasantry, many of whom were peasant-workers who combined seasonal work in the towns with farming. This massive discontent was greatly exacerbated during the First World War and facilitated the victory of the Bolsheviks in the Revolution of October 1917.

State Socialism (1917-1991): Social Identities, Work and Labour in a 'Classless Society'

The 1917 Revolution and the fall of the old regime opened up an era of socialism. The massive socio-economic and political changes the Bolsheviks brought about in the first decades of Soviet rule shaped the Soviet modernization project, which was ideologically anchored in the Enlightenment impulse to remake and improve society (Kotkin 1997). The ultimate goal of the socialist experiment was to achieve a classless society and eventually to put an end to the injustice and exclusion generated by capitalism. During the formative decades of Soviet rule, the search for a rational social order was fleshed out in a series of state-led policies: nationalization of the means of production, industrialization, collectivization of agriculture, urban planning, the spread of total public education and secularization. The hectic attempts to nationalize all industries were made in the 'heroic era' of the Civil War (1917-1922), when the Bolsheviks were trying to consolidate their precarious rule. After the Civil War, Lenin's New Economic Policies partially restored private trade and the market, but this liberal turn was phased out in the late 1920s, when Stalin rose to power. Stalin's socialism was marked by increased centralization and bureaucratization of the Party system.

The Stalin epoch is notorious for the magnitude of the violence it unleashed in the 1930s, including mass repressions, deportations, purges and fierce warfare against 'class enemies.' The focus on the dictatorial side of Stalinism was characteristic of the studies of the 'totalitarian school', which explained the efficiency of Stalin's order with reference to the terror and fear it generated. In polemics with totalitarian historians, 'revisionist' approaches sought to move away from equating Stalinism with totalitarianism by paying more attention to Stalinism' social base, that is, the new Soviet elite whose support was essential to Stalin's rule. In her study of social mobility and education in the 1920s to mid-1930s, Sheila Fitzpatrick (2002) traces the rise of the new political and managerial elite recruited from workers and peasants during the First Five-Year Plan (1928-1932). She argues that it was this stratum of upward engineering-technical personnel and industrial managers that endorsed Stalin's rule and pledged loyalty to the system. Their loyalty was ensured by a range of privileges and material incentives, such as housing, consumer goods, luxuries and leisure time. In a famous phrase of Vera Dunham's (1990), the later Stalin regime made a 'Big Deal', that is, proposed an alliance with the managerial-professional 'middle class'. This rapprochement between the regime and the middle classes caused a significant shift in values in that it restored material and private values at a time when the ascetic values of the socialist revolution were losing ground.

In Soviet Russia, the category of class replaced the old estate (*soslovie*) system of social classification and became a basic category of identity. In the 1930s, Stalin established three major groupings of Soviet society: workers, collectivized peasants and the intelligentsia. The last group was referred to as a 'stratum' (*prosloika*) and lumped together with two other groups, white-collar office workers and the Communist administrative elite (*nomenklatura*). Fitzpatrick (2000) points out the ascriptive use of Marxist class categories in Soviet Russia. She argues that, rather than reflecting the social and economic statuses of Soviet citizens, markers of class were ascribed to people through state-led class policies; in this sense, the Soviet invention of class had much in common with the pre-revolutionary system of estates that had defined the rights and responsibilities of citizens in relation to the state. While 'real' socioeconomic class remained elusive and indeterminate, in Soviet Russia social class was turned into a legal category that played a key role in the politics of class discrimination of the 1920s, when a class stigma was attached to various disenfranchised groups of Soviet citizens such as *kulaks*[5] priests, Nepman[6], and *meshchane*.[7] As a basic category of social identity,

---

[5] A category of affluent peasants.

[6] Urban private entrepreneurs at the time of the NEP, or New Economic Policies.

[7] In pre-revolutionary Russia, *meshchane* was the name for a social estate comprising the lower economic bracket of urban-dwellers, such as peddlers, servants and some artisans. In

class defined the citizen's legal status and opportunities: for example, the heavily stigmatized *kulak*s were deprived of voting rights from 1918 to 1936, while *bedniak*s (poor peasants) were exempted from agricultural taxes and were given a priority in admissions to higher education and recruitment to party offices. In the midst of collectivization, local soviets tended to ascribe class identities in a haphazard and informal manner (Fitzpatrick 1994). With the introduction of the passport system in 1932, the class position was institutionalized under the 'social position' entry of this main identification document. The principles of class identification changed throughout Soviet history, shifting from hostile class discrimination and class stigmatization in the early years of the revolution towards the equality-of-rights principle, proclaimed in the 'Stalin' Constitution of 1936. Even so, a tendency toward *soslovnost'* (estate system) permitted the social organization of the Soviet state. As Soviet peasants demonstrated the most clearly defined *soslovie* or estate-system characteristics, they did not possess the automatic right to passports and were restricted in their mobility. Unlike the other basic classes, peasants were obliged to provide labour and horses for roadwork and logging to the state. Simultaneously, they had unique privileges such as the collective right to use the land and to engage in individual trade limited to the '*kolkhoz* markets' in towns[8] (Fitzpatrick 2000: 37). Somewhat similar to Fitzpatrick's line of argumentation, anthropologist Caroline Humphrey (1983) describes the Soviet social order as a system of politically defined statuses that granted Soviet citizens with specific entitlements non-negotiable rights and social privileges.

From the onset of Bolshevik rule, the proletariat was proclaimed to be the new ruling class in Soviet society. As a socio-economic class, it included urban industrial workers and landless agricultural labourers. The rapid industrialization of the late 1920s led to a massive remaking of peasants into workers to staff the newly emerging industrial enterprises and construction sites. As Soviet-style proletarianization did not suffice in teaching former peasants how to work in industry, there was also a concentration on forging their political attitudes and allegiances (Kotkin 1997). In the Soviet state, work was cast simultaneously as a major civic right and an obligation: according to the 1936 constitution, no one had the right not to work. The socialist welfare state guaranteed full employment and offered a wide range of social benefits, including near-universal subsidies for housing, health care

---

the late nineteenth century, the term became derogatory, being equated with the supposedly philistine mentality of the petty bourgeoisie (Dunham 1990: 19-21). The Bolsheviks emphasized the pejorative sense of the word, which they usually applied to the category of urban white-collar workers (*sluzhashchie*) (Fitzpatrick 2000: 25).

[8] A *kolkhoz* was a form of collective farm in the Soviet Union.

and education; a broad system of retirement and disability pensions, sickness, maternity and child benefits; and special privileges for veterans and civil servants, as well as many other population categories. The majority of social and welfare functions were centred on the Soviet enterprise, which provided housing, kindergartens, allotments, leisure and health-care facilities to the members of labour collectives. It was impossible to obtain access to the most important forms of provision other than through the workplace.

From its very inception, the rapidly expanding Soviet industry suffered from labour shortages and irregularities of supply that jeopardized fulfilment of the Plan. During the First Five-Year plan, turnover and absenteeism increased dramatically as workers moved from one enterprise to another in a search of better wages, housing and food supplies. In order to curb unwanted labour mobility, the state outlawed job-changing and absenteeism from the late 1930s. However, the draconian labour regulations were rarely implemented in practice, as industrial managers and local legal officials tended to cover for departing labourers (Filtzer 2002b: 182-3). Criminal sanctions against job-changing remained in force until 1951, and it was not until 1956, after Khrushchev's 'Secret Speech', that anti-quitting laws were removed once and for all from the state's books. Khrushchev's policies marked a decisive break with the previous epoch of mass terror and forced labour. With liberalization of the labour law, the party-state turned to recruitment campaigns to mobilize labour to participate in the new grand projects of Khrushchev's era, such as the industrialization of Siberia and the Far East and the cultivation of virgin lands in Kazakhstan (Filtzer 2006: 162). The *gulag* economy that had provided labour power for Stalinist industrialization disintegrated after Stalin's death in 1953.

Many analyses of Soviet history concur in describing workers' quiescence and compliance with the regime, which was evident in the lack of collective resistance. Some scholars explain the Soviet Union's social stability and political quiescence with reference to the social contract theory (Breslauer 1978; Hauslohner 1987; Cook 1993). In this view, the regime ensured social consent and mass loyalty in exchange for a set of policy goods, including full and secure employment, stable and subsidized consumer prices, socialized health and educational services, and egalitarian wage and income policies.

Another approach explains the lack of resistance in the post-Stalin era as resulting from the regime's deliberate attempts to 'atomize' the working class. Filtzer (1996) argues that the party-state systematically undermined workers' solidarity and made it nearly impossible for Soviet workers to organize themselves collectively. He points out that, in the absence of collective organization, workers nevertheless opposed the regime through individual responses such as absenteeism, high labour turnover, alcoholism, go-slow and petty thefts of enterprise property – the types of behaviour that have usually been interpreted by scholars as evidence of disorientation and anomie. Given the high demand for labour power, the regime did not possess any potential sanctions against ill-disciplined workers, in particular the sanction of dismissal: 'if managers were too keen to punish absentees or "slackers", the worker could quit, leaving management in an even more precarious position than before' (Filtzer 2002b: 160). Thus, the chronic labour shortages that were inherent in the planned economy allowed workers to extract concessions from management and thus to ease the intensity of labour that came with the downward pressures imposed by the centre. Moreover, the irregular rhythms of Soviet production contributed to the lax work discipline in Soviet enterprises, since the chronic supply shortages and frequent equipment stoppages enforced idleness on a number of workers for long periods. However, disruptions to production and the ensuing losses of work time did not necessarily mean any reduction in the intensity of labour. To compensate for slack periods and stoppages, workers had to work overtime or perform work in rushes or 'storms', when a shop or enterprise would have to produce the bulk of its monthly or quarterly plan at the end of the relevant period.

Theorizing Socialism: The Economy of Shortage and its 'Dead Ends'

For the long time, the Soviet economy has been a controversial subject of analysis, being strongly enmeshed in political and ideological debates, and anchored in the rhetoric of the market versus the plan. In this section, I will outline how social scientists have contributed to the understanding of 'real socialism'.

Early attempts to understand the specific rationality of the socialist economy 'from within' were already being made by Western observers in the late Soviet era. Caroline Humphrey's (1983) insights into the *kolkhoz* economy are unique of their kind, as they were based on ethnographic fieldwork on two Buryat collective farms conducted in the 1960s to 1970s. Her findings highlight a specific rationale of Soviet production techniques in which considerations of profitability did not play a prominent role. The rationale that governed Soviet production was subordinated to the practical need to fulfil the state delivery plan. To this end, a collective farm might plan to make a loss that could be covered by state loans or lead to a reduced plan for the next year. Although collective farms sometimes created a 'surplus product' (a Soviet renaming of 'surplus value'), that is, a supplement to the obligatory delivery plan, it was in the interests of the *kolkhoz* management to conceal the existence of any surplus and avoid the pressure to increase the delivery plan. Typically the surplus was channelled into the grey area of exchange, being distributed through household economies or realized in gross terms by either sale or barter. Humphrey calls such surplus products 'manipulable resources', showing that they enabled *kolkhoz* managers to navigate the contradictions of the planned economy. The surplus could be paid in the form of 'in kind' wages and bonuses to the *kolkhoz* workers, whose pay and conditions of work varied greatly. 'Manipulable resources' allowed *kolkhoz* managers to establish relations of 'exchange' or 'debt' with workers by paying them over and above the regulated payment of wages. For their part, the *kolkhoz* workers were dependent on the farm's officials for a range of benefits, varying from supplying firewood in winter to permission for their children to leave the *kolkhoz* for further education. Another, informal way to dispose of a surplus product was to use it in negotiations for a reduced delivery plan or to obtain the means of production by relying on the help of various 'middleman', such as 'pushers' or *tolkachi*, who helped to obtain inputs or ensured the sale of *kolkhoz* products to state organizations.

An understanding of the Soviet economy as a system of bargaining for resources between enterprises and ministries is prominent in the work of Simon Clarke (1993a). Much like Humphrey, he challenges the idea of there being an irrational planned economy that would be viewed as defective by capitalist standards proclaiming the universality of the law of market value. Unlike capitalist systems that produce surplus value, socialist planning was not subject to the law of value but was primarily based on the production and circulation of use values. Clarke compares the socialist economy with the feudal system of exactions in kind that rested upon the allocation of productive resources by the centre (ibid.: 15). In a similar fashion, the American anthropologist Katherine Verdery (1991) places an emphasis on bargaining relationships between economic agents in state socialism. She locates the driving impulse of the socialist economy in the realm of distribution and the capacity of its actors to control resources, which she calls 'allocative (or redistributive) power'. In their everyday bargaining with the central planners, socialist managers resorted to a variety of subterfuges, such as padding out budgets and hoarding materials. By amassing resources, managers could enhance their redistributive power and exercise it in informal exchanges with other firms while obtaining the materials they lacked in order to fulfil the production plan. At the top level of political authority, the same principle of obtaining power by distributing resources was a key to the legitimacy of the Communist Party, which established its authority on the basis of promises of social redistribution and welfare. However, as this impulse to amass resources was at the heart of the planned economy, it caused imbalances between accumulation and redistribution. Heavy industry received the priority in the socialist economy since it allowed accumulation of the means of production more effectively and thus enhanced its allocative power. On the same grounds, the consumer sector was of secondary importance, as consumption and giving goods away ran counter to the bureaucrats' aspirations to strengthen allocative capacity and maintain bureaucratic control. In response to the endemic shortages of the socialist economy, consumers developed a variety of strategies to obtain consumer goods and services. These strategies included both illegal and quasi-legal means and in total comprised the 'second' or 'informal' economy, which was 'parasitic upon the state economy and inseparable from it' (Verdery 1996: 27).

The concept of the shortage economy has been widely adopted by many influential scholars of socialism. The sociologist Alena Ledeneva (1998) frames her study of informality and social networks in late socialism around the concept of the shortage economy. She shows that social networks (*blat*) were instrumental in mitigating the all-pervasive shortages and obtaining access to scarce material resources. In 2011 Tatjana Thelen initiated a debate about the adequacy of understanding socialism through the lens of the shortage economy approach, which was rooted in neo-institutional thinking. The concept was coined and popularized by the famous Hungarian economist and dissident Janos Kornai (1980) to illustrate the inefficiency of any bureaucratic regulation in comparison to market self-regulation. His theoretical model of socialism was built on the concept of soft budget constraints, that is, the neglect of the profitability principle that distinguishes socialist economies from capitalism, which operates on the principle of hard budget constraints. Thelen's criticism targets Kornai's theory and its repercussions for the anthropology of postsocialism. She captures the colonial underpinnings of 'socialism' and 'postsocialism' and problematizes the intensive transfers of Western knowledge to (post) socialist societies. The debate Thelen opened up has provoked further discussion, for example, about the role of local scholars in adopting metropolitan knowledge (Petrovici 2015). Such debates encourage us to look for new critical agendas and lines of argumentation that depart from equating Western capitalism with modernity and 'normality' and to allow 'voices from below' to tell their stories. In the next section, I will show how the narrative of a 'transition' has framed understandings of postsocialist change and Russia's subsequent failure to embrace capitalist modernity. This is followed by a critical analysis of postsocialism(s) in anthropology that suggests a different perspective on the 'transition' and challenges its normative assumptions by examining micro-structures and day-to-day life.

Russian Capitalism in the Macro-Perspective

The 1990s: The 'Transition' to Capitalism and 'State Capture'

In 1985 Mikhail Gorbachev, the last leader of the Soviet Union, announced *perestroika*, a set of reforms that aimed to liberalize the socialist system and included the first attempts to privatize state enterprises. The law on cooperatives was adopted in 1988. It allowed Soviet citizens to run private firms (cooperatives) that could operate under the protection of the Communist Party (KPSU) or Komsomol organization. Boris Yeltsin, Gorbachev's successor, championed the immediate transformation of Russian socialism into laissez-faire capitalism. With the financial support of Western agencies, such as the International Monetary Fund and the World Bank, Russia embraced a radical program of economic liberalization or 'shock therapy', which was announced on January 1992, some days after the dissolution of the Soviet Union (Åslund 1992; Pomer 2001). The Russian reformers, a group of young economists, expected the rapid liberalization of prices, the removal of subsidies and the sharp cuts in government spending to sweep away all the inefficient mechanisms of the planned economy and allow market mechanisms to bring supply and demand into line (Sakwa 2008: 283). The reformers predicted economic stabilization by the end of the year and promised gradual improvements in people's lives.

Yet this did not happen. The sweeping liberalization caused an explosion in prices, hyperinflation, a rapid erosion of real incomes and a sharp fall in production. It was not until 1996 that the macroeconomic indicators started to improve. Despite promising statistical indicators, many observers pointed to the serious structural problems of the Russian economy, reflected in dramatic demonetization, the rise of the hidden economy and a slump in tax revenues (Rutland 2001: 5-8). Gaddy and Ickes (2002) coined the term 'virtual economy' to show that market mechanisms did not work properly in Russia, as they were distorted by state support to inefficient industries. They argue that the Russian manufacturing sector took away value rather than added it, while the state subsidized inefficient industries by permitting tax arrears to build up, instead of letting such enterprises go bankrupt. In order to cover the costs of loss-making, the state redistributed the earnings of the value-producing centres of the economy, primarily the natural resources sector, to the non-viable sectors of manufacturing. The pretence of economic growth was sustained by overpricing output, which created the illusion of added value but in fact resulted in the increased indebtedness of enterprises, as reflected in endemic arrears of wages, pensions and tax payments. Gaddy and Ickes trace the roots of Russia's 'virtual economy' back to the Soviet economic model that subsidized enterprises by under-pricing raw materials. The authors argue that Russia remained a 'fundamentally not market-based economy', the market being only a pretence, whereas in reality the economy was sustained by its reliance on non-monetary methods, in particular barter.

Contrary to the reformers' expectations, bankruptcy in manufacturing was a rarity throughout the most turbulent years of liberalization, as was unemployment. The reformers expected inefficient and overstaffed state enterprises to rid themselves of excess labour once they were exposed to the external pressures of the market and its law of value. However, the managers of Russian enterprises strove to keep their workers and thus prevent mass layoffs. Amid the growing indebtedness of enterprises and the shortage of cash, unemployment rates stayed relatively low, peaking at just 13 percent in 1998 (Vasileva 2014: 116). In order to keep their workers on the payroll, managers gave them extended holidays, made in-kind payments or simply did not pay their wages, thus running up payment arrears. Clarke (1993b) argues that the strategy of preserving labour collectives served the interests of the 'industrial *nomenklatura*'. Under the new economic conditions, managers of former state enterprises strove to reassert their managerial control based on the existing pattern of social relations of production. Contrary to the intentions of the reform, enterprise managers made no attempts to restructure the social relations of production but rather stuck to the old familiar ways of running enterprises by maintaining supplies, reintegrating into regional political apparatuses and 'creating monopolies and conglomerates on a regional basis in an attempt to keep the market under control' (ibid.: 235).

For the vast majority of Russians, 'shock therapy' resulted in massive impoverishment and pauperization. In the face of plummeting living standards, people were thrown back on their own resources. In 1992, upon the launch of a large-scale drive for privatization by means of a voucher scheme, all Russian citizens were given vouchers which they could trade or bid for shares at voucher auctions in the former state enterprises. However, instead of dispersing former state property throughout society, as intended, most private assets accumulated in the hands of the *nomenklatura* and the managers of state enterprises (so-called 'red directors'). Both groups were able to benefit from privatization due to their access to insider information and start-up capital, which enabled them to buy up vouchers from ordinary citizens on a massive scale and thus consolidate substantial shares of property (Kryshtanovskaya and White 1996). The voucher privatization ended in 1994, but a large share of the Russian economy remained in state hands, including some of the country's most valuable companies. To continue privatization, the state launched a second wave in the form of loan-for-shares auctions that allowed conglomerates of Russian industrialists and financiers (known colloquially as oligarchs) to obtain the most valuable assets in the national economy – mainly oil and mineral producers – on favourable terms (Freeland 2000; Åslund 2007).

The Russian business elite exerted an enormous influence over the main political decisions throughout the 1990s by relying on close personal connections with state officials and policy-makers. For many political scientists, this interdependence between business and the state was indicative of the emergence of 'oligarchic capitalism' in Russia (Rutland 2001) and the corresponding weakness of the state in designing and implementing policies, a situation they call 'state capture' or the 'privatization of the state' (Hellman, Jones and Kaufmann 2003; Yakovlev 2006). Yakovlev points out that close integration with the state was only one of the strategies pursued by Russian entrepreneurs, one that co-existed with the opposite strategy of keeping a distance from the state. In this way, state capture refers only to those interest groups that sought special preferences and benefits from the government. The majority of entrepreneurs, particularly in the regions, preferred to keep their distance from the state so as to minimize the costs of doing business. For this reason, more market-oriented competition took place at the regional level, while the federal centres of decision-making became an arena for cut-throat competition for influence between lobbying groups (Yakovlev 2006: 1036).

Apart from the rise of the oligarchs and their interventions in state policies, scholars of the Russian economy recognize the state's low capacity to protect property and contractual rights. In times of legal vacuums and weak law enforcement, a range of criminal groups arose to provide protection services for business needs, such as 'roofing'[9] racketeering and contract murders (Volkov 2002; Yakovlev 2006). Moreover, the dysfunctional state could not ensure its own property rights through taxation: federal tax revenues fell from 25-30 percent of GDP in 1989 to 10-12 percent in 1997 (Rutland 2001: 7). As a result of tax shortfalls, the government resorted to issuing high-interest, short-term treasury bills (GKOs), which subsequently triggered the financial crisis of August 1998 (Sakwa 2008: 287).

The state's weakness, together with the controversial outcomes of privatization, have brought many observers to the unanimous conclusion that

---

[9] A roof (Russian *krysha*) is an informal protection arrangement facilitated through criminal gangs or state agencies.

the Russian transition failed to achieve its predominant endpoint, namely to produce flourishing private businesses and a healthy, pluralist democracy, as anticipated by the market reformers. The advocates of radical reforms blamed the irredeemably corrupt state and its rent-seeking government for the failure of the market transition in Russia (Hellman and Schankerman 2000). Åslund summarized this view as follows: 'Russia had embraced big-bang market reforms but collapsed in a corrupt mess' (2007: 129). Other observers blame the naivety of the reformers and their excessive reliance on 'simplistic textbook models of the market economy' (Berglöf et al. 2003). Critics of such simplistic understandings of capitalism have pointed out that the architects of the market transition failed to recognize the importance of social institutions and norms. By transferring assets to the private sector without 'regulatory safeguards', the reformers themselves increased the incentives and opportunities for asset-stripping and only succeeded 'in putting "the grabbing hand" into the "velvet glove" of privatization' (Stiglitz 2001: xviii). Instead of creating a competitive economic environment, rapid neoliberal reforms drove the economy into the 'institutional traps' of barter, mutual arrears, tax evasion and corruption (Polterovich 2001). As a response to the external shock of radical changes from above, the system chose an inefficient path of development, which some analysts related to a deeply rooted path dependence in Russia marked by repeated failures to undertake fundamental institutional change (Hedlund 1999).

The Putin Years: From 'State Capture' to 'Business Capture'

Since his accession to power in 2000, Vladimir Putin has imposed greater central control over Russia's federal system. By justifying his policy as a need to restore the vertical chain of government ('the verticality of power'), Putin strengthened the position of the federal government by limiting the powers of regional governors and reducing their rights and fiscal resources. The country was divided into seven large regions, each headed by a governor appointed by the president; most of the regional governments' legal rights have been abolished (Åslund 2007: 211-14).

As part of Putin's plan to establish the 'dictatorship of the law', the state simplified many regulatory procedures for business at the beginning of the 2000s. The number of activities that require licensing were reduced from 250 to 103. Under a new 'one-window principle', registering firms has been made easier, taking on average twenty-six days (Berglöf et al. 2003: 102-4). The tax regulations have been significantly changed in an attempt to alleviate the overall tax burden and boost tax revenues. The number of taxes was reduced from about 200 to 16; a progressive income tax from 12 to 30 percent was replaced by a flat tax of 13 percent; the payroll tax was cut from

40 percent to 26 percent; the corporate profits tax was cut from 35 to 24 percent; and several social taxes were merged into one. In 2000-2003 the 'simplified taxation scheme' was introduced for small-scale businesses, defined by the average number of employees not exceeding one hundred. If an entrepreneur chooses a simplified system, he or she is liable for a unified tax on either gross receipts at 6% or profits before income tax at 15%. Additionally, new laws cut the number of mandatory inspections for business.

Despite the state's efforts to boost business activities, small businesses continued to develop slowly, only accounting for 17 percent of employment (Rutland 2008: 1053). Bribe-giving and 'gift' exchanges between businesses and the state authorities persisted and even increased. In the regions, the local authorities have grown stronger owing to the increasing demands from business for property protection and contractual rights, which in the previous decade were mainly undertaken by criminal groups (Yakovlev 2006). By winning more support from local businesses, the regional authorities have consolidated their power by strengthening their capacity to penalize firms for tax avoidance. By that time, the widespread practice of tax evasion had shaped the business environment to such an extent that any new player entering the field would be compelled to break the tax laws. Since the 2000s, the formal rules turned into a new technique of rent-seeking through which the local authorities exerted their power 'to legitimately penalize' any firm for tax evasion. For instance, municipal officials could request a violator of the tax code to transfer a 'voluntary contribution' in order to fund the construction of a cathedral or the celebration of a municipal holiday in exchange for which administrators would condone the donor's non-compliance with the tax legislation (Yakovlev 2006: 1041). Moreover, the controlling agencies used business checks to extort money or certain goods by relying on arbitrary rule. For their part, business people responded to these abuses of administrative power by seeking informal alliances with state operators and the local authorities in an attempt to protect their rights (Golovshinskii et al. 2004).

Compared to Yeltsin's close relations with the oligarchs, Putin enhanced his control over the business elites. The state leadership has adopted a position of 'equidistance' from the business elite by promising that the state would refuse to revise the outcome of the privatization in exchange for big businesses staying out of politics (Tompson 2005). Those who did not comply were either forced into exile, like the media magnates Vladimir Gusinsky and Boris Berezovsky, or prosecuted, like Mikhail Khodorkovsky, the chairman of the oil giant Yukos. For many observers, the Yukos affair marks a watershed in state-business relations, a shift from 'state capture' to 'business capture' that ensures the state's control over the market (Yakovlev 2006; Åslund 2007; Rutland 2008).

Putin's model of state-oligarchic capitalism is seen as a highly ambivalent and unstable political project due to its dependence on the global oil market (Rutland 2008). Discussions of Russian capitalism typically point to the Russian economy's major ailments, namely the persistence of informal rules and of the rent-seeking behaviour of economic actors. Puffer and McCarthy (2007) point to the enduring importance of networks or 'clan' structures, which subsume the more formal, rule-based mechanisms that are necessary for the existence of a competitive market economy. They characterize the type of economic system that emerged in Russia as a form of state-managed 'network capitalism' in which various clan structures operate in the absence of the formally defined rules of the market game. Other scholars of politics stress the 'patrimonial' aspect of the Russian economy, a reference to an idea of Max Weber's. The concept of 'patrimonial capitalism' asserts that the Russian political economy has been shaped by neo-traditional forms of authority based on elaborate patron-client relationships (Becker and Vasileva 2017). Ivan Szelenyi (2016) argues that the patrimonial order, which has informed Russian developments in the long term, continues to shape the dynamics of the Russian capitalism.

Postsocialism 'From Below': The Social Consequences of Neoliberal Policy-Making

In contrast to the 'top-down' perspective of mainstream economists and political scientists, the view 'from below' allows a more ambiguous account of the transformations of planned economy to be portrayed. Anthropologists view critically the unidirectional and evolutionary underpinnings of the conventional transitional narrative, preferring to focus instead on the connection between macro-structures and everyday experiences of the transformation (Burawoy and Verdery 1999). In the anthropological perspective, concepts such as civil society, the state, private property, legality and corruption are not given and self-evident but need to be unpacked and reconsidered in the context of local processes (Hann 2002). In efforts to demystify the transition, anthropologists are equally sceptical of cultural explanations of postsocialism that portray Russian culture as an obstacle to any future change (Humphrey 2002: xx).

By problematizing the conventional narrative of the transition, social scientists have paid close attention to its unexpected outcomes and to the experiences of ordinary people. The themes of loss and change have been recurrent topics in research into the initial phase of postsocialism (Caldwell

2004; Bridger and Pine 2013). By examining a variety of 'survival strategies', this strand of literature aims to show that a retreat into subsistence production, a reliance on kinship networks and engaging in barter transactions had little to do with an omnipresent 'Soviet legacy' but were primarily responses to contemporary economic upheavals and a reaction to unregulated market reforms. Retreat to a primitive subsistence economy and a rejection of consumerism were among the most common 'defensive strategies' that were adopted as a response to destitution and the 'involution' of economic life in post-Soviet Russia (Burawoy, Krotov and Lytkina 2000). Entrepreneurial strategies were less common among working-class families due to the high risks involved and usually emerged under an economic compulsion to survive. Petty trade was the most popular occupation for those who had been laid off by failing enterprises.

In the face of severe shortages, general inflation and a chaotic legal situation, at the beginning of the 1990s local enterprises resorted to barter and a system of rationing. By issuing coupons, food cards or orders for certain categories of workers, local enterprises perpetuated unequal access to resources and increased people's dependence on the services offered by their workplaces (Humphrey 2002). Non-monetary exchanges between economic actors in open contradiction to market objectives proved to be efficient in times of economic crisis. Barter was crucial to maintaining production in a rapidly changing economic environment that caused a shortage of money. Barter transactions were heavily dependent on personal relations and established 'little pools of trust and mutual help' that fell largely out of the state's control (Humphrey 2002: 16).

Unemployment and the loss of income were just one side of the process of economic restructuring. Across Eastern Europe the deeper repercussions of unemployment included a loss of status, a loss of self-esteem and 'an incredible sense of loss of the sociality and close relations of the workplace' (Pine 2002: 96). In the context of deindustrialization and unemployment, large swathes of the population found themselves excluded from the public domain of production and were pushed back into the domestic domain, a process that Pine, writing about a similar situation in Poland, describes as 'a retreat to the household'. She argues that the retreat to subsistence production and kinship networks affected women to a greater extent than men, since the latter had more options in terms of casual work. The relocation of female activities from waged work to caring for the family deprived many women from individual autonomy and certain kinds of relatedness mediated through shared spaces and the everyday experience of labour under socialism.

In post-Soviet Russia, conversely, enterprises generally avoided making large-scale compulsory redundancies and strove to preserve the core of their 'labour collectives' instead. This partly explains why mass unemployment in Russia has not been predominantly a 'woman's problem' (Ashwin and Bowers 1997). Despite the predictions that women would gradually be pushed out of the labour market and would willingly relinquish the 'double burden' of working both outside and within the household, Russian women did not show any desire to abandon paid employment in favour of the latter. Aushwin and Bowers demonstrate that being a member of a 'labour collective' remains crucial to women's sense of identity. Moreover, female workers felt an emotional attachment to the workplace, seeing it as 'a release from the monotony of home life' (ibid.: 27; see also Alasheev 1995).

Ethnographies of post-Soviet enterprises investigate the changing ways in which the social relations of production and the organization of work have been reshaped by successive economic restructurings. Changes have been evident in the growing significance of monetary incentives, the increased fragmentation between different categories of workers and the emergence of new meanings of work and styles of management (Clarke et al. 1993; Clarke 1995; Ashwin 1999; Dunn 2004; Kesküla 2014; Kofti 2016). In her study of postsocialist transformations in East Germany, Thelen (2005) shows that the demise of socialist redistribution and the growing social inequalities at work led to a reduction of social relationships among workers and the vanishing of interpersonal trust and familiarity from the workplace. Relations of trust shifted into the realm of the family and private life instead, reflecting the broader move towards the 're-traditionalization' of social ties whereby 'kinship ties are becoming more important for communication and for solving difficulties than other ties' (Thelen 2005: 24).

The contraction of the welfare system and the withdrawal of the state form another aspect of loss that has been addressed by anthropologists. Humphrey (1999) and Anderson (1996) conceptualize changes in the postsocialist welfare infrastructure as a change in regimes of citizenship. The socialist system granted civic rights on the basis of one's position within the complex and hierarchical structure of Soviet society, whereby work and residential units were the primary sources of one's entitlements. Belonging to nesting social categories (e.g. war veterans, women, married couples), as well as to a certain labour *kollektiv*, defined one's own bundle of civic entitlements, which were allocated preferentially and mediated through an intricate system of civic documents such as the *propiska* (residence permit) and internal and external passports. The erosion of multiple citizenship regimes in post-Soviet Russia through their reduction to a single dimension has been experienced by many as a loss of collective entitlements and has provided a basis for popular resistance to the Western ideals of civil society and democracy, the latter coming to be seen 'as the antithesis of civic entitlement and of civilization itself' (Anderson 1996: 114). Likewise, Hemment (2009) points out that the recipients of 'categorical benefits' in the Soviet Union were not stigmatized and marginalized as 'welfare recipients' in the liberal welfare state; on the contrary, social provisioning under socialism was dignified and embraced the majority of Soviet families. Hemment traces the ambivalences of Putin's welfare politics and the resulting hybrid type of welfare, which she calls 'Soviet-style neoliberalism'. Taking some radical steps in the direction of liberal welfare politics (e.g. pension reform, the 'monetization' of social benefits and the liberalization of housing and utilities charges), the state at the same time resurrected Soviet forms of citizenship and the statist regime of welfare (e.g. increased state spending on public assistance projects and the 'maternal capital' programme). The key feature of 'Soviet-style neoliberalism', according to Hemment, is that ongoing neoliberal restructurings are typically obfuscated by the vocal commitments to Soviet-era cultural forms and the partial shift towards statist social welfare, energized by the mobilization of anger over the earlier neoliberal reforms of the 1990s: 'the Putin administration advanced liberalizing reforms at the same time as it rhetorically distanced itself from them' (ibid.: 36). In another study, Melissa Caldwell examines local understandings of social assistance and support among the recipients of foreign aid projects. She argues against narrow utilitarian understandings of poverty as a scarcity of material resources, for it is social scarcity – the lack of extensive social resources – that frames the understanding of poverty in Russia. In her research on Moscow soup kitchens, she shows that the food-aid programmes offered their recipients not only material assistance but also a sense of social solidarity and of group membership in their projects.

Privatization is another theme that anthropologists have engaged with critically. Criticisms have been lodged against the standard liberal model of property rights, its ideological underpinnings and its claims to universal applicability (Hann 2007). Anthropologists argue for more multifaceted understandings of privatization as embedded in and encompassing social processes whose end point is unknown. From the anthropological perspective, property is more adequately described not in terms of rights but as a process of making certain kinds of relationships. Verdery (2003) argues that a system of values and power relations is key to understanding the transformation of one form of property into another. In her study of the unmaking of socialist property in Romania, she investigates how the new regime of value justified its claims by promoting new values in relation to kinship, land and the new forms of inequality.

Douglas Rogers (2015) attends to the regional level of privatization in his study of the oil sector in the Perm region of Russia. His scrupulous account of the intersection of the oil industry with cultural production provides rich insights into processes of state formation and corporate formation, the complex layers of state–corporate entanglement and the return of the Soviet-era cultural intelligentsia to Russian politics.

These socio-economic transformations have produced a new logic of social differentiation and class structure in the new Russia. The low-inequality society that characterized Russia under state socialism shifted abruptly to become one of the most unequal societies in the world (Novokmet, Piketty and Zucman 2018). Under capitalism the former 'heroes of labour' faced rapid declines in their status and material lives. The change from 'veneration to denigration' in relation to workers (Kideckel 2002) and the symbolic impoverishment of manual labour overall (Walker 2012) have been connected to the wider global shift from 'a society of producers' to 'a society of consumers' (Bauman 2005). In the context of symbolic and economic dispossession, postsocialist workers are increasingly turning to right-wing politics and nationalist discourses to voice their disapproval of neoliberal globalization (Kalb 2011). However, nationalism and support for right-wing populism were not universal responses among impoverished workers in Europe. For example, it was not an option for Russian-speaking miners in Estonia, who could not embrace the discourse of Estonian nationalism and instead turned to a discourse of hard work to maintain their dignity and justify themselves as worthy citizens (Keskülä 2015). Vanke and Polukhina (2018) document further the unmaking of the post-Soviet working class by showing how the memories, skills and experiences of Soviet industrial workers are being erased and made 'invisible' by urban activists who are actively reshaping industrial spaces in Russia and remaking them in line with the now dominant middle-class lifestyles and identities. Morris (2016) calls for a different perspective on the trajectories of post-Soviet workers. Not denying the processes of dispossession and the demise of labour, he challenges thinking about industrial spaces and blue-collar work solely in terms of decay, marginality and economic precarity, instead proposing to investigate how workers are making their lives 'habitable' and even 'comfortable' in the new conditions. While the informality of labour may be read as a sign of precarity, Morris shows that many workers actively reject formal employment, making informality a 'normal' response to the uncertainty and contingency associated with formal work.

With the expansion of capitalism and its hierarchies of value, the former 'heroes of socialist labour' gave way to the new 'heroes of free market ideology' – the aspiring middle-class subjects (Walkowitz 1995: 163-5). The domination of the new privileged class has been built symbolically on the values of entrepreneurialism, modernity and the 'good life'. The research interest of social scientists shifted accordingly to exploring middle-class identities, cultures of consumption, gendered class trajectories and forms of social mobility. It has been shown that the members of the urban middle-class tend to construct their identities through symbolic renunciations of Soviet-era experiences and modes of thinking and instead strive to embrace more 'modern' – that is, 'European' and 'Western' – standards of the 'good life' (Shevchenko 2002; Patico 2008; Rivkin-Fish 2009; Zdravomyslova, Rotkirkh and Temkina 2009; Salmenniemi 2012b). However, despite such distancing and devaluations of the Soviet past, scholars of postsocialism have noticed striking similarities connecting the social imagery of the post-Soviet middle class with Soviet ideas and practices. Examples include the significance of the notion of culturedness (*kulturnost'*), approval of egalitarian values and reliance on social networks in managing everyday life. The politics of culturedness, made manifest in the attempts of the socialist state to inscribe relatively high standards of individual consumption marked by simplicity, moderation and propriety, have continued to shape lifestyles and consumption patterns after socialism (Patico 2008; Gurova 2012). The logic of Soviet consumption underpinned the consumption style of the new Russian elite, for it was not the quality but the 'quantity of style' that distinguished the flamboyant lifestyles and 'mindless' conspicuous consumption of the New Russians from less well-off Russian consumers (Oushakine 2000).

Conclusion

This chapter has aimed to provide the essential background to the social, economic and political history of Russia. Analyses of (post)socialist political economies have rarely been free from the political and ideological implications that underpin the debate between the virtues of the market versus those of the planned economy. The new spiral of the Cold War in the period of the Russian takeover of Crimea has revived the rhetoric of East-West confrontation and inevitably impedes analyses of Russian neoliberalism, which neglect the fact that Russia has been deeply incorporated into the global economy and actively partakes in global accumulation and dispossession (Morris 2017). In this chapter, I have brought out the major discussions in the social sciences that frame the understandings of Russia's socialist past and its capitalist present.

Anthropology and its preference for studying 'from below' not only enrich the institutional vocabulary of the macro-theorists, but also have the potential to engage critically with the latter's models and put forth new critical agendas that go beyond socialist – postsocialist dichotomies. In the following chapter, I will focus on a dimension that is rarely addressed among political scientists and economists, namely the realm of morality and value, and trace its historical developments and transformations in Russia specifically.

Chapter 3
Russia's Moral Background: Orthodoxy, Soviet Values and Multiple Moralities of Postsocialism

The Study of Morality in Anthropology: Social Norms, Freedom and Conflicts over Values

This chapter gives a brief overview of Russia's moral background by discussing a particular repertoire of concepts and practices that have historically informed and underpinned the realm of morality in Russia. However, before going into details about particular articulations of morality, I will briefly discuss how morality has been conceptualized in anthropology. There are certain themes that have gained particular attention and provoked debates in the anthropology of morality, a relatively new field of inquiry that invites a critical re-examination of a long-standing subject in the social sciences – the category of the moral.

One such question is how we should understand moral action. When the realm of morality is seen through a Durkheimian perspective, it is conflated with the reproduction of social norms, obligations and rules that organize social collectivities and dictate codes of individual behaviour (Robbins 2009). Laidlaw (2002) argues against the view of morality as comprising law-like obligations and instead suggests seeing moral acts as based on free and reflexive choices. In his ethnography of moral life in Papua New Guinea, Robbins seeks a way to reconcile both approaches by arguing that conscious choice and freedom (what he calls the 'morality of freedom') may coexist with the routine and unreflective reproduction of social norms (the 'morality of reproduction'). Drawing upon Louis Dumont's theory of value, Robbins views values as forces that organize cultures and articulate which elements are valued more than others, thereby structuring them into hierarchies of values. But in contrast to Dumont's harmonic image of culture, Robbins's approach to culture as a hierarchy of values is more dynamic and historical. He argues that in times of cultural change the routine cultural reproduction of values becomes problematic and value conflicts inevitably arise. Situations of conflict invite social actors to make reflexive choices and act freely by choosing between conflicting values.

Thus, moral decision-making becomes possible as a result of cultural change when people are forced to navigate and solve conflicts of value. Such moments of 'moral breakdown' provoke social actors to call into question traditional, fixed and unproblematic rules of life and to work consciously on their moral personhood (Zigon 2011). Where values are in open conflict, people tend to formulate most clearly the moral frameworks within which they evaluate situations and act according to such evaluations (Heintz 2009: 13). Robbins admits that new, more stable structures of values may arise as soon as the period of cultural change and conflict is over (Robbins 2009: 70). In post-industrial societies, this stability and harmony of values seem unlikely to be achieved. As Max Weber famously pointed out in his classic works, a conflict over values and irreconcilable contradictions between different spheres of values lie at the heart of the modern complex societies in which multiple and conflicting hierarchies of values coexist (Terpe 2016).

This book draws upon an approach to the notion of the moral economy that brings the economy and analysis of class into the study of social norms and values (Thompson 1971; Scott 1976; Edelman 2005; Palomera and Vetta 2016). According to this approach, these are structural inequalities and group interests that constitute dynamic constellations of values and account for both value conflicts and harmony (see Introduction for a more detailed discussion of the moral economy approach).

In the following sections, I will provide a brief historical overview of Russia's moral background by tracing the major discourses and practices that pertain to the institutional level of morality and its public articulations. I start my overview with the moral system of the Russian Orthodox Church, which has been a central arena for shaping individual moralities and public discourses in Russia for centuries.

Russian Orthodoxy: Otherworldly and Ascetic?

In his historical overviews of world religions and economic ethics, Max Weber did not pay much attention to Orthodoxy (Weber 2004, 2009). Even though he developed an intense interest in Russia, he was primarily concerned with studying recent political developments in the aftermath of the Russian revolution of 1905 and did not make any attempt to incorporate religion and ethics as he did in his famous analyses of Hinduism, Confucianism, Buddhism, Islam and Western Christianity (Ertman 2017). Eventually, Weber lost his interest in the Russian political drama (Hann 2011: 14). Without any systematic examination of Orthodox tradition and history, he considered Eastern Christianity to be too mystical and otherworldly to be able to induce social change comparable to the Protestant impact on Western rationalization and modernization (Makrides 2005: 182). According to Weber, Orthodoxy was openly mystical, ascetic, sentimental, traditionalistic, communitarian, anti-rational, more focused upon ritual and eternal salvation, and less concerned to engage with the world. Historically, the Orthodox Church has not shown any interest in transforming the world but rather has fostered a communitarian spirit and other-worldly orientations, thus standing in the way of modernization and progress (Buss 2003). The broader political implications of this view are evident in the marginalization of those countries in the EU that have mostly Orthodox populations, such as Greece or the Balkan states, which are considered culturally underdeveloped, alien to the West and incapable of achieving a breakthrough to modernity (Makrides 2005: 185).

In his critical engagement with such simplistic stereotypes of Eastern Christianity, Makrides appeals for a detailed historical and social analysis that would shed light on the particular responses of Eastern Christianity to the modernizing influences coming from the West. He argues that, notwithstanding of its proclaimed hostility to the 'spirit of modernism', the Orthodox Church has not remained unchanged and static but has undergone considerable transformations throughout its history (ibid.: 196-8). It would be misleading to see Eastern Orthodoxy as an ultimate barrier to economic development, taking into account the economic achievements of Balkan merchants and Russian Old Believers. Moreover, Eastern Christianity is not a monolithic entity but consists of various branches that incorporate an array of teachings, not uncommonly contesting each other. Last but not least, Makrides reminds us that there are more types and modes of rationality than those found in the Western variant of modernity alone (ibid.: 196-200).

The anti-modern orientations of the Orthodox Church and its otherworldliness are usually substantiated through references to the ideals of contemplative monasticism and personal salvation as the key to Eastern Christianity. Kenworthy (2008) argues against the stereotypical equation of Russian Orthodoxy with passive acceptance and escapism from the world. Instead he strives to infuse historical dynamism into discussions of Orthodox morality by tracing how various actors both within and outside the church disputed the meanings and purposes of contemplative monasticism. Kenworthy points out that actual monastic life has never been confined to the narrow goal of individual salvation but has usually embraced the needs of whole communities of believers, for example, by praying for the community, providing spiritual guidance to the laity and undertaking social activities in the world. Thus, the pure anchoritic tradition of absolute renunciation of the world was rarely observed in practice, even though it retained its ideal appeal within the Orthodox tradition, as in other 'world religions'.

The socialist period represented a particular turning point in the history of Russian Orthodoxy. During World War II Stalin granted some concessions to the Church, but two decades later his successor, Nikita Khrushchev, phased them out during the anti-religious campaign of the 1960s. Khrushchev's onslaught against religion aimed to neutralize the Church as an ideological competitor of the state. As a result, the Church strengthened its focus on its liturgical activities, as it could no longer take on an active social role under socialism. By undercutting the Church's social influence and reducing religion to a purely private affair, the Soviet regime succeeded in strengthening the Church's other-worldly orientation. Although after the Soviet Union collapsed the Church enjoyed a resurgence of religious freedom, it nevertheless continued to place a strong emphasis on liturgical activities to the neglect of its active social role. Rather than developing an ideology of social service, the Russian Orthodox Church places a great emphasis on the restoration of church buildings (Kenworthy 2008: 42-50).

In 2000, the Orthodox Church issued the *Bases of the Social Concept of the Russian Orthodox Church,* a voluminous document clarifying its stance on a variety of secular topics related to the state, the law, culture, the economy, bioethics, etc. This endeavour to engage with a new set of issues and concepts that the Church had never addressed before became 'an important step toward entering into dialogue with the contemporary culture' (Makrides 2005: 201). In the *Bases of the Social Concept*, the Russian Orthodox Church asserts its positive relationship with the world by striving to divorce itself from the mystical-ascetic tradition and catching up with developments in Western theology. In doing so, however, the Church faced a fundamental dilemma in how to adopt the world without losing its institutional identity, built as it is on the language of tradition (Agadjanian 2003b). As a result of these conflicting trends, the novel message of world-affirmation has been outweighed by the world-rejecting stance reaffirmed by the Church in the face of globalization and the perils associated with it. Ultimately, the *Bases of the Social Concept* conveys highly controversial messages undermining its initial effort to incorporate the world within the Orthodox theological framework (Agadjanian 2003a).

One of the sections of the *Bases of the Social Concept* deals specifically with the economy, and more particularly with the issues of work, payment, profit and justice. The document legitimizes profit-making activities, unless they are motivated by pure self-interest or violate the norms of religious morality. Interestingly enough, the document explicitly refers to Weber's work in asserting an essential difference between the Orthodox understanding of work and the thesis of a specific Protestant ethics, which establishes a causal link between the accumulation of wealth and salvation. In general, the Russian Orthodox Church's attitude to the economy draws upon an array of controversial Biblical examples, making it rather difficult to use the *Bases of the Social Concept* as a practical guide for everyday life (Köllner 2012: 66-7).

When the realm of Orthodox morality is explored ethnographically, scholars aim to understand how Orthodox mores and teachings are being played out on the ground and how they inform social action. As Köllner (2012) demonstrates, the Orthodox clergy in contemporary Russia tend to view business and money-making as inherently immoral activities, secretive and opaque in their essence. For their part, business-people associate priests with the monastic ideals of asceticism, renunciation and sharing. Both clergy and business-people assess each other's honesty and morality by drawing upon these mutual perceptions. Accordingly, the other-worldly orientations of Orthodox priests are not given *per se* but are sustained and reproduced by the laity in their evaluations of the Church's relevance to modern society.

Caldwell (2011) questions the applicability of Weber's typology of religions to an empirical study of Orthodoxy. She does not regard other-worldly and this-worldly orientations to be opposite ends of the spectrum, but argues that the same social action may embrace both orientations. When religious practitioners seek to establish relationships with a deity, they direct their actions to another world. However, the same action can be simultaneously directed to this world, for example, to the needs of a social community, as in cases of giving and sharing. Elsewhere, Caldwell (2010: 339) points out that the recipients of Orthodox charitable programmes perceive the Russian Orthodox Church as an institution of entitlement, a 'state-like civic institution with a moral imperative to provide for the needy'. Such expectations fuel public dissatisfaction with the Church, which is seen as incapable of satisfying the needs of its constituents or of taking on the role of benevolent provider. Caldwell's research highlights the relevance of these broader social concerns and this-worldly orientations to the bulk of ordinary religious practitioners: 'From a theological standpoint, Orthodoxy may well be oriented toward otherworldly experience, but from the perspective of ordinary people, Orthodoxy is an institution embedded within a this-worldly domain of real-life needs and circumstances' (ibid.: 346).

Tocheva (2017) echoes Caldwell's point about the embeddedness of religion in the broader dynamics of social and economic life. In her study of Orthodox parish communities in post-reform Russia, she argues that taking a more inclusive approach to religion would help in 'thinking through the edges of the parish' and capturing the entanglement of parish life in society at large (ibid.: 9). To this end, she proposes the notion of 'street-level Orthodoxy' as a more inclusive theoretical framework that embraces a heterogeneity of actors, positions and spaces within the church.

Thus, anthropological approaches to the sphere of religious morality stress its embeddedness in the broader field of social norms and strives to get away from the view of religion as an isolated and separate arena of institutionally sanctioned values. Due to their focus on religious practices rather than on theology and textual analysis, ethnographic studies of religion show that the familiar Weberian dichotomies cannot be applied uncritically to Eastern Christianity.

For many centuries, Eastern Christianity has been the primarily source of meanings and values in Russia. When the Bolshevik revolution occurred in 1917, the secular institutions of the Soviet state took over the Church's capacity to create meanings and social solidarity. Therefore new moral understandings and models of personhood emerged in Russia under communist rule.

Soviet Morality: Between Private Aspirations and Collective Values

The fall of the monarchy in 1917 and the Bolsheviks' accession to power initiated a new wave of cultural change marked by self-conscious attempts by the new power-holders to dismantle previous hierarchies of value and produce a new morality based on Marxist theory and the ideal of social equality. The first post-revolutionary decade became a period of drastic innovations, social and cultural experimentation and utopian projects rooted in the moral economy of the Russian peasantry on the one hand, and the rich tradition of the socialist radicalism of Russian intellectuals on the other (Stites 1991). During the early years of revolutionary reconstruction, the attempt to establish a new proletarian morality gave rise to a plethora of collective institutions, social movements and artistic associations that proclaimed communal ideals and rejected private aspirations. The experiments with communal life, the liberation of sexual norms and the search for new artistic forms were among the early attempts to create a proletarian culture and suppress the 'philistine' and 'vulgar' morality associated with the former bourgeoisie. Yet these energetic efforts to articulate new values and enforce cultural change remained quite marginal and did not gain much popularity beyond the new cultural elite (Fitzpatrick 1992).

In the Stalin period, revolutionary principles lost their attractiveness, and there was a return to more traditional or middle-class values. Some Party leaders and the young communist intelligentsia saw this 'great retreat' from revolutionary ideals as a betrayal of them. In her seminal book, Dunham (1990) identifies this shift as a new tacit agreement (what she calls a 'big deal') between the regime and the middle-class ethos. The new cohort of upwardly mobile communist intelligentsia, the so-called *vydvizhentsy*, provided a social base for the Stalin regime and demonstrated public and private loyalties in exchange for material incentives and privileges (Fitzpatrick 1992). The values and aspirations of Soviet technocrats and skilled workers were in sharp contrast with the mores of self-sacrifice and asceticism of the previous heroic phase of revolution (Dunham 1990: 18).

The growing embourgeoisement of Soviet society was also evident in the revival of traditional family values, respect for the Russian past, and appreciation of the classics of nineteenth-century Russian literature and music (Fitzpatrick 1992). The turn towards consumerism was promoted within the framework of culturedness (*kulturnost'*), which became 'the fetish notion of how to be individually civilized' (Dunham 1990: 22; see also Hessler 2000; Gronow 2003; Donahoe and Habeck 2011). Culturedness as a process of acquiring proper conduct and manners legitimized the concerns about possessions and status that had been condemned in the early years of the revolution as part of a bourgeois lifestyle. In the Stalinist discourse, a reference to cultural levels and education provided a way to conceptualize the hierarchy and privileges of the Soviet intelligentsia – a social group that embraced all citizens engaged in non-manual labour, but also served as a euphemism to designate the upper strata of society, the new Soviet elite (Fitzpatrick 1992: 217-18). When rationing was in force from 1929 to 1935, the new Soviet intelligentsia enjoyed priority access to the supply of material and cultural goods. Their privileges were not openly publicized, and the networks of distribution they had access to were closed to the general public. At the same time, while the language of revolution and its anti-elitist agenda had not completely disappeared from the public discourse of morality, it coexisted with manifestations of privilege, social hierarchy and acquisitive consumerism. In this way, Soviet morality embraced contradictory hierarchies of values which coincided with the divisions of class and gender: the taste for luxury and middle-class values did not apply to all sections of society but was primarily associated with the elite, while the working classes and the peasantry were encouraged to follow a different set of norms and values (Fitzpatrick 1992: 233-7). This coexistence of conflicting logics of value remained visible until the end of the Soviet era, even though the value given to equality and the commitment to build a classless society were proclaimed as paramount in the official moral discourse.

The Foucauldian approach to morality, with its focus on the practices and techniques of moral training, provides another lens for the study of the moral domain of Soviet Russia. Applying a Foucauldian framework to the formation of the Soviet individual, Kharkhordin (1999) traces the genealogy of Soviet morality back to Eastern Christianity, arguing that the monastic ritual of public penance and its central component – a revelation of one's sins in public – were unreflexively adopted by the Bolsheviks, who harnessed Orthodox penitential practices in establishing Soviet collectivism. In Stalin's times, the practices of collective self-criticism were institutionalized by Party activists in the course of the Party purges (*chistka*); in late socialism, they were normalized and ritualized through the mechanisms of collective social organization. According to Kharkhordin, horizontal surveillance and admonition not only permeated social life within the official realm of discourse, but also underpinned all social institutions, including networks of friends, informal groups, subcultures and movements of dissenters. As a result of the total collectivization of life, the dominant type of Soviet individual was split between two spheres of life – the visible public sphere, and the hidden intimate sphere. In order to protect themselves from pervasive mutual surveillance, Soviet citizens sought to escape into the secret sphere of their intimate lives, where they could practice suspect behaviour they would have avoided in public. According to Kharkhordin, the fact that the sphere of private life in the Soviet Union originated in dissimulation and secrecy set it apart from Western conceptions of private life that were rooted in a different set of values and background practices.

This rather bleak vision of Soviet collectivism as a site of mutual surveillance and self-policing is predicated upon the Foucauldian perspective that places too much emphasis on techniques of domination and control and does not leave room for studying autonomy and ethical freedom (Laidlaw 2002: 321). This is why Kharkhordin's analysis of the Soviet Union's discursive order fails to explain the popularity of collective forms among rank-and-file workers (Alasheev 1995; Vladimirova 2006). Critics also note that his reliance on prescriptive sources sheds only limited light on the transformation of social control during the era of the thaw and overlooks the spaces for individual autonomy that opened up in the wake of the post-Stalin transition (Unfried 2001; Platt and Nathans 2011: 310). Although personal life in the late Soviet era was 'neither completely "private" not fully autonomous', it nevertheless allowed ordinary Soviet citizens to develop alternative ideas and values and dissociate their actions from officially sanctioned expressions and discourses (Platt and Nathans 2011: 311).

In the era of the thaw, the state's interventions in the sphere of morality were aimed at strengthening the 'spiritual needs' (*dukhovnie potrebnosti*) of Soviet citizens. To reinvigorate moral incentives, the state launched a series of campaigns promoting family and workplace morality and opposing drinking and 'hooliganism'. The codified standard of ethical behaviour – the *Moral Code of the Builder of Communism* – was adopted at the Party Congress of 1961. But discrepancies and concomitant tensions between institutional morality and individual behaviour became increasingly palpable in the post-1956 era. This gap became significant when various groups of dissenters emerged among the 'generation of the sixties' (Shatz 1980; Bergman 1992; Nathans 2007) and the rise of *samizdat* publications, that is, unauthorized reproductions of censored and underground publications (Komaromi 2012). However, the discrepancy between the official discourse of the state and private life was not necessarily expressed in explicit criticisms or anti-Soviet attitudes; rather, this disjuncture was visible in a growing multiplicity of attitudes and behaviour that diverged from the officially sanctioned ethical standards, as evidenced in attitudes to divorce (Field 1998) or in intellectual diversity in the humanities and social sciences (Firsov 2008). Yet the state still set the limits to this growing plurality of views and beliefs. Platt and Nathans suggest there was an implicit social contract according to which the regime tolerated a degree of autonomy in private life for the sake of social stability. They call such autonomy 'imaginary', as it was granted on the condition that people would refrain from open political dissent (ibid.: 319). Millar (1985) also suggests the existence of a social contract during the Brezhnev epoch. According to this tacit agreement, the regime tolerated the expansion of small-scale private economic activities, networks of informal exchange and even petty theft and the personal use of government property. Drawing an analogy with the Big Deal proposed by Vera Dunham, Millar calls the social contract of late socialism a 'Little Deal' and argues that it partly enabled the regime to offset the inefficiency and mal-distribution of the Soviet retail system and ensure a more equal distribution of real consumption.

The rise of consumerist aspirations and acquisitiveness in mature socialism went hand in hand with increases in the standard of living and was partially espoused by the authorities. Khrushchev's leadership brought popular prosperity to the centre stage of domestic policies in delivering the promise to increase material well-being and in stressing the link between material abundance and communism. In contrast to the more exclusive model of Stalin-era consumption, the mass construction of individual housing and the mass production of consumer goods in the Khrushchev era targeted the majority of the Soviet population. Khrushchev's successor,

Leonid Brezhnev, took up the same political commitment to prosperity by declaring his intention to improve the living standards of the toiling masses (Gurova 2006; Chernyshova 2013; Vihavainen and Bogdanova 2015).

However, the open orientation towards consumption was never free from contradictions. On the one hand, the Party legitimized aspirations for a better material life and linked material well-being to notions of modernity and progress. On the other hand, Soviet propaganda depicted the dangers of consumption and materialist excesses associated with philistine mentality and immorality (Chernyshova 2013). In order to control rising consumer expectations, officials strove to redefine the socialist norms of consumption. The Soviet media propagated patterns of proper consumerism based on the rational needs of 'cultured', quality-seeking consumers and expected Soviet citizens to avoid over-indulgence and unhealthy preoccupations with things – so-called *veshchism*. Thus, Soviet shoppers received mixed signals from the authorities in relation to consumption and material abundance.

However, it was not only contradictory signals that multiplied the ambivalences of late socialism and questioned the publicly sanctioned moral order. In addition, the official discourse of the late Soviet era dramatically lost its force and its capacity to influence people's minds. According to Yurchak (2006), the official public language – the Soviet 'authoritative discourse' – became increasingly hollowed out from within and excessively ritualized. Yurchak argues that this ideological hollowness was a key condition that made the collapse of socialism possible 'without making it anticipated'. He contends that the last Soviet generation constructed alternative social realities on the margins of official social spaces, living outside or beyond (*vnye*) the Soviet official discourse. Without intending to undermine the existing order, the last Soviet generation in fact created the conditions for the discursive shift and the collapse of the Soviet Union by simply living *vnye* and being indifferent to the semantic content of the official discourse. *Stiob* – a form of deflationary irony – allowed Soviet citizens to take up positions beyond the Soviet discursive order without articulating any political or social concerns.

Among numerous critics of Yurchak's 'postmodern' interpretation, Platt and Nathans (2011) question the resolutely apolitical character of alternative spheres of meaning that thrive on the margins of official discourses. They criticize Yurchak for taking the political indifference of 'normal people' at its face value and representing their apolitical attitudes as being normal and effortless. For Platt and Nathans, the lack of political meanings was not natural but rather conscious, representing a self-restrained attempt to align with the tacit agreements imposed by the regime in exchange for the ability to create zones of individual autonomy. When the

Soviet Union collapsed, the state-initiated reforms released the restrained political potential concealed within the zones of autonomy that had comprised 'the imaginary private sphere' of the late Soviet era.

In her critical reflections on Yurchak's book, Kormina (2015) notes that the author misconstrued the 'authoritative discourse' of late socialism by representing it as a monolithic and fixed entity. Kormina draws attention to the fact that Soviet religious policies and the rise of ethnic nationalism created other versions of public discourse that are overlooked in Yurchak's book, which focuses on a rather specific category of 'normal people', namely the young and educated technical intelligentsia from Leningrad. In the following section, I will outline this other dimension of the official Soviet discourse by delineating the contours of the Soviet secular project and discussing its far-reaching social and political effects.

Soviet Secularism and the post-Soviet 'Religious Revival'

The Bolsheviks' anti-religious politics drastically reshaped the boundary between religious and secular in Russia. Drawing upon Marxist teachings, Soviet rulers viewed religion as an ideological tool obscuring and facilitating social exploitation and therefore to be eradicated in the new classless society. Besides, the builders of socialism criticized religion as a force of inter-communal strife and division. In her study of atheist propaganda in the Volga region, Luehrmann (2011: 31) demonstrates that Soviet-era atheists sought to replace the religious fragmentation of local communities with a state-centred vision that followed the logic of 'the political theology of the sovereign'. As religion had long served as a marker of communal identity in the Russian Empire, the Soviet atheists equated religion with the social boundaries that prevented local communities of Mari, Tatar and Russians from merging into 'a union-wide public of strangers' (ibid.: 48). Ultimately, 'religion as cohesion' had to be replaced with a system of newly invented Soviet rituals stripped of any reference to non-human forces.

Soviet rituals were mainly seen as a form of political socialization and a means of increasing group solidarity (Lane 1981). The first Soviet rituals were invented and put in place already in the early years of the revolution, their aim being to replace the major Orthodox rituals with secular analogues such as 'Komsomol Christmas' and 'Komsomol Easter'. The invention of rituals reached its peak in the 1960s, when the renewed campaign for secular festivals was launched as part of Khrushchev's anti-religious crusade. The newly established Institute of Scientific Atheism, a branch of the Soviet Academy of Science, conducted a series of ethnographic and sociological surveys in order to assess the level of religiosity on the ground. The survey results showed that the regime's atheist propaganda was failing to reach its objectives, as the numbers of baptized Soviet citizens who attended churches and venerated icons remained alarmingly high (Smolkin 2009). Since then, a number of new rituals had been invented and put into practice all over the Soviet Union. Cultural workers or *metodists* were put in charge of Soviet cultural management in the form of republican and local commissions (Luehrmann 2011). The *metodists,* who were put in charge of creating rituals, wrote the scripts for future events, selected the music and poetry, created the name of the ritual and gave it a date in the calendar. If a newly created ritual was approved by the local commission, it was rehearsed, discussed again and then introduced on a republic-wide scale. As a result, a plethora of Soviet rituals emerged in the 1960s celebrating the major events of the individual life-cycle and public events such as initiation into social or political collectives (e.g. Komsomol), obtaining a passport, induction into the armed forces, initiation into the working class, *subbotniks*[10], and military-patriotic rituals such as Victory Day or the Day of the Soviet Army and Navy (Lane 1981).

As for the age-old annual holidays embedded in particular religious traditions, Soviet cultural workers strove to turn religious holidays into 'folk customs' belonging to a particular ethnic 'culture' but not to a religion (e.g. Latvian *Ligo*, Ukrainian and Belorussian *Ivan Kupala*, the Tatar festival of *Sabantui,* the Mari *Agavajrem*, etc.). Through such secular adaptations of seasonal celebrations, atheist activists sought to separate potentially progressive ethnic 'culture' from harmful and backward 'religion'. Paganism, being recast as a folk tradition, therefore occupied a special place in the hierarchy of cultures, as it was regarded as a less harmful vestige of a more democratic past compared to the coming of a more oppressive Christianity and Islam (Luehrmann 2011: 47).

Such efforts to eliminate religious symbolism and turn it into a secular concept of 'culture' have had far-reaching effects. From the mid-1950s, religion was removed into the public domain of museums and integrated into the wider discourse of national culture (Kormina and Shtyrkov 2015). This secularized version of religion was also introduced into the system of Soviet education, being inserted into the framework of Marxism-Leninism and suffused with patriotic rhetoric. Moreover, religion as a cultural heritage was enthusiastically supported by some Soviet intellectuals, who voiced their concerns about the decaying churches that had come to symbolize the vanishing pages of Russia's great national history. This wave of paradoxical 'Soviet nostalgia for religious life and especially for the great Orthodox culture' was transformed into a vast social movement for the preservation of

---

[10] *Subbotnik* is a voluntary-compulsory community workday on a Saturday.

historical monuments. The bulk of such monuments were Orthodox churches located in the remote north-west regions that had strong associations with the pre-modern past and surviving folk traditions (ibid.: 33).

The rise of interest in Russia's national cultural heritage in the late Soviet period paved the way for the current 'religious revival' in the aftermath of *perestroika*. Kormina and Shtyrkov argue that the numerous grassroots initiatives to restore church buildings that mushroomed in the early years of the transition were primarily motivated by the same impulse to preserve the 'authentic' pre-modern past, rather than stemming from religious motivations as such. Not uncommonly the enthusiasts of the 'religious revival' did not exhibit any particular religious commitments whatever, though they might have developed them further through participation in the liturgical life of the churches they had restored (see also Tocheva 2011).

Kormina and Shtyrkov's study echoes Luehrmann's idea that the post-Soviet religious resurgence occurred in continuity with the principles of Soviet secular training. For Luehrmann, such continuities – or 'elective affinities' – between secular and religious forms are predicated upon the argument that 'the religious and secular spheres are not governed by fundamentally different ethics or rationalities, but intersect in the lives of individuals and communities' (Luehrmann 2011: 218). In her study, she illustrates how the complementarity of secular and religious forms survived fairly intact under socialism. Normally atheist propaganda targeted the young and middle-aged, but tolerated even intensive religious practices among the older age groups. As a result, it was not unknown for some Soviet citizens to turn to religion after retirement without being stigmatized, and many devoted atheists underwent the same transition in the post-Soviet years (ibid.: 202-10).

While the mainstream narrative proposes to see religion and secularism as two different domains, Luehrmann argues that there is a 'constant back-and-forth between the dynamics of secularization and theologization' (ibid.: 16). She reframes the dynamics of the post-Soviet 'religious revival' as a process of 'recycling', arguing that various post-Soviet religious actors have utilized the didactic approaches of Soviet atheism, sometimes seeking 'to emulate and recreate Soviet educational networks', and sometimes keeping 'a tension-ridden distance' from them (ibid.: 218).

Building a Class-Based Society: Multiple Moralities after Socialism

Jarrett Zigon (2011) addresses post-communist transformations through the concept of 'moral breakdown', positing a radical problematization of previously unreflected practices and discourses. In the previous sections of this chapter, I have shown that in the period of mature socialism the Soviet regime had not completely precluded the existence of alternative values and meanings, but had striven to seal and encapsulate them within the sphere of the individual's private life. After the state gave up its control over the realm of values, this led to an explosion of moral debates and the emergence of competing moral conceptualizations, both secular and religious. In this section, I will explore the link between the struggles over competing moral values and the process of class-making. In other words, I will explain which conceptions of social justice and moral worth accompanied the processes of marketization and to what extent they have been contested by those groups whose life chances were substantially limited by the emerging inequalities caused by the market reforms.

The decade of rapid and uncertain change in the 1990s, with its sharp social polarizations, economic instability and criminalization of everyday life, provoked a general perception of the market transition as one of moral confusion and decay (Ries 2002). Manifestations of moral breakdown were numerous and difficult to ignore. They included 'growing socioeconomic disparities, the plight of lower-income people, the intrusion of socially deviant activities such as graffiti and drunkenness into public space, piles of trash and other refuse, the lack of public decorum, environmental degradation, and political and financial malfeasance' (Caldwell 2011: 61). While media reports decried the spirit of cynicism and moral degradation that was infiltrating the social and moral fabric of the new Russia, masses of ordinary people tried to make sense of ongoing structural changes by endowing money with destructive agency and blaming it for devastating effects and breaches of social relations (Ries 2002). Drawing upon Bloch's distinction (1973) between long-term and short-term morality, Ries argues that the major moral conflicts of the transitional era would be better described in terms of an inability to find some way of reconciling the two dimensions of social life: the long-term morality of collective values, and short-term considerations of making profit. In this conflict between morality and the market, Soviet ideologies about the honour of work, the evil of speculation and the fetishistic power of money have been persistently evoked in making moral claims against money and its potential to corrupt the social fabric. The mystification and demonization of money as 'an agent of spiritual and social corruption' went hand in hand with the paradoxical romanticizing of street mafias, perceived as new providers of social and moral order and a substitute for the weak state that had gradually withdrawn from its social obligations by cutting back on basic social entitlements (ibid.).

The emergence of the middle, entrepreneurial and business classes created new social inequalities and led to radical rearrangements of gender roles and identities. The ideals of appropriate masculinity and femininity have been entangled in new configurations of power and the consolidation of the 'bourgeois' values of the incipient middle class, 'defined through possession of resources, opportunities of income, and mode of consumption' (Gapova 2002: 658). Restructurings of the labour market led to the re-domestification of women and their displacement from public life into the household (cf. Pine 2002 on Poland). The new conceptions of masculinity were redefined in terms of access to material resources and a man's responsibility to provide for his family (Gapova 2002; Gal and Kligman 2012). Capitalism legitimized male dominance, for the market economy was gendered as an exclusively masculine project built upon cultural models of successful masculinity (Yurchak 2002; Yusupova 2016). Yet the emergence of new discourses that advocated male superiority coexisted with Soviet imperatives regarding female employment and the practical necessity of earning a living that forced many women to participate in wage work and endure the double burden of work and domestic duties (Ashwin 2006).

Gender rearrangements reflected one aspect of the newly emerging regime of value underlying the class-based society and market economy. A few works on postsocialism shed light on how the new system of reward and social inequalities have been legitimized in the Central and Eastern European (CEE) countries and the former Soviet Union. They show that symbolic constructions of the past played a significant role in both shaping and contesting the emerging system of new inequalities. Gapova (2002) argues that post-1991 democratization projects in Belorussia and the rise of nationalism are better conceptualized though the lens of class, since national issues were not just an expression of national feelings but served as vehicles articulating certain group (class) interests. She points out that the project of 'Belorussian independence' was rooted in the language of market values and aspirations to embrace a Western-type of prosperity articulated through a commitment to such 'noble' values as freedom, democracy and human rights. In contrast to the independence project, the post-communist elites in Belorussia promoted a nationalist project based on Soviet patriotism that articulated and mobilized the social discontent of those 'have-nots who lost more than they found in the brave new world' (ibid.: 652). The link between the rise of national sentiments and class formation has been explored by Kalb (2011) and Kesküla (2015) in relation to other parts of Eastern Europe.

Along with projects promoting a national identity, consumption represented another venue in which to display and practice social distinctions. The creation of class subjectivities by means of consumption has been well-documented in other parts of the world. It was noticed that social memories of the past added specificity to post-Soviet practices of consumption. According to Rivkin-Fish (2009: 82), aspiring middle-class Russians claimed their entitlement to material privilege by positioning themselves within the 'narrative of long-standing victimization of the intelligentsia by the Soviet state'. By asserting their belonging to the imagined community of the 'intelligentsia', educated Russians invoked many of the moral values that underlay the symbolic privileges and authority of the Soviet cultural elite, including the values of 'culturedness', high education, honesty and moral righteousness. This type of class genealogy enabled educated Russians to distinguish themselves from the supposedly uneducated and apathetic masses of the working classes on the one hand, and the stereotypical 'new Russians' on the other. Paradoxically, however, many of those educated Russians who justified practices of exclusion and social inequalities were themselves marginalized from the benefits of market reforms and experienced material losses because of marketization (see also Patico 2008). Rivkin-Fish argues that associating themselves with the values of the cultured intelligentsia helped educated but impoverished Russians to partially offset the dispossession they experienced in the market economy.

The entrepreneurial class was symbolically represented by the figure of the new Russian man – the butt of endless jokes, gossip and scandal. In jokes and stereotypical images, the Russian nouveaux riches are shown as physically fit men, with shaved skulls, dressed in crimson suits, wearing massive gold neck-chains or gold crosses on their chests, driving expensive cars and being accompanied by women easily available for sex (Oushakine 2000). Such clichéd images attributed vulgarity and bad taste to the Russian nouveaux riches, as was evident from their mindless consumption and excessive manifestations of wealth. In other words, the New Rich men in Russia had 'money without culture' and experienced problems in obtaining cultural refinement (Sampson 1994). In his study of 'symbolic struggles' among the Hungarian and Romanian nouveaux riches in the early years of the transition, Sampson treats the processes of acquiring cultural capital by the new entrepreneurial elites as an essential part of class formation. As cultural refinement or its absence connoted different ideologies of wealth, the 'symbolic struggles' between the old and new elites could better be described as a cultural revolution that resulted in a profound restructuring of cultural principles and practices. In Russia, the new ideology and aesthetics of success, manifested in the flamboyant lifestyles and conspicuous consumption of the new Russians, significantly lacked novelty of meaning (i.e. quality), representing rather the 'quantitative intensification' of former objects and status symbols, such as golden jewellery or cars (Oushakine 2000). Given the focus on the 1990s, these studies reflect on the initial period of class formation in the wake of the market reforms. More recent research on symbolic struggles and class identities among the Russian elite, by contrast, reveals more variegated cultural representations of the entrepreneurial class that came to displace the notorious image of the businessmen as a criminal, firmly associated with the epoch of 'wild' capitalism in the 1990s (Cohen 2013; Salmenniemi 2016).

Conclusion

This chapter has aimed to provide the essential context of Russia's moral background with a focus on both religious and secular moral discourses and practices. The chapter traces the major dynamics and developments of institutional morality that were articulated by key religious and secular institutions in Russia, whether by the Orthodox Church or the Soviet state. Both institutions strove to define what should be considered paramount values. Institutional moralities were not absolute, but rather were constantly negotiated and contested by social actors reinterpreting the Russian Orthodox Church's moral theologies or the Soviet state's official ideologies. I also showed that institutions do not produce a single totalizing morality but include a range of moral positions and not uncommonly send mixed signals to their audiences. The fall of socialism in 1991 generated cultural change and gave rise to new values that underpinned the transition to a class-based society and a market economy. The new regime of value based on market principles of exchange claimed to be universal and natural. Its moral hegemony has been sustained and reinforced by those social actors who framed their actions in terms of resistance to socialism and sought to gain new privileges in the market-oriented society.

The link between morality and class-making is central to this book, as it allows us to see how individual moral dilemmas and the language of values interact with market constraints. In the ethnographic part of the book, to which I now turn, I will explain this link further by examining local meanings and practices among those actors who actively partake in accumulation and act within the different scales of value that are being inserted into multiple forms of social relationships.

Chapter 4
Smolensk and the Regional Economy: Mapping the Business Landscape

Compared to other Russian regions, Smolensk oblast ranks among the relatively poor peripheral provinces that cannot balance its budget without federal subsidies. In a 2015 report, Smolensk oblast came 62nd out of 85 Russian regions in its level of economic development, thus approaching the bottom of the table.[11] In contrast to regions that thrive on the basis of their natural resources, the Smolensk region does not possess any oil or gas reserves, nor has it been successful in attracting foreign investment, unlike the neighbouring Kaluga region, which accommodates a cluster of automotive industries, including such transnational car giants as Volkswagen and Skoda. Smolensk still bears the title of the 'Diamond Capital' thanks to the diamond-faceting industry that developed here from the 1960s. However, this industry has been severely weakened by international competition, and nowadays the Smolensk economy is reported to be heavily dependent on state defence contracts and transfers from the federal budget.

Another of Smolensk's titles, 'The Shield of Russia', points to the city's historical role in defending Russia's western boundaries. Although its location on border has meant it has incurred severe damage and losses in times of war, nowadays the region can capitalize on its advantageous geographical position as a trade and transport hub. In what follows, I aim to provide an overview of the regional economy and state policies in relation to the private sector and thus provide an entry into understanding the wider constellations of the political, economic and civic structures that have a bearing on business activities in the region. To do this, I will trace the major economic transformations in the province over the last century with a particular focus on post-Soviet developments.

---

[11] https://riarating.ru/infografika/20160615/630026367.html (accessed 11 March 2020).

Pre-Revolutionary Years and the Soviet History of Smolensk

Smolensk, with a population of circa 330,000, is located on Russia's western border, 360 kilometres west-southwest of Moscow. It is one of the oldest Russian cities, its history dating back to the ninth century. It was caught up in political struggles with Lithuania and Poland in the fourteenth to seventeenth centuries, occasionally being incorporated into its powerful western neighbour, the Grand Duchy of Lithuania, and being obliged to adopt Magdeburg Law because of that incorporation. Roman Catholicism was propagated in this period, and the religious landscape of the city continues to be shaped by diverse churches and movements, although here, as elsewhere in the country, the Orthodox Church strives to play a leading role as a national religion for all Russians.

In tsarist Russia, Smolensk province remained largely agrarian and, like most central Russian regions in the nineteenth century, it faced overpopulation and a growing shortage of agricultural lands. As a result, over sixty thousand peasants left the region at the turn of the twentieth century in search of new arable lands in sparsely populated Siberian regions (Golichev et al. 2013: 52-8). In Smolensk province, the number of individual smallholders who held enclosed lands outside the commune (*khutora*) was one of the highest among the neighbouring regions, and their number continued to grow until 1928, when the Soviet state introduced collectivization (ibid.: 81). By 1937, 97 percent of peasant households had been turned into collective farms or *kolkhozy*, with 98,000 peasant households being reorganized into two thousand settlements (ibid.: 83). The early Soviet history of the region is well-documented due to the classic work of Merle Fainsod (1958), an American sovietologist whose research draws on the Smolensk party archive, which had been captured by the Germans during World War II.

Before the revolution, the major enterprise in Smolensk province was a cotton factory that accounted for a quarter of the region's industrial output (Golichev et al. 2013: 86). During the first decades of Soviet industrialization, over three hundred new industrial enterprises were built in the region. One of the largest projects was the Smolensk linen factory. The story of its heroic construction, which depicted the enthusiasm and self-sacrifice of two thousand workers, was perpetuated in the official Soviet canon (Smirnov 1968). Young people from Smolensk took part in labour mobilizations outside the region and joined the biggest construction sites in Ukraine and Kazakhstan, and at Magnitogorsk, Chelyabinsk, Kuznetsk and Komsomolsk-on-Amur.

Plate 1. The shopping mall 'Galaktika'.

The 1930s opened up a golden age of large industrial enterprises being developed within the framework of central planning. The city's specializations included aircraft and instrument engineering, power-generation, textiles, diamond-faceting and the production of construction materials. Major changes began in the second half of the 1980s, when 'perestroika' introduced the elements of a market economy. After 1991, most state-owned enterprises were privatized. Many factories have closed entirely, while the survivors have undergone massive layoffs, declines in production and the comprehensive degeneration of working conditions. The aircraft plant and several large manufacturers producing machines and equipment for the aircraft and military industries went into decline in the 1990s, but since the early 2000s they have bounced back again due to increased state procurement and the growing demand for military equipment. The several garment factories continued to operate but were not particularly viable. The linen industry could not survive global competition, and the city's linen factory was closed in 2005. After its closure, the factory was turned into a shopping mall, a transformation that represented a common aspect of the transition in Russia, namely rapid expansion of the sphere of exchange at the expense of production (Burawoy 2001). Various local actors took up trade in the 1990s. In the next section, I will briefly examine the rise of petty trade in Smolensk, drawing on the accounts and personal histories of those who ventured to dive into the new world of mercantile capitalism.

The 'Wild' 1990s: Petty Trading, Criminal Gangs and Quick Fortunes

The austere environment of the 1990s prompted many Smolensk urban dwellers to abandon state employment and enter the realm of petty commerce. Local 'shuttlers' or itinerant traders (*chelnoky*) travelled abroad to nearby countries like Poland, Romania or Belorussia to buy consumer goods there and sell them on street corners or in open-air markets back in Smolensk. For the most part, these transfers included simple consumer items like clothes, homeware, cigarettes and electronic goods, but other 'shuttlers', mainly men, delivered cars to the local market by travelling abroad, purchasing a car there, and then driving it home and selling it in the market.

As elsewhere in Russia, some entered trade because of absolute necessity and the lack of other job opportunities, while others were attracted by the potential to make a profit (Humphrey 2002: 70). Dina, the daughter of a *kolkhoz* chairman, started to travel to Poland in the mid-1990s to supply her own shop in Smolensk with baby wares. In her recollections, the 1990s features as a golden age of trade, a time of quick returns and big profits. At the time the demand for baby commodities in the domestic market was so high that it took Dina just a couple of days to sell off a batch of goods brought from Poland. The only constraint that stood in the way of her rapid accumulation was a lack of capital and the limited capacities of her car, in which Dina, accompanied by her husband, made trips to Poland. Later the couple set up a small manufacturing plant to produce baby wares on the spot. Eventually, Dina developed her own brand of baby clothes and moved into wholesale.

Plate 2. Kolkhoz market, the biggest open-air market in Smolensk.

Along with successful stories of accumulation, many more traders failed in business and had to return to wage employment. This was particularly the case for those who came from less privileged social and economic backgrounds than Dina and who could not count on the skills, networks or capital resources of their parents. Masha, a machine operator and a mother of three, turned to petty trade because she was unable to live on her meagre salary from the state garment-manufacturer. She started travelling to Romania, while her husband and two teenage sons helped her by selling what she brought back in the local open-air markets in Smolensk. After five years working as a shuttler, Masha closed her business because she could not afford to pay dues in return for protection, known in Russian slang as a 'roof' (*krysha*). As a result, she was pushed out of the market by a gang of Azeri criminals who controlled private commerce in her market area. In contrast to Masha, Dina never had to deal with the local criminal gangs that proliferated in the 1990s and that brought most businesses under their control, especially in trade (Volkov 2002). This was because Dina's husband worked as a musician at a restaurant frequented by a powerful city gang. The gang members treated Dina's husband as 'their' musician, a relationship that provided Dina with a degree of protection. What is more important, Dina was acquainted with the leader of this criminal group, since they both came from the same small town and used to play together in early childhood. This personal connection with a powerful criminal fraternity ensured that Dina and her husband were immune to their violence, in contrast to the majority of ordinary traders like Masha.

In some cases, criminal gangs recruited male traders to 'collect the tribute' from other business operators in return for protection. One of them was Sergey, a successful and adventurous wholesaler and the owner of several kiosks in the city during the 1990s. One gang choose him to assist them in collecting payments because, as a former athlete, he was physically fit and thus well suited to participating in organized violence. In his passionate account of his involvement in 'violent entrepreneurship' (Volkov 2002), Sergey conveyed an image of the 'honest bandit' (Ries 2002) who had helped petty traders settle disputes and enforce contracts, punishing and intimidating violators only after thorough investigation. Sergey considered himself lucky because the gang eventually allowed him to quit racketeering since his criminal duties took up all his time and did not leave him any to take care of his own kiosks.

From the 2000s, the state regained monopolistic control over organized violence, and the power of organized criminal groups began to wane. The majority of violence-managing agencies and militant gangs disappeared from public spaces and moved into the underworld or successfully adapted to the new order by cooperating and merging with the state apparatus to varying extents (Stephenson 2015). But even in the late Putin era, ordinary citizens in Smolensk occasionally resorted to the protection and enforcement services provided by criminal gangs. For example, one machine operator, who was employed in a private garment factory, confessed that several years ago she had appealed to a criminal gang, and her problem, which she preferred not to reveal, was successfully resolved.

At the time of my fieldwork in 2015-16, a number of business owners reckoned that the state security services had replaced these mafias, pointing out that their agents acted in even more predatory ways than the street bandits, who at least had a code of honour and saw themselves as upholding social justice. As rumour has it, any well-functioning and viable business could be taken over by the Federal Security Service officers, given Putin's presidency's enormous support of them. It is hard to say to what extent such hostile takeovers posed a real threat to the small-scale businesses in Smolensk since none of my interlocutors had first-hand experience of this sort, but the rumours about the predatory behaviour of the secret services were pervasive in the business milieu, and the issue was also widely discussed in the regional and national media throughout the 2010s.[12]

In the collective memories of many Russians, the 1990s are widely portrayed in terms of the rupture of the earlier structures, lifestyles and identities that had created uncertainties and wrought havoc in people's lives. In the stories of the first cohort of business people, those who started their ventures in the 'wild' 1990s (*likhie devjanostye*), uncertainty was interpreted in two ways. On the one hand, it was equated with a hostile environment, a pervasive mafia and an inadequate business infrastructure that worked against small-scale capitalism. On the other hand, the lack of protection and regulation opened unprecedented opportunities to get rich for those who could take risks in those times of adventure capitalism and react immediately to the changing circumstances. The subsequent cohort of entrepreneurs, those who started their businesses under Putin's presidency, tend to see themselves as creating proper modern enterprises within a more 'civilized' institutional framework, while many of their predecessors from the 1990s and early 2000s were frowned upon as being stuck in scenarios of 'wild' capitalism that had nothing to do with genuine business rationality and efficiency. The new cohort of entrepreneurs, especially the young, were more willing to educate themselves on business matters, to learn from the gurus of self-help literature and to work on their personalities, driven by a desire eventually to become full-fledged subjects of global capitalist modernity. This 'symbolic struggle' between the older and younger generations of private entrepreneurs[13] took the form of a certain conflict over values that problematized the moral framework of doing 'wild' business – risky, aggressive, ruthless, criminal and mafia-like, and predicated on alliances with state functionaries and extensive bribery (cf. Sampson 1994; Cohen 2013). In the next chapter, I will detail this emergent moral framework with its focus on economic efficiency and personal talent and discuss the new dilemmas and questions that were spawned by its implementation in Russia.

The next section will outline the state's measures in support of entrepreneurship. I will review the government's policies and existing programmes of support while simultaneously keeping an eye on the micro-level and discussing more mundane forms of the engagement of state actors with local entrepreneurs.

---

[12] For more details of corporate raiding and property redistribution in Russia during the 2000s, see Sakwa 2011, Osipian 2012 or Rochlitz 2014.

[13] I attribute this clash in values to the generational divide in a very loose manner since the supporters and opponents of each moral framework could be found in both cohorts.

State Practices and Policies in Relation to Small Businesses

At the official level, the growth of small private enterprises is declared to be a priority of Russian national policies. To date, the small and medium-size private sector in Russia comprises 21 per cent of the economy, less than in the advanced economies.[14] The overall number of active small and medium-size businesses in the region was approximately 23,300 in 2015. Of these, 13,700 were individual entrepreneurs, that is, did not form a corporate body, and the remaining 9,600 were companies.[15] The majority of small enterprises were engaged in trade, public catering, real-estate services, construction and manufacturing (see Table).[16]

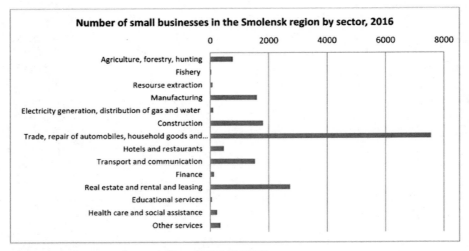

Source: Smolenskstat, Key performance indicators for 2016, 23.06.2017
http://sml.gks.ru/wps/wcm/connect/rosstat_ts/sml/ru/statistics/enterprises/small_and_medium_enterprises/

Table. Number of small businesses in the Smolensk region by sector, 2016.

---

[14] http://www.gks.ru/wps/wcm/connect/rosstat_main/rosstat/ru/statistics/accounts/ (accessed 25 July 2020).

[15] In Russia, four types of companies are recognized legally and organizationally: the limited liability company (OOO), the cooperative limited liability company (TOO), the closed joint-stock company (ZAO) and the open joint-stock company (OAO). The new legal category of self-employed was introduced in Russia in 2017. The definition of it status and taxation are still pretty much work in progress, being subject to legal change, and so far the number of self-employed have not been represented in the official statistics.

[16] *Smolenksstat*, the regional branch of the state-run statistical agency, *Rosstat*: Available online, http://sml.gks.ru/wps/wcm/connect/rosstat_ts/sml/ru/census_and_researching/researching/statistic_researching/ (accessed 25 July 2020).

In the 2000s, the Smolensk municipality launched a programme aimed to promote a wide range of entrepreneurial activities. Initially this government programme targeted small businesses from all sectors, providing them with direct support in the form of cash grants; no proper accountability was required. As a result, many unscrupulous recipients claimed that they were going to start a business but instead used a cash grant to purchase a private car or go on a vacation. Others created shell firms just to be able to receive a subsidy. To prevent this misuse of public funds, the government tightened its control over subsidies and limited their support to the production and farming sectors, thus excluding a vast majority of businesses in trade and services from government assistance. Ever since then any candidate applying for a subsidy has had to provide a detailed business plan and is held accountable for its implementation. Also the number of cash grants fell significantly in favour of indirect incentives. The revised programme partially reimbursed a firm's expenditure on purchasing equipment or acquiring electricity. Besides this, small businesses could obtain a loan at 8% interest for a maximum of three years. Given that the average interest rate for business loans amounted to 28%, the state loans were more affordable than a standard bank credit. While many regarded banks' interest rates as too high, some businesses sought alternatives to expensive banking services by resorting to subterfuges, such as taking out consumer credit or mortgages and using this money for business purposes, or simply borrowing money from friends and relatives.

    The amount of paperwork and the requirement to submit a business plan dissuaded many from applying for a subsidy. The very concept of a business plan was unfamiliar to farmers engaged in small-scale agricultural businesses, and they were appalled at the prospect of getting caught up in paperwork during the high season. Having friends or relatives who could assist in writing applications and reports could facilitate access to subsidies. A professor of economics at the local university helped his daughter write a business plan when she decided to apply for a subsidy. Whereas the professor treated the business plan as an essential step in starting up a business, his daughter was openly sceptical about this, saying that 'she merely kept everything needed in her head'. For her, a business plan was nothing more than an official requirement she had to comply with in order to receive a grant. After she had obtained the subsidy, her father again helped her in accounting for the money she spent.

    The requirements of the audit culture related to subsidies not only covered writing reports and business plans, it implied more intensive forms of checking among those businesses that received subsidies. Kristina, a former shop assistant, was among the first applicants to receive a cash grant of sixty thousand roubles when she set up her first pet shop. During the following year, in which she was held accountable for the grant money, her shop was checked numerous times by the monitoring agencies. Owing to this intensive checking, Kristina was constantly under stress, given the enormous number of regulations governing sales of pet goods. One such check found a violation and fined Kristina for selling drug products for pets without having a license to sell medicines. As a beginner, Kristina was unfamiliar with this requirement. Eventually, she was taken to court for this violation. She said that after going this hard experience she would never apply for a grant again. This concern, that accepting a subsidy would attract the unwanted attention of government agencies, increased the general reluctance to engage in such programmes. Even though Kristina could fulfil the terms of the programme, she felt immensely relieved when it ended and the state loosened its grip on her nascent business. The government grant of sixty thousand roubles was insignificant set against the loan of five hundred thousand roubles that she and her husband had taken out with a bank. Thus, in her case the subsidy was not a real incentive given the massive paperwork involved and the increased attention of the monitoring agencies.

It is not surprising that mature businesses were the main beneficiaries of the subsidy programme. Experienced in all the ins and outs of financial accounting and checking procedures, such companies had better chances of acquiring a government subsidy. Polina, a professional auditor, had acquired solid experience in accounting before setting up her own business. Unlike Kristina, who was a schoolteacher by training, Polina had no issues with writing business plans and financial reports. Besides, her extensive network of friends from business and public administration facilitated her negotiations with the monitoring agencies. Due to her extensive experience and connections, she was able to obtain two subsidies totalling 450,000 roubles. With this money, she reimbursed her expenditure on furniture and equipment that she had purchased for the new office of her advertising agency. Polina admitted that there was no urgent need for this injection of cash, since her growing company was doing well. Even so, she wanted to take advantage of the free money, given especially that providing financial statements and other related obligations was not a burden to her.

Since the mid-2010s, government policies have changed in favour of big business and the goal of attracting large investments in the region. In 2015, two industrial parks were established in Smolensk oblast that received enormous funding from the regional and federal budgets. It was announced that one of the parks would accommodate innovative enterprises producing composite materials, while the other would provide modern industrial facilities for a variety of industries.[17] Although at the time of my fieldwork the two projects only existed on paper, they were touted as highly promising undertakings with the potential eventually to bring prosperity to the region. In comparison to these grand projects, which were flagged because of their 'innovation' and 'technology', small-scale economic activities, concentrated overwhelmingly in the retail and service sectors, have been relegated to the background. As soon as 'investment support' (*investpodderzhka*) was proclaimed as a new priority, incentives for small businesses were reduced. With this shift in policies, the government aimed to promote industrialization and attract large-scale investments in the region.

This orientation in respect of industrial development coincided with a turn toward import-substitution polices nationally. These policies resulted from the political crisis following the annexation of Crimea and were aimed at reducing imports from Western countries. Although the sanctions mainly affected food imports, the Russian government implemented a wide range of import substitution policies aimed at modernizing the national industrial base. Overcoming Russia's dependence on high-tech products imported from the West was the most ambitious goal to achieve, as this demanded enormous investments on a long-term basis and a significant reorganization of domestic industry (Tolkachev and Teplyakov 2018). The Smolensk region lagged far behind other Russian regions in the development of high-value-added industries. According to the 2015 survey, which measured the innovation indexes of Russia's regions, Smolensk oblast ranked 56th out of 83 regions, with Moscow, Tatarstan and the neighbouring Kaluga region occupying the top three places (Gohberg 2017). The project of the two industrial estates mentioned above promised to boost the development of high-grade technologies in the region. However, for the most part local experts argued that innovations were extraneous to regional development. A professor of economic geography in Smolensk complained that local industries had been following the traditional path of development in neglecting technological innovation, so that their products could not compete with imported goods. For him, this lack of innovative ambition represented the major problem of regional development, inasmuch as it hampered modernization and did not allow the regional economy to benefit from Smolensk's favourable geographical position as a transportation hub linking Moscow with the rest of Europe.

In discussing these new policies and regional development generally with entrepreneurs, I was often told that, regardless of the local government's apparently good intentions, its projects were unlikely to come

---

[17] https://smolinvest.com/platforms/industrial-parks/safonovo/ (accessed 11 March 2020).

to fruition. The reason was endemic corruption. Many businessmen believed that the industrial parks had been created with the sole intention of laundering money. This profound distrust of the ruling class was reinforced by the mundane experience of interactions with state actors. The practice of bribery was reported as ubiquitous by many business-owners, although some sectors were exposed to it more than others. Extortion of money was common practice in the construction sector. When applying for a building permit, a construction firm was expected to pay a bribe to the building office in order to avoid red tape. Lev, the owner of a small construction firm, suffered continuously from payments being solicited by staff in the building office. Although he did not resist these approaches in practice, Lev felt humiliated having to pay 'those bastards' working in public offices. As a technocrat, he treated bribery as a serious deficiency in the system of governance and was supportive of those strong measures against corruption that had been implemented in some South Asian countries.

However, many business-people accepted the necessity of bribes in anticipation of acquiring political patronage. According to the logic of patronage, entrepreneurs did not just respond to the illegal soliciting of bribes but invested it in nourishing paternalistic ties with government authorities. However, although this was a quite common expectation, it was not shared unanimously, and some businesses openly rejected the idea of patronage. Elena, the owner of a firm providing legal support to businesses, witnessed a lot of entrepreneurs become disappointed with the lack of reciprocity they expected to receive on the part of state bureaucrats. She said that some of her clients had been giving bribes for years to customs or tax officials, counting on their assistance and advice. As long as businesses performed well, public officers were supportive of them, but when their clients faced any serious problems and expected their patrons to help, the latter often proved unwilling to cooperate. This taught Elena never to rely on bribes and inclined her to put her trust more in the law. Her rule of thumb was 'One should obey the law, do all paperwork properly, and not to give others a chance for nit-picking'.

Elena's decision to end informal exchanges with public officials and stick to the rule of law resulted from her suspicion of state actors and their readiness to stick to the tacit rules of paternalistic arrangements. At the same time, bribery was so deeply embedded in the broader norms of reciprocity that it was not easy to remove all informality from one's relationships with officials and stick entirely to the rule of law. Andrei's story illustrates this. Andrei ran a landscape firm that sold plants and offered landscape projects to private houses and dachas. When Andrei set up his business, he became acquainted with a public official whom he occasionally consulted about the intricate bureaucratic regulations regarding landscape projects. Andrei considered their relationship to be one of 'semi-friendship' (*poludruzhba*) and acknowledged it by giving small discounts to his 'semi-friend' when the latter bought plants from him. To Andrei, exchanging little favours in this way was a normal practice between friends. However, when the same official ordered a whole design project for his dacha, Andrei charged him the full price. He noticed that his client immediately became sad and looked extremely disappointed when he had to pay him. At this point it occurred to Andrei that actually his earlier practice of giving the official a discount had acted like a bribe and had been tacitly solicited in exchange for advice in business matters. Andrei realized that in asking for the full price for the design project, he had violated this tacit agreement, making him very anxious about any penalties that might follow from the monitoring agencies as a consequence. Luckily, this incident had no consequences for him, except that his special client made a complaint about one of the plants he had bought from Andrei and asked to exchange it or have his money returned. Andrei felt relieved that after this incident his 'semi-friend' never showed up at his shop again. Being an advocate of 'honest' and 'transparent' business models, Andrei nevertheless could not avoid a feeling of ambiguity that made it difficult for him to disentangle illicit practices from the accepted norms of reciprocity and friendship. The example of Andrei, who got caught up in the ambiguities of his friendship with the public official, like other local businessmen's expectations of political patronage, foreground the embedded aspects of informality, as is evident in the everyday social life of the state and private businesses (cf. Morris 2019). I will follow up the point about embeddedness further when discussing different levels of the informalization of work in the private sector.

Wages and Employment in the Private Sector

Given that this research mainly investigates small businesses with employees, this section will provide a brief overview of the local labour market and employment patterns in the private sector. Since the 1990s the private sector has been the main source of employment for a growing number of people (Clarke 1999). According to the 2015 Statistics Digest, small firms employed approximately 83,000 people in Smolensk oblast, or 16% of the working-age population of the region (Shunin 2015: 119).

As elsewhere in Russia, the flow of migrants from the former Soviet republics brings diversity to the local labour market. The highest proportions of migrants come to Smolensk from neighbouring Belorussia (4,527 in 2014), Ukraine (2,015), Uzbekistan (1,717), Tajikistan (770) and Moldova (705) (Shunin 2015: 29). Although there are no statistical reports on immigrant labour in Smolensk, my own observations indicate that migrants from the former Soviet republics occupy predominantly low-level jobs in trade and construction. Belarussian and Ukrainian traders bring goods such as clothing and food produced in their home countries and sell them at various trade fairs and in open-air markets. Belarussian construction workers are particularly valued in the local market, as they are seen as more skilful, reliable and disciplined than other ethnically defined migrants, especially those from Central Asia. The Central Asian traders reportedly control the biggest open-air market in the city and are known for their small trading ventures in fruit and vegetables.

The outflow of population from the region is primarily driven by the better prospects of work and pay in Moscow and St Petersburg. Between 2002 and 2010 the region lost more than fourteen thousand people (Golichev et al. 2013: 132). In 2014, 2,762 people left Smolensk oblast for Moscow, 3,585 for the Moscow region and 1,065 for St Petersburg (Shunin 2015: 31). In that year, the average monthly income in Smolensk was 21,821 roubles (ibid.: 47), less than half that in Moscow, where it averaged 54,504 roubles.[18]

However, regional out-migration was not linear but included repeat and return movements. Some former Smolensk residents returned to their home city, having lived and ''worked in Moscow for years. Acknowledging decent pay and better economic opportunities in the capital, they could not adjust themselves to the metropolitan lifestyle and the gigantic size of the city, which demanded long commutes to work and increased living costs. In the end, rent ate up a substantial proportion of working incomes in Moscow, while in Smolensk many had their own apartments. To settle in the region around Moscow so as to cut the cost of renting was a common strategy on the part of working migrants, but it too meant longer commutes to work, sometimes as long as three hours in each direction. As a result, some out-migrants opted to return to Smolensk, especially when they started their own families and it became more difficult to proceed with the same hectic lives when they had children.

Others chose to work in Moscow sporadically while keeping their residence and primary employment in their home city. Zakhar, an ambitious young lawyer, headed a department at a state institution in Smolensk, where he earned 13,500 roubles monthly. As this was a rather modest income, Zakhar supplemented his formal earnings in the public office by occasional jobs in Moscow as an organizer of wedding ceremonies. Entertaining guests for five hours brought Zakhar an extra 20,000 roubles, more than his

---

[18] https://www.gks.ru/free_doc/new_site/population/urov/urov_11sub.htm (accessed 11 March 2021).

monthly income in Smolensk. Zakhar kept this additional job a secret, thinking that it might tarnish his reputation as a lawyer. At the same time, the earnings from his casual job in Moscow were essential to his making a living in the provincial city, even though Zakhar had a senior position in the public office. The proximity to Moscow (it took five hours to travel by bus from Smolensk) and a network of wealthy friends in the capital allowed him to earn additional income without leaving his primary, respectable employment in the state sector.

As well as illustrating the striking gap between the poor periphery and the wealthy centre, Zakhar's story illustrates another feature of the Russian labour market, namely that the state sector generally offered a poor level of pay. Consequently, the private sector attracted many with promises of higher pay. However, informality has been a firm condition of this promise so long as higher salaries could be guaranteed because the work was unregistered. Although a few businesses proudly stated that they paid their workers 'white' (i.e. registered) wages, the overwhelming majority of small firms in Smolensk offered 'grey' forms of employment. The 'grey' jobs were regarded as a trade-off between informal ('black') and completely formal ('white') employment. While almost all employers claimed they would be happy to register their workers and pay them 'white' salaries, they complained about not being able to afford to pay social insurance contributions on earnings which amounted to approximately 40% of their salaries. For the 'grey' forms of employment, the formal, registered part of a salary normally represented the minimum wage[19], whereas the bulk of the salary went undeclared and might be several times higher than its registered element.[20]

According to local entrepreneurs, such semi-formal arrangements were beneficial to both employer and employee, since they significantly reduced the tax burden and resulted in higher incomes. The firm had to pay lower social insurance contributions and withhold 13% of income tax only from the registered part of the salary. Although 'grey' wages set the norms in the small-scale private sector, some employees worked completely informally, receiving their 'black' salaries in cash. This applied particularly to elderly workers who sought informal employment in order to qualify for receipt of full pension benefits. In many cases, a degree of informalization was negotiable with the employer, and the same employee could change her status several times while working in the same firm. As a rule, a newly hired

---

[19] In 2015, the monthly minimum wage in Smolensk was 5,965 roubles, or nearly ninety euros.

[20] The proportion of registered to unregistered salary in 'grey' schemes varied in every firm, but the registered part cannot be below the minimum wage.

employee would start to work informally and, after some months of probation, would be registered at the minimum wage, receiving the rest of her remuneration off the books (the 'grey' scheme). Casual and temporary workers were rarely registered at all, whereas a highly skilled, permanent, respected worker could be rewarded with 'white' employment, which served as an incentive to work in a firm. Thus, the gradations of informality often reflected the particular status of the worker, fixing his or her positionality within the hierarchies of power and authority in the workplace.

Dualist or legalist perspectives on informality foreground the division between legal–formal and illegal–informal economic activities. More anthropologically inclined perspectives complicate this view by demonstrating the difficulties involved in untangling the formal from the informal in everyday life (Morris 2019: 13-14). These difficulties multiply when one realizes that the state usually plays an active role in facilitating and enabling informal economic activities by conniving at them and turning a blind eye to them (ibid.: 16). 'Grey' and 'black' wages are a typical example of an open secret, given how ubiquitous and widespread these practices are throughout the country. Yet, some business-owners reported that they were regularly called into the tax office to explain 'why your workers are paid so low'. The tax officers were well aware that the minimum wage comprised only a part of the real earnings, and therefore their question was not about low salaries as such; rather, it signalled the authorities' concerns about illicit practices of employment, and they urged such firms to switch from 'grey' to 'white' wages. Dina, the owner of the small garment factory mentioned earlier, became angry every time she had to pay a visit to the tax office and face interrogation about only paying her workers the minimum wage. The reason she got angry lay in the mixed signals the state's regulatory bodies sent to small businesses. For the most part, the state tolerated the payment of 'grey' and 'black' wages in the private sector and turned a blind eye to it. The local authorities shared an understanding of the precarious economic conditions in which many small firms operated, and informal employment was seen as a coping strategy enabling a large number of small enterprises to stay afloat. However, once in a while the state activated its control function in order to reduce the level of informality. It was apparent that Dina was not afraid of being fined or prosecuted for paying her workers off the books to top up the minimum wage. Seeking advice, Dina even consulted the prosecutor on this issue and was advised to file a complaint against the tax office if they persisted in their request that she increase the proportion of formal earnings. Paradoxically, the prosecutor described the actions of the tax office as illicit, while Dina's intention to continue paying 'grey' wages was tacitly acknowledged. This example illustrates how tacit agreements with local state actors and their ambiguous roles complicate the legal perspective on informality.

It was more than just financial benefits that business-owners derived from informal employment. Admittedly, it was easier for the employer to sack a worker who had no contract. The Russian labour laws were described by many business-owners as over-protective and as giving too much power to the worker. For example, Dina, mentioned above, admitted that she was afraid of her workers because the existing labour regulations ultimately took their side. 'They are always right, while I am always wrong', she said, summing up the essence of the labour laws. In particular, she was concerned by the law that prohibited the dismissal of pregnant female workers. Dina blamed some of her pregnant workers for taking advantage of this law to refuse to do their jobs, being aware that Dina cannot dismiss them while they are pregnant. Dina complained that she had no other means to control such workers than to 'appeal to their consciences'.

On the other hand, several business-owners considered contractual relations between employer and employee to be more reliable than verbal agreements that did not entail any legal responsibilities. Workers who were formally employed and had a permanent work contract were required to provide their labour books (*trudovaya knizhka*) to their employer, personal documents containing all the workers' employment records, with an entry giving the reason for the termination of previous contracts. In cases of theft, regular absenteeism, alcoholism or any other serious violation, the employer could indicate this in the labour book, which would make it much harder for the worker to find a new formal job. Since the labour book was the primary source for the calculation of pension amounts, this allowed the employer to use it as a tool to discipline his or her workers.

Complaints about poor work discipline and bad work ethics were a recurrent topic in the narratives of local business-owners. Such complaints mainly concerned unskilled employees, especially those who had come from the countryside and regional areas. Their rural backgrounds and reliance on a subsistence economy were considered the main sources of their poor work ethic and lack of ambition. Olga, a businesswoman who migrated to Smolensk from Norilsk in 2010, was struck by the local habits and attitudes to work that she encountered in the city. The first thing she noticed after moving to Smolensk from the Arctic was that the city's streets were full of people idly walking around in the daytime. She found a striking contrast here between the busy and industrious lifestyle of Norilsk and the idleness that seemed to reign over Smolensk. However, since setting up a chain of clothing stores and hiring several shop assistants, she acquired a better sense of local habits. Her shop assistants, all of them young girls who had migrated into the city from the surrounding region, regularly showed up late or were absent from work. On one occasion, Olga pointed out to one unreliable girl that the latter was fully dependent on her job, having no other sources of income, no husband to rely upon and no accommodation of her own. Olga wanted to discipline the girl by promising to give her a bad report in her labour book, which would hamper her future formal employment. 'How are you going to survive then?', Olga asked her. To her surprise, the girl was not at all intimidated, just shrugging and saying that she would go back to her parents' village and live off their potato crop. After this incident, Olga became convinced that this philosophy was at the core of the local idleness in Smolensk, making people lazy and relaxed, as they could always count on their subsistence economy as something to fall back on when jobless. For Olga, Norilsk, her home town, represented a perfect environment for nourishing strong attitudes to work, as this northern city is located in the permafrost region, precluding any agricultural activities and leaving wage work at a local industrial enterprise as the only option to make a living. Olga claimed that the harsh Arctic conditions and extremely limited opportunities to earn a living were conducive to fostering subjects with 'strong characters', whereas the productive lands of the Smolensk region and the abundance of informal economic activities engendered what she called a 'relaxed mentality' and lax work discipline.

The subsistence economy was indeed widespread among the local population. Not only did migrants from rural areas cultivate their own private plots, but many urban dwellers were engaged in subsistence farming. While Olga frowned upon the subsistence economy for making people less dependent on wage work, for a large number of employees, growing potatoes and other vegetables was essential to supplement their modest wages. Those who possessed large enough plots sold their produce in the local market. At the beginning of the farming season, a large proportion of machine operators in Alpha, a local garment factory, especially elderly women, headed to their garden plots and dachas after working hours and at weekends. In times like these, talk about soils, seeds, sprouts, plant watering and weeding dominated the shop floor. Some women even brought sprouts to the workplace and left them on a windowsill so that they could take care of them during working hours. One machine operator, a woman in her late sixties, took a furlough for the whole summer, as she regarded her work on the land as more important than her informal and underpaid job in the factory.

Attempts to enforce better work discipline took various forms. As Olga's story illustrates, a formal contract and punitive measures could not ensure work discipline alone. Many employers attempted to introduce a range of monetary and non-monetary rewards to instil 'harmony' into their work collectives and reduce labour turnover. Such attempts ranged from creating elaborate workplace rituals and symbols to taking up the functions of the welfare state by paying benefits to workers from the firms' funds, such as childcare allowances. However, these measures mainly targeted the core groups of employees who were engaged in high-skilled jobs. Small businesses also provided on-the-job training, as it was often difficult for the local labour market to fill skilled jobs. For example, one IT company organized various contests and competitions among students at the local technical university, and then recruited the winners and trained them extensively on the job in how to work with the relevant software.

The oil-price crash and the sharp devaluation of the Russian rouble at the end of 2015 worsened the economic performance of the regional economy and hit small businesses in particular. The depreciation of the rouble had a negative impact on those firms that depended on imported goods. As a result, many firms increased the prices for their products and services and suffered a decline in sales as a result. Some businesses accumulated arrears of pay, cut back on salaries or laid off workers. At the same time, it was not uncommon for Smolensk's entrepreneurs to stress the positive impacts of economic instability, saying that the crisis prompted them to try out new solutions that they would probably never have done otherwise. For example, one local manufacturing firm decided to set up a new shop in the region, and an advertising agency opened a branch in Moscow after suffering a sharp drop in demand in the local market. Certainly, not all businesses had the resources to expand, and a great many simply hoped to wait out the downturn. Employees in private firms were far less optimistic about the deteriorating economic situation, since their real incomes fell, and some lost their jobs.

Conclusion

The aim of this chapter has been to look at the broader frame of the local business landscape and thus shed the light on the underlying practices, legal norms and state policies that implicate the workings of small businesses. I started with a brief look at the local history of Smolensk by tracing major economic developments in the province before and after the revolution in 1917. Owing to the modernization project launched by the Soviet authorities in the 1930s, this predominantly agrarian region was transformed into a heavily industrialized economy, with leading industries such as aircraft, equipment manufacture, textiles, garment manufacturing and diamond faceting. After the collapse of the Soviet Union, only some of these big industrial enterprises were able to survive the transition to the market, while a number of industries were closed down and ceased to exist, as happened to the linen industry. Not until 2014 did the Russian government become concerned about the demise of the national industrial base and initiate policies aimed at modernizing domestic industries.

Over the first decade of the market transition, the first cohorts of local entrepreneurs were mainly involved in petty trade, for which they travelled abroad to Poland, Romania or Germany. Only a lucky few were able to succeed and accumulate wealth, while a large number of shuttlers failed and moved back to wage employment. Since the early 2000s, petty traders have been removed by the big players, and the newly built shopping malls have gradually supplanted the earlier open-air markets. But as in the previous decade, most local small businesses were concentrated in the retail and service sectors. Government programmes offered subsidies to petty entrepreneurs, giving a priority to agricultural businesses and manufacturing. I have shown that the state's resources and capacity for provision was a subject of constant negotiations between state bureaucrats and local business-owners. Such negotiations were embedded in broader norms and moralities of exchange, so that it was not always that easy for entrepreneurs themselves to draw a sharp line between illicit and licit practices.

Similar informal negotiations prevailed in the employment sector. I will describe such negotiations between employers and employees in the next chapters. Here my aim has been to outline the general patterns of wages and employment within the private sector. I have briefly discussed the different degrees of informality, ranging from 'black' to 'white' jobs with 'grey' in between, and have touched on the aspects of work discipline and surveillance of work by officials. Overall, therefore, this chapter has provided a general backdrop to a more detailed discussion of values, to which I turn in the following chapters.

Chapter 5
Family-Based Firms: Reconfiguring the Value of Family Ties

'I believe that relatives should not work together at the same...not even in different departments of the same firm'. This was how Mikhail, the owner of a small-scale enterprise and a lecturer at one of Smolensk's universities, phrased his 'firm rule' regarding the recruitment of kin. Elaborating on this general norm, which he claimed never to have violated in the course of his entrepreneurial career, Mikhail explained why owners are so averse to any form of family involvement in their businesses:

> When you need to take some unpopular decisions, it may become difficult, because you are depend on these people, socially and morally. Really, never hire your relatives in your firm.

Like many other petty entrepreneurs in Smolensk, Mikhail advocates separation between the two spheres of life of family and work on the grounds that they are driven by different logics of value, or 'sphere-specific logics' in Weberian terminology (Terpe 2016). According to Mikhail, family commitments that dictate one set of moral orientations inevitably bind and restrict his entrepreneurial action, the latter presumably being guided by rational, profit-maximizing considerations that are entirely legitimate within the world of work, but questionable and even shameful when confronted with the language of family values. When the boundary between work and family is not respected, relationships with close relatives are sure to be damaged. This seemingly common-sense wisdom is widely held not only by business-owners but by ordinary people as well.

The idea that one has to maintain a distance between family and work echoes the market discourses of global capitalism that encourage such separation and therefore drastically reformulate the value of family ties in the context of work and labour. The imperative to remove family and kinship ties from the realm of the economy is promoted by the popular business literature, which instead praises personal responsibility and autonomy as the core of entrepreneurial agency and enshrines the principle of maintaining a clear-cut boundary between work and family (and sometimes friendship) as a dogma.[21] Historically, the participation and cooperation of family members was pivotal to the rise of capitalism: family-run enterprises were prominent during the Industrial Revolution in Britain (Hall and Davidoff 2002; Barker 2016), as well as in Russian Empire (West and Petrov 2014; Ulianova 2015). During the Soviet period, production and reproduction were closely interlinked through the socialist system of welfare. The post-1991 marketization of the economy started the opposite trend of disembedding one's private life from one's work (Dunn 2004; Thelen 2005; Keskūla 2014). Under neoliberal modes of governance, work has increasingly been redefined as based on contractual, utilitarian obligations between autonomous individuals, while the ideals of social protection, emotional attachment and family-like reciprocity are being expelled into the sphere of private life, with the family taking over the major costs of social reproduction. Keskūla (2014) examines this shift in her analysis of a mining company in Estonia, where the employment of family members became an object of harsh criticism, as family-friendly policies have been equated with nepotism and corruption since the transition. Keskūla demonstrates how the newly promulgated corporate ethic of transparency clashed with long-standing Soviet moralities and labour policies that encouraged labour dynasties and thus furthered the embeddedness of family relations in the workplace. Given my focus on the low end of the private sector, I will discuss to what extend the same disembedding tendencies and re-evaluations of family ties are visible among small-scale business operators in provincial Russia.

What struck me when I became immersed in the field is that many entrepreneurs evinced a degree of uncertainty in deciding whether the family was a resource for their firms or rather a liability. Some, like Mikhail, expressed a strong aversion to any form of family involvement in business. The majority of my interlocutors rarely applied the notion of family business to their kin-based economies. Many associated family enterprises with other cultural and ethnic traditions, whether exotic Japanese businesses or family-oriented ethnic entrepreneurs from the Caucasus and Central Asia. Filial succession and intergenerational depth were commonly seen as key features qualifying a firm as a family-based enterprise, while the majority of my informants were first-generation business-owners. Moreover, the concept of 'family business' (*semejnyj biznes*) was not recognized in either public

---

[21] Many Western business-success manuals have been translated into Russian since the 1990s. Together with their Russian equivalents, this sort of prescriptive literature is especially popular with business people of the younger generation (up to forty years old) seeking advice from the 'gurus' of capitalism.

discourse or official taxonomies, adding to the sense of 'otherness' of such categorizations.

At the same time, I quickly learned that family ties played a crucial role for small businesses and entrepreneurs, many of whom relied extensively on the assistance of relatives and in-laws. Despite the ambiguity of a kinship-based economy, many businesses strove to mobilize kinship moralities, especially the ethic of reciprocity, to generate trust and loyalty in their relationships with their workers. The vanishing of trust from interpersonal relationships and with regard to social institutions in general has been well-documented in studies of postsocialism. Shlapentokh argues that Russians demonstrate a 'fatal mistrust of social institutions' that is among the highest in the world (2006: 155). His diagnosis of 'a climate of mutual distrust' in Russia corresponds to those media reports that bemoan 'the moral degradation' of society (ibid.: 154). Many ethnographies have added to this bleak picture by documenting the shift in conditions of interpersonal trust since the demise of socialism. In her study of the post-communist transformation in East Germany, Thelen (2005) argues that relationships of trust have not entirely disappeared in postsocialist restructurings but have shifted into the realm of domestic life involving primarily relatives and core family members. She assumes that these rearrangements have led to a 're-traditionalization' of social life, as 'kinship ties are becoming more important for communication and for solving difficulties than other ties' (ibid.: 25). It is this shrinking of relations of trust to the size of the family group that accounts for the entrepreneurial desire to deploy family connections in business. Accordingly, family ties also feature as a resource that enables business-owners to create trust and loyalty in the workplace in times of 'fatal mistrust'.

However, the growing importance of family networks and the shift towards a re-traditionalization of social relations since socialism clashes with the ethics of transparency and the drive towards the disembeddedness of the family from work. These two logics imply different configurations of public and private, rational and emotional, impersonal and personal. In what follows, I will trace how these controversial dynamics are being played out on the ground in the context of small private firms. How do entrepreneurs in the Russian provinces negotiate the value of family ties in their daily lives? Do they consider family members to be a resource their firms can use or a liability? How do these practices of evaluation correspond to larger occupational and class structures, patterns of ownership, gender norms and family law?

The 'Family Trap': Family Business as a Dilemma

Before setting up his own firm in legal and business services in 2009, Oleg had worked as a top manager in various banks and manufacturing companies in Smolensk and St Petersburg. Like Mikhail, whom I introduced briefly at the beginning of this chapter, Oleg upheld the ideal that neither relatives nor acquaintances should ever be hired. Echoing Mikhail's concerns about the 'tough decisions' a boss has to make, Oleg projected his concerns into the domestic sphere. He argued that the overlapping of work and family life would inevitably be to the detriment of family relations, especially for a couple: 'A woman at work and a woman at home – these are two different things. You would cease to perceive your wife as a woman. Besides, when you get home, it would be difficult to switch from the daytime mode into the evening mode.'

The irony of Oleg's situation is that his wife works alongside him, having the responsibility for the company's second office. Responding to my surprise over this gap between theory and practice, Oleg admitted that this certainly violated his rule, but then stated that the whole arrangement was purely temporary. He explained that it was his own initiative to offer this job to his wife when a regular employee took maternity leave. He thought this would be a good opportunity for her to get to know the company, which might become crucial one day if some misfortune were to happen to him ('an air crash or something else'). Driven by a practical concern to secure an income for his family, Oleg was ready to put his managerial principles on the back burner.

This paradoxical gap between the ideal of not using family labour but relying on family networks in practice was a recurring theme in my encounters with Smolensk's entrepreneurs. To overcome this contradiction, they would explain this deviation by referring to personal circumstances that forced them (only 'temporally', as in the case of Oleg) to violate their principles. In this section, I will dwell on this gap between the desire to draw a clear-cut boundary between family and business and the systematic failure to realize this value in practice.

Much like Oleg, another interlocutor, Sasha, was struggling to balance his family commitments with business rationality. Sasha, an affable and energetic young man in his mid-twenties, started his first venture in food services together with a friend. Later the two friends reinvested the capital in a second project, a chain of local sushi bars which they managed collectively with a third associate. Sasha tried to ground his entrepreneurial career on the solid basis of his business knowledge. In his preoccupation with 'self-development' and 'personal growth', he relied on the popular business literature, business training sessions and his networks of personal contacts.

When I mentioned my interest in studying family firms, Sasha was eager to discuss this issue with 'an expert', expecting me to give him advice with regard to his own predicament on this matter.

One situation that bothered him very much was the fact that his elder brother had been pushing him to start a new business project with him as a partner. A successful manager in an international company, his brother was 'hassling' (*dostaval*) Sasha with an idea for a joint venture (Sasha said this happened after his brother read an American bestseller in business advice literature, Rich Dad, Poor Dad by Robert Kiyosaki). Finally, after a year of hesitation, Sasha succumbed to this idea, although still not sure he was making the right decision. His major concern was that this collaboration would damage his good relationships with his brother and even his parents, as Sasha expected the morality of kinship always to be at odd with the tough norms and ethics of business. In addition, he also feared that loyalty and solidarity with his family would inevitably restrict his decision-making and conflict with his business goals:

> I constantly fight with my friends [business associates – DT] but… We can fight because the emotional level is a bit different. Whenever I fight with my friends, it stays between us. But when it comes to my brother, this also embraces our relatives, because he has a wife, children… our parents as well, which is a mess (*kasha-malasha takaja nachinaetsja*). (…) For me it is easier there [with non-related partners – DT] because there… well, I can talk honestly with my friends, I can tell them anything as it is… in living colour. But I would offend my brother by talking in this way.

I wondered why Sasha had made this decision at all if he still has so many anxieties about the family project. Sasha shrugged his shoulders: he just succumbed to his brother's pleas. Having said this, he rushed to provide a more rational argument, returning to the norms and values of the sphere of economics: 'Well, also… I… as they say, KPI [Key Performance Indicators – D.T.], cash in hand above all else. I also want this… this is worth doing. I see that this has potential, there will be another asset. I certainly want more prospects, to make money, that's about it'. But the prospects of creating a new asset did not remove his anxieties, and Sasha still had many worries about his family-based project.

It is not only men who have to deal with such anxieties. Anna, a manager in her husband's firm, a business coach and an environmental activist, draws upon solid business theory to rationalize her conjugal partnership. As in Sasha's case, I met Anna in the Business Club, where she was giving a public lecture announced in the local social media. Anna was actively involved in the Club's educational activities and regularly organized public lectures and reading groups there on business-related topics. It was at one such gathering that she presented a book by Ichak Adizes, an American popular writer in management and organizational theory, whose insights on what it means to be an 'ideal executive' framed Anna's own vision of the division of managerial responsibilities in a company. In this book, Adizes pushes back against the idea that a perfect manager should be able to implement a diverse range of managerial tasks himself. For Adizes, a good manager is one who can identify his lack of skills in certain areas and compensate for this by delegating such duties to subordinates or business partners.

Drawing on Adizes's theory, Anna framed her involvement in her husband's company as contributing her strong points (the role of *administrator*, in Adizes's terms) to supplement his weak points, which she identified as a lack of self-discipline. She believed that it was this division of managerial duties that explained the success of their growing IT company. Later on in the interview she explained further why she and her husband were a 'perfect match' as business partners. For Anna, her husband, together with another business associate of his, exemplified good entrepreneurs in Adizes's terms, for they had entrepreneurial vision and could set larger goals for a firm. However, they dramatically lacked self-discipline and the capacity for routine work:

> They have generated a lot of ideas (*ponapridumyvali kuchu idej*) but never implemented even half of them. And they needed someone… What are my strong points? I get up and do things. I get up at seven o'clock and do everything, step by step. This is an administrative or disciplinary function, right? To put in order, to give impetus to move, to work.

But even reformulated in the language of economic efficiency, Anna's 'perfect match' with her husband faced the typical pitfalls that accompany any confusion of the obligations of business and kinship. Being well aware of 'family traps', in Anna's words, she asserted her willingness to quit the company the moment familial duties interfered with economic logic and prevented the firm's growth. Saying this, she portrayed her future withdrawal from the company as inevitable and as following the 'objective' laws of economic life-order discovered by the management analysts:

> Surely, there are some shortcomings [of doing business together – DT]. First, all our, uh… accumulated patterns of behaviour and relationships, they are being transferred here. Everything that annoys me at home with Pavel [the spouse – DT] irritates me at work as well. The same with him, right? For sure! At times it is hard to restrain myself when I feel that I am right or he feels that he is right.

> Certainly, it does matter... But I am prepared for this because if... I do not know, if the company is growing further and outgrows me (*pererastet menja*), for instance, huh... in this case, I will definitely quit the company. I will quit it easily and reassign my responsibilities to someone else. Otherwise it may cause a problem. Of course, it would be difficult for Pavel to tell me like this, 'Look, Anja, it is time to quit. You are already... you are not useful anymore (*pol'zy ot tebja net*), leave us.' He won't dare put like this, hence I am going to monitor the situation myself. Otherwise this may bind us, because it is a classic example of a managerial trap which is precisely called a family trap. (...) I believe that it is better not to work with relatives if possible.

According to this logic, the efforts to reconcile family commitments with business rationality are never enough; rather, family involvement is viewed as a concession made under certain constraints that have nothing to do with true business rationality. In their efforts to rationalize entrepreneurial action, Russian business-owners tend to downplay familial responsibilities and to disentangle them from the sphere of economic rationality, at least discursively, if not in practice. When family and work overlap, the binding power of relationships of kinship must be neutralized and reformulated in the language of business utility, thus transforming family ties into a business asset and enhancing the productive capacities of family-based economies.

What is missing in such narratives of enlightened entrepreneurs is the rhetoric of merit that is usually mobilized by the critics of kinship-based economies. Lima (2000) shows how financial elites in Portugal invest a great deal of capital in equipping their sons, the future inheritors of their businesses, with the most prestigious academic training. Getting a prestigious degree has a very important symbolic meaning, as it conveys a message that intergenerational succession is not just 'a simple process of filial descent' but is based on the personal merits of successors who get 'the best possible professional skills' through education (ibid.: 170-2). In her study of family firms in the Italian silk industry, Sylvia Yanagisako (2002: 90) points out that a second generation of Italian silk-producers sought various means to reassert their entrepreneurial independence, 'transforming themselves from sons created by the father to generative fathers who create firms and families'. In the case of Russian entrepreneurs, what lay behind their suspicions of family labour did not have that much to do with the lack of particular work skills and capacities on behalf of their family members. Rather, it was the general desire to assume an entrepreneurial attitude and to claim one belonged to the global capitalist modernity that would simultaneously designate a distance from the attitudes and legacies of the socialist and postsocialist pasts. Those of my interlocutors who regularly congregated in the Business Club shared this general aspiration to engage with 'true' capitalism and distance themselves from the 'uncivilized' and 'wild' forms of doing business that were notorious in the 1990s.

The desire to be modern and efficient managers was not the only reason for suspicions of kinship-based economies. Admirers of the Western business literature and those who did not show any interest in developing entrepreneurial attitudes both agreed in their concerns about family businesses at the point of family conflicts. There was a wider anxiety that bringing together business and the family would break family ties and lead to estrangements between family members. In the next section, I will examine why Russian entrepreneurs nevertheless turn to relatives for assistance, despite this not being the first choice for many of them.

The Family as a Pool of Flexible Labour

As in many other capitalist contexts worldwide, the family unit provides businesses with a pool of cheap (unpaid or underpaid) and flexible labour, whose responsibilities and duties towards the firm are embedded in norms of reciprocity and mutual assistance. In small enterprises, family members usually straddle the blurred boundary between labour and capital, their flexible involvement enabling small firms to survive the early, formative years of business (Yanagisako 2018).

Anna, who casts her marriage alliance as a 'perfect match' between business partners, could not easily define her duties in the company run by her husband. She said her responsibilities were loosely those of development directors or project managers in 'respectable companies'. Pointing to the fluidity and vagueness of her duties, she concluded that her major task was to compensate for deficiencies in managerial control on the part of her husband: 'When something somewhere goes wrong (*chto-to gde-to provalivaetsja*), I have to find out why and take some steps to improve it.' Anna joined the company right after her husband, the head of the firm, had bought the enterprise from a competitor and merged it into the bigger venture. As a result, the company's workforce doubled to fifty employees. At that point Anna's husband asked his wife 'to help them out' in undertaking a reorganization that would ensure the successful merger of the two companies. Before that, Anna had been employed as a human resources manager in a big bank while simultaneously managing her own small kindergarten, which she sold as soon as her two daughters started a school.

For Anna, the flexible arrangements of her new job allowed her to dedicate more time to raising her children, the household and social activities. As she worked on a part-time basis, usually from home, she could afford to invest more time in the domestic sphere than the average working mother. Anna raised two daughters of early school age and made their education and upbringing her great priority. To provide her daughters with the best educational and care options, she took an extra-mural university course in psychology so as to learn how to be a good mother. She dropped university as soon as she felt she had obtained enough knowledge about child psychology and channelled her upbringing of her children into a more practical mode: that is, she opened her own private kindergarten, as she was dissatisfied with the quality of childcare in Smolensk's existing preschool institutions. Drawing on her parents' savings, she purchased an apartment for the kindergarten. However, the kindergarten did not yield much profit and was burdensome to maintain, so Anna closed it down soon after her own children started school. Apart from domestic life and childcare, Anna was visible in the local social media and actively participated in public events related to business education and ecological initiatives in the region, such as waste recycling.

Thus, being employed in her husband's family firm allowed Anna to spend more time at home and sustain a middle-class lifestyle centred around values associated with education and knowledge. In addition to her job in the family business, Anna generated an income by renting out the apartment that had become vacant after she had closed her kindergarten project. However, it was her husband who was the family's main provider.

Their middle-class lifestyle established a desirable pattern for harmonizing work and family, but for many small enterprises aspiring to upward mobility, such ideals were out of reach. The fact that Anna was able to benefit from her employer's flexible arrangements was due to the earning capacity of their growing IT company, which provided accountancy services to a prosperous Moscow clientele. In many other small and less-capitalized firms, the flexible labour of family members implied exploitative rather than more relaxed conditions of employment.

When it comes to research into family firms in capitalist economies, anthropologists tend to draw attention to the darker sides of familial mutuality that mask the exploitation of family members in various forms (White 2000; De Neve 2008). In her study of Turkish home-working, White (2000) argues that the ethics of gift-giving and expectations of familial reciprocity justify the forms of control and subordination that exist between family members. Since material exchanges within a kin group are deeply imbued with a sense of solidarity and mutuality, it is more problematic to recognize relations of exploitation when family members are involved. Here I would like to draw attention to another side of family-based enterprises and show that they also function as a safety net for those relatives with a weak position in the labour market, for example, being unemployed or needing more flexible work schedules so as to combine employment with childcare. For them the family firm may provide a temporary or permanent employment solution and thus be of benefit to them. Not every small enterprise has enough resources to become a 'buffer against failure' (White 2000), and a certain level of viability and capitalization is required for this to happen.

I will illustrate this point using the example of Alpha, the garment manufacturing firm I mentioned earlier, which, over its rather long history, has served as a resource for two generations of family members to fall back on in times of crisis. The owner, Lidia Alekseevna, an uncompromising woman in her sixties, started the enterprise in 1992 soon after the privatization reform was set in motion.[22] Over the two decades of the company's existence, various members of Lidia's nuclear family have worked in the company in different capacities. When in the mid-1990s her husband, an aircraft engineer, faced severe payment arrears in his aircraft enterprise, his wife 'took care of him' (*pristroila*) by providing him with the odd job in her factory. She put her husband in charge of book-keeping, as reliable accountants were in great demand at that time. Lidia was more than satisfied with his services, but as soon as the aircraft industry slowly began to recover after 1998, her husband sought to withdraw from being an accountant. The family enterprise was not his last resort – as an aircraft engineer, he had more opportunities to market his skills in the local private sector. At that time, he took several odd jobs in the growing construction sector and made calculations for local construction firms. Finally, when a system of electronic book-keeping was introduced in the late 1990s, he took this as a good excuse to quit the family enterprise. As soon as he left, however, his teenage children took over book-keeping responsibilities in the family firm.

When the children grew up, they chose different forms of involvement in the garment firm. Lidia's son opted for an independent career in Moscow, where he studied at the university and then took an engineering job. However, Lidia's daughter Alina stayed in the industry and continued to work at her mother's firm. In a manner typical of the second generation of business-owners, Alina portrayed herself as someone who had 'grown up in the business' (Yanagisako 2002: 90): even in her early childhood years she took on some simple tasks, like doing an inventory in a warehouse, and then proceeded to more sophisticated tasks as a teenager, such as managing the books, packing goods and acting as night watchman. She described her early

---

[22] See Chapter 6, where I discuss this case in detail.

engagement with the firm as if she had been destined to take over the business in the future. But this narrative overlooks the fact that Alina had actually made other educational choices but failed in pursuing them. After finishing school she planned to become a doctor, but her poor academic performance did not allow her to enter the prestigious medical institute. Eventually Alina enrolled at the university in Moscow and, having obtained a degree in design, moved back to continue working in the family enterprise as a manager. This appointment coincided with another critical event in her personal life: she got pregnant and was faced with the prospect of raising her child alone. Alina's managerial tasks covered a very wide range of responsibilities. She joked that the term 'general worker' (*raznorabochaya*) would describe her duties more accurately, 'manager' being too vague and misleading. Her major task was to substitute for any absent employee in case of need. Indeed, when I started work in the firm, Alina combined her administrative duties with a cutting job for several months while they were looking for a new worker for the cutting room. Given labour turnover and unexpected sick-leave, it was crucial for the firm to have such a versatile employee to ensure deadlines were met. At the same time, her flexible and rather relaxed schedule benefited Alina, as it allowed her to balance motherhood with waged work more effectively.

Finally, Alina's boyfriend also benefited from the family enterprise when he lost his own job. Being between the jobs, he showed up at Alpha whenever Alina asked for help. These were occasional requests to carry out tasks firmly associated with what were perceived to be male responsibilities, such as throwing out heavy bags of production waste, shovelling away snow in front of the entrance area or making minor repairs. As soon as these occasional labour inputs turned into more regular assistance, Alina asked her mother to pay her boyfriend for his work. Several months of such occasional assistance, combined with the boyfriend's failure to find a new job in his field, gradually changed into more regular employment, and Alina's boyfriend (later her husband) started to accompany her on her visits to clients and her business trips to other cities.

This example shows how a family firm may link emotional and material exchanges, that is, one's moral obligations towards one's family with the principles of the market and making a profit (Narotzky 2015). In post-reform Russia, after the state withdrew from its promises of social protection, networks of kinship took over the role of a buffer against failure. For the two generations of family members, Alpha has served as such a buffer, protecting disadvantaged relatives from the adversities of the labour market by granting them employment opportunities when jobless. At the same time, the men in the family did not seek regular employment at the factory and tried to remove themselves from working under the supervision of the women once a job crisis was over. Gender stereotypes and conceptions of gender-appropriate work played a certain role in these sporadic engagements with the family enterprise on the men's side. The garment industry has a particular gender profile associated with 'female' professions, which are deemed less prestigious and are paid less than 'male' jobs (Kozina and Zhidkova 2006; see also Collins 2009). According to Alina, her brother evoked this gender stereotype when explaining his lack of interest in working at the garment factory, saying 'clothes are not my thing'. The prevailing gender conventions could add to male unease about working in a 'female' enterprise and the need to subordinate oneself to the control of wives and sisters, that is, of those who posed a threat to their masculine selves and questioned their authority within the family. Once men had better employment options to choose from in the labour market, they opted for their own projects outside the family enterprise and the female power that came with it.

However, the gender configuration of labour I observed in Alpha was rather unusual outside the garment manufacturing sector. In most family-based firms it is men who run the firms and exercise control over other family members, usually their wives, siblings or parents. Gender hierarchies and family mutuality allow male entrepreneurs a great deal of flexibility when it comes to rewarding family members for their work. It was not easy to acquire access to this information, since many male owners found it shameful to admit that family workers are systematically unpaid or underpaid. Only once was an expectation that such labour should be free expressed bluntly.

Zakhar, a young lawyer, had recently set up a firm in legal services. He did not conceal the fact that his mother regularly cleaned his office for free, regarding the job to be one of her family obligations within the household. Similarly, Zakhar encouraged his girlfriend to quit her job in the bank and help him out with the firm. The assistance he requested from her took the form of an unpaid job in his office. He expected that she would take care of secretarial duties and that her unpaid labour would help the firm survive the early phase of accumulation. However, unlike Zakhar's mother, his girlfriend was not responsive to his urging, preferring to pursue her own, safer career in the banking sector.

My other male interlocutors were typically more reserved in revealing the conditions under which their partners and other relatives worked for them. Participant observation and interviews with other family members often helped to provide a more nuanced picture of family assistance. When I interviewed Vadim, the owner of two businesses, I cautiously inquired whether his 'civic' wife, who was doing round-the-clock shifts at his hostel, was getting paid. Without hiding his irritation, Vadim assured me that of course she was remunerated for what she did. However, during my prolonged stay in the hostel, I learned that Natasha, Vadim's partner, was not paid regularly, unlike other, non-related employees, although she worked longer hours and was supposed to fill in for any worker at the reception desk. However upset Natasha felt about being short of cash, she was ready to put up with her underpaid job in light of massive indebtedness that loomed over her husband. She felt it was her moral duty to help him pay off his substantial debts, which partly consisted of loans from a friend that Vadim had used to invest in his second business and partly of unpaid alimonies for two children from his first marriage.

Thus, the flexible labour of close family members was crucial for many small businesses with limited financial resources in order to ensure their viability in the market. Like the Italian manufacturers around Lake Como studied by Yanagisako, Russian family firms convert family labour into capital by drawing on the unpaid or underpaid labour of family members (Yanagisako 2018). The new middle-class ideals of gender relations in post-Soviet Russia facilitate this process by making women more inclined to collaborate in men's risky projects because of a sense of moral obligation towards the family. Given the conditions of uncertainty and precarity that many firms face at an early stage of their existence or in cases of indebtedness, relations of care and expectations of mutual support enable the exploitation of female labour. Once a firm reaches the stable phase, it can benefit disadvantaged family members and give them a buffer against failure in the sense that it provides family members with side-jobs or even permanent employment.

However, the low cost of family labour is not the only factor that matters. What makes family members so attractive to small businesses as employees is the quality of trust and reliability that comes as integral part of the morality of kinship. In what follows, I dwell on this demand for trustworthy relationships in business circles and show how this encourages business-owners to rely more on family ties.

Other Family Resources: Trust and Loyalty

The issue of theft and its persistence in the context of labour frequently popped up in my encounters with Smolensk's petty entrepreneurs. The commonest complaint of this sort was about workers cheating on their bosses. Pilfering from the workplace, under-reporting the costs of transactions and fiddling the books were among the most widespread forms of cheating that allowed workers to appropriate a part of their firms' surplus value. Less often, customers also engaged in cheating by not paying for goods and services and disappearing into thin air after requesting delays in payment.

Pilfering and theft are nothing new in the context of labour in Russia. Similar clandestine practices penetrated collective institutions in Soviet times. Despite its illegality, pilfering was rarely prosecuted under Soviet rule, and even acquired a degree of legitimacy due to the peculiar conditions of socialist economies and their property regimes. Verdery (2003: 67) demonstrates that Romanian villagers working on a socialist collective farm did not regard their regular removal of produce from the *kolkhoz's* fields as theft. Rather, they treated such unofficial appropriations to be 'their right to take from the collective', a view also held by many farm managers, who condoned such practices for the sake of cementing good relations with their workers. Ledeneva argues that this 'sense of "entitlement" to a share of state resources' survived after socialism and legitimized numerous informal practices of 'petty privatization of the state' by post-Soviet actors (Ledeneva 2008: 131, 134).

These historical continuities and shared experiences of the Soviet past may imply that postsocialist workers are more inclined to cheat and outwit their employers compared to their counterparts in Western advanced economies, where private property rights have historically been more entrenched and better defined. This, however, would be a gross exaggeration. As Gerald Mars (1994) reminds us in his study of 'normal cheating' in the Anglo-Saxon world, examples of occupational crime are abundant in Western contexts, though they have been significantly less examined there. In his research, Mars identifies a category of 'fiddle-prone jobs', namely organizational arrangements that make acts of 'normal cheating' easy to perform. He argues that minor fiddles provide additional 'perks' for occupations and constitute a 'covert reward system' that may substantially supplement the formal system of rewards. Drawing on the assumption that occupational crime is not a uniquely postsocialist phenomenon, I will discuss how small businesses protect themselves from the risks associated with theft and prevent the drain on their resources.

In their responses to theft and pilfering by their employees, business-owners have developed a number of strategies that can be summarized as three patterns of control. The simplest way to reduce opportunities for pilfering is for the owner to perform the 'fiddle-prone' tasks himself. Ultimately, this strategy implies that no worker can be trusted, so it is usually used as a last resort or a temporary solution. Vadim, the owner of two businesses, the stamp firm and the hostel, revealed that his worker had been stealing materials from the firm, especially the expensive foreign-produced paints used for colouring plastic signboards. It transpired that this worker was providing colouring services on the side more cheaply than Vadim. His workshop was safely insulated from the main office space, being located in an otherwise deserted basement – a typical example of a 'fiddle-prone' work environment. The nature of the materials used also added to the fiddle-prone nature of the job, given that it was difficult to measure how much ink one needed to paint a signboard. When he discovered the thefts, Vadim dismissed the violator and filed a lawsuit against him, though he lost the case due to a lack of sufficient evidence and of witnesses prepared to confirm that an occupational crime had taken place. From that moment on, Vadim has painted the signboards himself.

However, rather than reducing one's labour force, a more common solution to tighten managerial control is to introduce some organizational change, for example, to do more accurate accounting of materials or cash given out to workers. Sasha confronted cheating among his workers from the very moment he set up his first business in petty trade, selling corn snacks on the streets and in the shopping centres. When recruiting salespeople for his snack business, Sasha was inspired by the idea of only hiring old ladies, typical Russian *babushki*, who would trigger a feeling of 'grandma warmth', conjure up associations with homemade food and thus attract more customers. After a thorough selection procedure, Sasha hired a bunch of saleswomen, all of them nice *babushki* in their fifties or sixties. Pretty soon, however, he had sacked all of them for misreporting. He found that his *babushki* were regularly understating the real amounts of products they sold. This led him to introduce stricter record-keeping of the corn supplies given out to workers.

Some entrepreneurs can afford to introduce technological changes that reduce opportunities to fiddle. Switching to cashless transactions and formalizing payments were among the most common measures to control the flow of money within a firm. An owner of a fitness studio was aware that his personnel, responsible for collecting payments for fitness services, tended to collude with clients in making cheaper deals and kept no record of this. To put an end to unreported transactions, he installed a computer system that recorded each payment, a measure that promised to reduce the number of unregistered payments.

However, technologies, however sophisticated, cannot guarantee that employees will not find room for manoeuvre or new workarounds to 'beat the system'. Besides, computerization does not suit all working arrangements, leaving some jobs more 'fiddle-prone' than others. This means that relations of trust are in high demand among employers. As Lev, one of my interlocutors, put it, cheating is not only an issue in enterprises like McDonalds, where all the work operations are highly streamlined and formalized. However, once work tasks become more complicated and workers retain some autonomy, cheating is an ever-present possibility. Lev, an owner of several businesses in construction, also had first-hand experience of dealing with cheating: some of his real-estate agents regularly misreported the size of the commission payments they received from clients. Lev said it was nearly impossible to strengthen managerial control due to the independent, difficult to monitor nature of their work.

Thus to confront cheating in this 'fiddle-prone' occupation, Lev resorted to the third strategy I will describe here, namely making use of family networks. Lev hired two close relatives, a brother and a nephew, for positions as real-estate agents. However, his family-friendly policy was ultimately not successful, since he faced another dilemma, namely having to deal with a lack of occupational ability on the part of certain family workers. Lev complained that his relatives demonstrated no desire to work, and therefore their trustworthiness did not pay, as they could not meet the main requirement for the job – to be active and independent workers. Lev was annoyed that his relatives did not show a glimmer of entrepreneurial spirit and that he had to 'spell out' (*razzhevyvat*) each and every work task to them, making him feel like a 'nanny' at work – a position Lev could not tolerate, as he was a vigorous supporter of the idea of the 'employee-entrepreneur' (Voss and Pongratz 2003).

Even though it was not successful in Lev's case, the tactic of relying upon kinship networks to prevent fiddling at work and other occupational crime was widespread among business-owners. In this sense, kinship solidarity serves as a mechanism of 'alternative enforcement', an extra-legal means of combating occupational crime and observing the terms of formal contracts (or verbal agreements if there is no formal contract) by relying on relational mechanisms of kinship solidarity. In the majority of practical situations when fiddling is uncovered, the only penalty against violations of trust is to dismiss the worker (consider Vadim's attempt to put up a legal fight, which came to naught). To avoid the costly outcomes of occupational crime, entrepreneurs prefer to make use of the family as a resource and the horizontal relationships of trust that are built into kin networks. In a similar way, circles of close friends may provide the same level of trust, such trustworthy insiders figuring prominently among business associates or informal money-lenders.

However, trust is required not just to secure business assets from theft and misreporting: it is also vital in contexts where economic agents not uncommonly walk on the edge of legality when exploring legal loopholes and possibilities for tax evasion (Ledeneva 2006). In this case cooperation with key employees is crucial to protect a firm and keep its secrets from monitoring agencies and other outsiders. Bookkeeping falls into the category in which the demand for trust is particularly high due to the high stakes involved. It is not surprising that many small businesses tend to entrust managing the books to members of their family.

In post-Soviet Russia, accountancy has routinely been related to tax avoidance. This places accountants under pressure to satisfy the demands of business-owners to minimize the tax burden by exploiting defects in tax legislation and searching for legal loopholes in it. A competent accountant is supposed to follow ongoing up-dates in legislation and creatively engage with tax regulations so as to 'legalize' tax avoidance on paper (Ledeneva 2006). In Smolensk, highly skilled and experienced accountants have been always in great demand in the private sector: for example, Vadim recruited his bookkeeper from a friend, another entrepreneur, who carelessly boasted about his hardworking and reliable employee. Accordingly bookkeepers may gain considerable power due to their structural position in a firm that results from their intimate knowledge of how far the 'paper' level of transactions diverges from the real one. By sharing such secrets with an owner, accountants can derive powerful leverage enabling them to resist managerial control and enjoy special benefits that are unavailable to regular workforce (the accountant in Vadim's firm was the only registered employee among six other workers working informally). On the other hand, this type of dependence on an accountant's ability opens up wider possibilities for abuse and cheating, as a skilful accountant may use his or her knowledge against the employer.

The story of Polina (35 years) and her uneasy entrepreneurial career sheds more light on the risks associated with bookkeeping. Polina started her working life rather early, in her late school years, as she had to help her poor working-class family get by. However, her background did not prevent her from obtaining a university degree in accounting in the late 1990s. Since Polina had to pay for her university education, she combined her studies with a number of informal part-time jobs that included trading in an open-air market, being a bus conductor, working in the elections for a local deputy, being a secretary in a legal firm and doing accountancy jobs for small businesses. After graduation, Polina started working in an advertising agency. Her talent and hardworking habits were acknowledged by her superiors, and she was rapidly promoted to the top of the accounting hierarchy, being given the position of finance director.

Having worked for several years as a worker for wages, Polina decided to quit and set up own business. Not without hesitation, she stepped on to the risky entrepreneurial path because of the precarious situation she faced after becoming pregnant. Since most of her wages from the advertising agency went undeclared, Polina was only entitled to quite meagre maternal benefits, based on the smaller, official part of her salary.[23] Moreover, at that moment she broke up with her boyfriend, and the prospect of being a single mother added to her general sense of insecurity. To set up a business was her way of obtaining access to maternal payments, given that as the firm's owner she could give herself a high salary and consequently was eligible to obtain somewhat better social benefits.

Polina in fact set up two firms, one to provide outsourced accounting services, the other, which was set up collectively with three of Polina's work-mates from her previous job, specializing in advertising. She persuaded her friends to quit their current jobs and start a joint venture with her, Polina herself being the overall director. She was also the only one to provide any start-up capital. To that end, Polina took out a loan, which she used to rent an office and buy the necessary equipment.

When her child was born, Polina, a single mother, supervised her nascent joint venture somewhat less closely. From time to time, her associates handed her some money as her share, pulling it out of their pockets. Polina never asked her business partners to show her the books, as she had complete trust in them. It was not until her maternity leave was over that she discovered the books had been fiddled. As soon as she started to work at her full capacity again as the director of the advertising agency, she spotted huge discrepancies in the account books. It did not take her much time to figure out that the actual company profits had been falsified and understated in an obvious way. She realized that her partners had been cheating her all the time that she had been on leave. Feeling betrayed and not wishing to continue doing business with her associates, she withdrew from their joint venture and focused entirely on her second business, of which she was the sole owner.

Apart from her own painful experience of broken trust, Polina learned more about fiddling the books from second-hand sources. In providing accounting services for other businesses, she came across far more complicated cases than her own. She was especially appalled by one case of fiddling that forced a business into bankruptcy and closure:

---

[23] As a financial director, Polina was paid around 60-70,000 roubles (approx. a thousand euros), though the officially declared part of her salary comprised only the minimum wage of four thousand roubles (approx. 50 euros). This amount entitled her to receive maternity benefits ranging from twelve to twenty thousand roubles a month (approx. 170 to 280 euros) during the first six months of her maternity leave.

Polina: We had a lot of interesting cases related to the Prosecution office and other stuff. One client contacted us about... I still remember him, he's a taxi-driver now – his own accountant destroyed his business. His business was ruined by his accountant. He ran a furniture factory, making furniture. It was a small factory. He contacted us, saying, 'Girls, there is a problem – I have a feeling that my accountant is stealing a bit (*podvorovyvaet*), but I can't figure out how much she is taking'. I think she [the accountant – DT] was already pregnant at that time. (...) Anyway, we started auditing the books and found a huge amount of money. That is, if he made a profit of three million roubles, eight hundred thousand of it had been transferred to her account. It's just crazy! We helped him write a complaint to the Prosecution office, but the girl was already on maternity leave and had pretty big belly. He could not get his money back, his company went bankrupt, and he switched to taxi-driving. A short time afterwards he gave me a lift as a taxi-driver, since he had gone bust... This is the same old story, but it was too late to change anything...

DT: Do you mean there was no way to get the money back?

Polina: Of course there was no way to do this! She has not even been prosecuted because she was a single mother raising a child alone, and given her financial status she could not transfer this money back, end of story. She just did not have any assets. I guess she either transferred her assets (*perepisala*) into someone's else name or there were some other scenarios, I don't know, I didn't go into it any further. But I remember that we had this experience and that it was quite crazy.

Polina said that she had never felt hiring family members was a good idea, but these incidents made her rethink the value of family ties. A new case of 'betrayal' occurred when a key employee quit her job. This girl did most of the accounting services in Polina's firm, including operations for their 'VIP' client. Polina said she did not mind her employee changing jobs; what she regarded as a betrayal was the fact that she took with her Polina's 'VIP' client, who had secretly offered her employment in his company. Both the former employee and the VIP client concealed their real motives from Polina, and she only learned that they were working together by accident.

After this incident, Polina appealed to a family member and asked her brother's wife Marina to work as an accountant in her firm. She stressed that Marina's loyalty was a key quality in her considerations: 'I knew that Marina would never leave me, that she would never cheat on me (*nikogda ne podstavit*), that she would just quietly do her job'. During our interview,

Polina referred to Marina as '*svoi chelovek*' (literally 'own person'[24]), a popular idiom widely used in both the Soviet and post-Soviet periods to designate 'an affiliation with particular social circle of trusted people' (Ledeneva 2008: 122). These circles of trusted insiders ('publics of *svoi*') determined the specifics of public life in the late Soviet era (Yurchak 2006) and were indispensable in exchange of favours, or *blat* dealings (Ledeneva 1998). For Polina, the circle of trusted people initially consisted of her work mates, but after a chain of betrayals she came to realize the moral value of family ties and placed her trust in close family members instead.

Relationships between the 'people of the circle' are built upon an ethics of solidarity and mutual obligations. Following the imperatives of reciprocity, Polina promised Marina that she would reciprocate her loyalty with the secure and stable working conditions that she could guarantee her as an employer: 'Under no circumstances will I ever dismiss Marina! Even if the firm is falling apart, Marina would be the last person to leave this organization. That's my responsibility'. Moreover, Polina accepted Marina's lack of accountancy skills and patiently supervised her professional growth and gradual on-the-job training. In passing, Polina hinted at some 'serious mistakes' that Marina had made recently because her professional skills were not sophisticated enough. However, it was reliability and commitment that were the crucial qualities of Marina's work, and Polina was ready to tolerate imbalances in their reciprocal relations, in accordance with the logic of the long-term morality of kinship (Bloch 1973). When speculating about the firm's future, Polina said that she considered Marina's two children to be among the heirs of the firm, along with her own seven-year-old son.

In return, Polina expected her sister-in-law to do more work, which she represented as voluntary contributions made by Marina on her own. When Polina expanded her business by setting up an advertising agency, she had limited financial resources and required cheap labour. For this reason, she occasionally asked Marina to help her male workers make souvenirs, and Marina did this so well that this job was eventually made her permanent task: 'Since then Marina has been making St. George ribbons with delight. If something else is required, she is always willing to give us helping hand in production. Her motor skills are incredible. Guys have problems making small things, and we put aside small items for a while. But sometimes we make small things, and Marina is our ultimate help in these matters'. Also Marina is responsible for keeping order in the office kitchen, coming in earlier every morning to put away the kitchen utensils. It goes without saying that any time Polina needs an extra pair of hands to assist her in buying work

---

[24] Another version of the same phrase is *nash chelovek*, 'our person'.

materials in local retailers, she picks Marina. For Polina, these ancillary tasks are woven into the wider performance of *svoi* sociality, which is based on intensive communication, the sharing of ideas and spending time together. For her part, Marina has never objected to carrying out multiple tasks going far beyond her immediate bookkeeping responsibilities. As Polina describes Marina's role in her enterprise, 'she does all the legwork (*vsegda na podhvate*)'.

Kinship morality is also mobilized to secure the position of employer in times of crisis – when Polina did not have enough capital to pay her employees' wages, she first of all delayed Marian's pay: 'At the moment we have some difficulties in paying wages. Marina says, "There is no need to hurry to give me my wages, I understand everything, no worries. You can give me just part of it now, like ten thousand roubles (ca. 150 euros) to get by. Never mind, the rest of the money you can give me later." Marina always does me favours (*idet navstrechu*)'.

Polina is well aware of the restrictions that reciprocal obligations impose on her managerial control. Like many modern managers who frown on the idea of working together with family members, she has reservations about the binding power of family reciprocity. To overcome this predicament and reassert her managerial power, Polina blatantly puts aside family sentiments when, she says, she 'squeezes' Marina 'like a lemon', meaning that she exploits her close relative no less than any non-related employee in the firm. In fact, she claims that as an employee Marina is even more subordinated to her control than the other workers, since her close working relationships with the latter are projected into the domestic sphere. To demonstrate this, Polina promised that after our interview was over (we finished late in the evening, around 11 pm) she would call Marina and discuss her mistakes in accounting, 'because there are mistakes, there are serious mistakes, which she does not see, and I want her to correct them as soon as possible'. This extra control over a family member indicates that the imperatives of efficiency remain strong and are not overridden by the norms of family reciprocity.

Despite all the ambiguities that working with family members may involve, Polina was satisfied with her decision to hire a family member. Moreover, she took her friendly-family policy further and hired her brother, Marina's husband, to manage her firm's production site. As a middle-class women, Polina had difficulties in managing blue-collar male workers, as this required her to change familiar patterns of management and introducing stricter and harsher methods of supervision, which she found to be less appealing (she attempted to remain a 'good boss') and which undermined her femininity (for her, being tough with workers meant adopting a masculine posture). Thus, Polina delegated control over the production process to her brother, for whom the working-class norms of masculinity were a habitual environment, and he soon managed to impose his authority and win the consent of his male subordinates.

The story of Polina's firm illustrates the gradual process which led this employer to reassess the value of family ties after her previous relations with non-related employees and associates had failed to guarantee the qualities of trust and caused her material losses. In his research on industrial labour in India, De Neve (2008: 240) argues that the moral content of kinship is not inherent in any relationships of kinship but has to be activated and mobilized by the employer, since 'reliability does not flow automatically from morality and morality itself does not flow automatically from kinship'. Accordingly, 'kinship' and 'relatedness' are very flexible and malleable constructions that may lead to highly ambiguous economic outcomes when deployed in the context of work. Whereas Polina has managed to deploy kinship morality in relation to her family members and exploit their loyalty in relation to specific tasks in her firm, Lev, whom I mentioned above, could not achieve the same effect, as his loyal but somewhat slow-witted relatives proved to be unsuitable in their capacity as real-estate agents.

Fictive Kinship and the Authority of the Collective

Not only did Polina rely on the labour of her close kin, she also strove to stretch kinship morality to cover unrelated employees. In doing so, she evoked the metaphor of 'company as family', saying that she treated all her workers as family members. Her dream was to create a family-like close-knit community that would unite like-minded individuals. However, this attempt to impart a family feeling to her company was mainly addressed to a particular category of workers, her white-collar female employees. Her male employees at the production site have been far less affected by the discourse of family.

To accentuate the family metaphor and make the office space look more like home, Polina set up a fully-fledged kitchen area in the office space. She treated the kitchen as a symbol of inclusion and equality at work. To insert a kitchen was a deliberate choice for which she gave up her own office. In addition to everyday habits of commensality, the kitchen area was a place where her office workers usually socialized after working hours on Fridays, drinking and playing board games. Drinking on Fridays was one of the many rituals Polina introduced in the workplace. Each day in the office was devoted to a particular topic: for example, Wednesday was reserved for managing conflicts. To this end, the workers formed what they called the 'common court' to discuss collectively any situation of conflict at work. If there was no conflict to sort out, there was an alternative agenda for Wednesday – each worker was expected to say 'thank you' to one of her colleagues and thereby acknowledge her work in front of the whole work team. Every season Polina arranged a 'creative' photo-shoot for the office girls, placed their pictures on the office walls and even fixed print-outs of them on the shutters of the office windows. Polina proudly stated that they had also made three short movies featuring her work team and had composed an anthem mentioning the names of each office girl and giving a glimpse of her role in the work team.

Much like 'real' kinship, such attempts to turn non-related employees into fictive kin seek the same practical outcomes – to discipline workers, secure a stable labour force and prevent labour turnover (De Neve 2008). For Polina, to be 'like relatives' with her subordinates invoked the image of a loyal and reliable workforce. She was proud to say that, after splitting from her former associates and quitting her first business, her employees did not abandon their boss, but followed her and helped her to set up a new firm, even though it entailed more risk for them than staying in their previous place of work. In the same fashion, Polina expected that a sense of obligation would keep her workers in her firm in the midst of the financial crisis that hit her advertising business in 2015. In the aftermath of the crisis, the firm cut its prices for its services in order to stay afloat and wait out the economic turmoil. This resulted in frequent delays in payments and the laying off of five people, which reduced the overall number of employees to 23. Polina said that even this number made them the largest work team in the city comparing to other advertising firms, which rarely employed more than ten people. When one of her male workers from the production site quit the firm because of wage arrears, Polina felt insulted and expressed her resentment in openly moral terms: she had paid him a good salary in the days when the firm prospered, but as soon as it faced hardships and she had to introduce 'brief delays' in payment he left in search of better job opportunities. Her outrage reveals her expectations of long-term obligations on the part of her workers, who are supposed to tolerate delays and imbalances in reciprocity (Bloch 1973). Given that the worker had rejected such long-term obligations, Polina concluded that he had never in fact been 'our' person (*nash chelovek*). This incident shows that employers' preoccupations with building close and lasting bonds within a firm may prove to be 'nothing more than wishful thinking' and may not affect workers or bind them to a firm (De Neve 2008: 235).

What makes this postsocialist example different from Indian (De Neve 2008) or Japanese cases (Kondo 2009) is the culturally specific ways in which Polina instilled the values of family morality in an attempt to create ties of relatedness among her employees. Whatever the source of her managerial inspiration, the notion of a labour collective (*kollektiv*) consisting of a circle of *svoi* people formed her image of social relations at work. To reproduce this type of *svoi* sociality in the workplace, Polina made attempts to redefine her relationships with her workers in a more horizontal manner by overriding the vertical hierarchies of subordination. As mentioned above, she refused to have her own office and instead preferred to settle down to work (*pristraiivat'sja*) somewhere at an empty desk or on the kitchen table. Her idea to put a kitchen in the workplace highlights the values of familiarity and *svoi* sociality, reflecting the fact that the kitchen has occupied a central role in creating ties between *svoi* people in both the late Soviet era and afterwards by engaging in rituals of hospitality and commensality (Pesmen 2000: 164-6; see also Ries 1997).

To accentuate the horizontal principle of her management style, Polina instructed her workers not to address her by patronymic[25] and preferred to recruit her peers (the majority of employees were in their late twenties and early thirties). When hiring a worker, she inquired about his or her interests and hobbies so as to make sure that she shared similar values with them, of which a commitment to self-education was central. Her crucial concern was the unity of the labour collective, and any newcomer was expected to blend into the work team, that is, 'to get into the collective' (*vzhit'sja v kollektiv*), ideally by 'screwing themselves into the team like a small screw'. For her part, Polina portrayed her leadership as driven by a sense of responsibility towards her labour collective. These people were 'the weight on her shoulders', who propelled her to develop the firm more efficiently, as this directly affected the livelihoods of her workers and their families. When the crisis sprang up at the end of 2014, Polina became extremely pessimistic about the firm's ability to survive the coming year. She said that it was her own labour collective that nudged her to shed her pessimism and search for new solutions to the task of navigating the firm through the turbulent years. The solution proved to be rather expensive and risky, for Polina decided to expand and set up a new branch in Moscow in the hope of attracting wealthy Muscovite clients with cheap Smolensk prices.

For Polina to supervise a work team of over twenty people made it possible for her to implement her ideal vision of how relationships at work should be organized. Even though this vision was influenced by the idioms of Western corporate culture, it had nevertheless been interpreted and read through the lens of specific post-Soviet experiences. Polina's appeal to restore the sense of the collective nature of an enterprise corresponded to the

---

[25] To add a patronymic after a first name is a normal way of addressing people of higher status or age in Russia.

feeling of loss and of the reduction of social relations in the workplace that many post-Soviet workers experienced with the transition to capitalism. In her research on postsocialist workplaces in East Germany, Thelen (2005) demonstrates that the reorganization of work after reunification with West Germany provoked a sense of nostalgia for the quality of the social relations that had characterized working lives under socialism, when workers used to spend more time together and shared personal matters with each other. In this sense, the metaphor of 'company as family' that Polina deployed in her enterprise aimed to restore this vanished multi-functionality of workplace relations and the level of familiarity between co-workers that recalled the socialist work collectives of the past. Even though Polina, being in her mid-thirties, did not have any personal experience of working under socialism, she shared a feeling of nostalgia for the socialist past and followed some of the moral imperatives that were at the core of the socialist project. She said that if the Soviet Union had not disintegrated, she would most likely have wanted to pursue a career in Komsomol, the Party youth organization, because she enjoyed organizing people and orchestrating social activities. She was particularly attracted by the type of work known in Soviet official language as *obshchestvennaya rabota*, or work for the benefit of society. In the capitalist period, her desire to benefit society was accordingly channelled into an attempt to enhance the quality of social relations at work by creating a kinship-like community. Her preoccupation with team-building gave Polina a great deal of job satisfaction, while the other, more pragmatic aspects of managing the firm bored her.

The desire to bring about social change and benefit society underpinned another endeavour that Polina pursued, along with running an advertising agency, namely the *Smolensk Business Club*. Setting up the club was the idea of her boyfriend, a local intellectual, historian and activist. Polina endorsed this idea with her money and energy. The organization aimed to bring together local entrepreneurs and provide them with a platform for networking and communication. But it also invited anyone who was interested in 'intellectual' leisure activities, such as playing chess, discussing books, watching movies or participating in public lectures covering a variety of topics, ranging from marketing to mathematics. To keep the club going was a serious financial burden for Polina, but she did not want to give it up and hoped to find a way to commercialize it and turn it into a profitable venture. The club had a clear mission to popularize the idea of entrepreneurialism, and Polina believed that opening a business was the only way to overcome 'the catastrophe' of the precarity of working life and cope with deteriorating living standards in the region.

Polina's commitments to the local community hint at the broader implications underpinning her attempts to 'impart a family flavour' to the workplace (Kondo 2009). However, the metaphor of the company as family turned out to be problematic. Male workers from the production site occupied a marginal position in the work group, and their class-otherness invited different methods of regulation and stricter forms of control. Contrary to the rhetoric of family unity, the principles of *svoi* morality did not manage to transcend the class divide between the blue-collar and white-collar workers, but rather strengthened the inequality of employment statuses within the workforce. In this sense, the morality of *svoi* sociality reproduced the major ideologies and principles of work that predominated in the era of flexible capitalism (Mollona 2009; Kjaerulff 2015).

Conclusion

The idea of the family-run enterprise has proved rather tricky in Russia. The concept is non-existent in the public discourse, nor is it visible in the state's statistics or regulatory documents. Because of the lack of an established taxonomy and normative framework, the concept has become a matter of individual choice and inclination. In this role, the idea of doing business with relatives is surrounded with a lot of ambiguity. I conceive this ambiguity as corresponding to the difficulties involved in evaluating the value of family ties, given that more than one standard of value is operating at the same time. These different realms of worth dictate their own sets of obligations and responsibilities – personal, intimate, social, market, contractual, etc. As Narotzky (2015) points out, a family enterprise is a site where different regimes of value overlap with each other to the point that it becomes practically impossible to differentiate between care and money-making, reciprocity and market exchange, emotional and monetary transfers, 'love labour' and wage labour. This high degree of value enmeshment translates into the inability of social actors 'to define their actions in terms of stable categories', that is, to relate the action to a particular domain of value (ibid.: 193). This lack of clarity generates anxieties for some social actors, while for others it becomes an instrument of exploitation. Narotzky argues that the removal of clarity and the overlapping of different realms of value not only pertains to family-run businesses but underlies the workings of present-day flexible capitalism in general and its 'new moral hegemony based on the blurring of value regimes' (ibid.: 194).

I find these conceptualizations extremely useful for understanding the sorts of dilemmas that Russian small businesses have to grapple with. In this chapter, I have unpacked the particular anxieties and tensions that the idea of a family-based enterprise give rise to among Russian entrepreneurs. At the same time, I showed why small businesses nevertheless rely on kinship networks and how they negotiate ambivalent value domains in everyday practice.

Many Russian entrepreneurs express a desire to draw a sharp boundary between the realms of care and the household on the one hand, and of market exchange and profit-making on the other. To realize this ideal compartmentalization of different value spheres, they prefer to separate family from business. However, this ideal division is not easy to sustain in practice in a context in which household economies and systems of provisioning are tightly interwoven with capital accumulation. As Narotzky illustrates in the case of family farms in Spain, the responsibility for a family and the responsibility for a firm converge once family incomes are capitalized. It is not surprising that attempts to insulate the family and household from a firm's economy repeatedly collapse in practice.

For business-owners, the desire to draw a clear-cut boundary between family and business draws upon two types of narrative. The first one emphasizes the idiom of love and care, while the second argues from the point of view of capital. The capital narrative reproduces the logic of capital and draws upon the Western model of social personhood that aspires to personal autonomy from any sort of social commitment or moral obligation that may hamstring entrepreneurial agency in the workplace (Rose 1992; Dunn 2004). This narrative comes to the fore in the accounts of young (or would-be) entrepreneurs aspiring to upward mobility. They enthusiastically respond to 'the pervasive spirit of entrepreneurialism' (Ikonen 2013) by striving to remake themselves as modern capitalist subjects in the hope that this personal transformation will launch them into economic progress and upward mobility. From this point of view, the family should be separated from business so as to enable entrepreneurs to express their agency more freely and not be bound by moral obligations in the process of accumulation. However, such ideals of autonomy cannot easily be applied to the ambiguous arrangements of small businesses, connected as they are to the realm of household and family through transfers of money, emotions and labour. For some business-owners the failure to reconcile value and actual practice creates anxieties, while others demonstrate a great deal of savvy in their attempts to adapt Western theories to their particular needs and experiences. The sorts of difficulties experienced by enlightened Russian entrepreneurs in realizing their ideals correspond to Narotzky's (2015) scepticism about value potential serving as a moral guide for action in the present-day world, one dominated by global capitalism.

However, despite the desire to keep the family and the firm at a safe distance from each other, many small businesses are complicit in blurring these two value domains when they seek the assistance of relatives and spouses and generate capital by relying on cheap and flexible family labour. Long-term reciprocal obligations within a kin group facilitate relationships of exploitation and normalize requests to perform unpaid or underpaid work, especially at the early stages of capital accumulation or in cases of indebtedness. Another aspect of family reciprocity comes into play when a firm becomes viable and can serve as 'a buffer against failure' for disadvantaged family members with weak positions in the local labour market, such as single mothers and unemployed or underemployed family members. In this way, family-based enterprises combine both sides, benefiting social reproduction by granting family members better prospects of making a living, while possibly turning into sites of exploitation.

This chapter has shown that the long-term morality of loyalty to kin is evoked to fix constantly collapsing relations of trust between capital and labour. By relying on family labour, entrepreneurs seek to protect their businesses against various forms of occupational cheating and theft that may incur substantial material losses, especially when it comes to managing the firm's finances. I conceive this reliance on extra-legal and therefore alternative mechanisms of protection as a form of 'alternative enforcement' drawing upon long-term obligations of kinship and restrictive norms of *svoi* morality in order to protect private property from theft and misreporting. The metaphor of company as family, invoked in attempts to turn unrelated employees into family members, enables business-owners to strengthen work discipline and control, as in their relations with 'real' kin who work for them. At the same time, I have shown that under postsocialism the metaphor of company as family takes on additional meanings and ironies in that it evokes Soviet-era experiences of work, rather than just mimicking Western idioms of corporate culture. Yet, regardless of its point of reference, metaphorical kinship reproduces the logic of capital accumulation by instilling discipline in workers and strengthening the fragmentations between different groups of workers.

What does all this mean with respect to the concept of the family firm? Does the notion of 'family business' exist as an emic category in Russia? While some small businesses do describe themselves as family-run enterprises, this is a rather fragile description, capturing a momentary balance achieved in negotiating the different logics and values evoked in a kin-based economy. Those who struggle to achieve this balance generally avoid this term, regardless of how many family members actually work in their firms.

Chapter 6
Small Garment Manufacturing: Between Precarity, Creative Work and Developmental Hopes

The *Galaktika* shopping centre was opened in the 2010s and quickly turned into the most remarkable, yet controversial symbol of late capitalist modernity in Smolensk. Many city-dwellers felt excited to find this huge, glittering, Western-style shopping centre in their provincial city, accommodating shops selling popular Western brands of clothing, a supermarket, several cinema halls, courses for children and a dozen restaurants. Middle-class urbanites felt relieved that they no longer had to commute to Moscow at weekends to shop. The new shopping area proved to be the most vibrant centre of leisure activity in the city, attracting crowds of visitors every day of the week. The open-air Kolkhoz market, located just a five-minute walk from *Galaktika*, has shrunk since the 1990s, but it has remained popular with the poorer segments of the local population and rural residents. The sharp contrast between the two shopping places – the dirty and insecure area of the open-air market, and the shiny surfaces of the shopping mall – convey an idea of the progress and modern development that the city has undergone in recent decades.

Yet the shopping centre proved controversial because it had been constructed within the walls of a former linen factory that had closed in the mid-2000s. In Soviet days, linen cultivation and textile manufacturing were among the major industries of the region. Drawing upon the Hungarian experience, the regional Party authorities planned to restructure and amalgamate the textile manufacturing, but the complexities of bureaucratic coordination and then the collapse of the Soviet Union disrupted these plans for further developments in linen manufacturing (Klimenko 2001). When in the mid-2000s the linen factory went bankrupt, the local press accused the top management of deliberately bankrupting the state-owned enterprise and draining its capital into their own pockets.²⁶ As a local reporter put it, the linen factory, founded in the 1930s, remained immune from the 'barbaric' German bombings of World War II but could not survive the 'barbaric' era of the market reforms introduced by its own state. The factory symbolized the heydays of the Soviet industrialization project, and its conversion into a shopping centre was met with indignation by many of those city-dwellers who were in no rush to erase the memories of Soviet industrial modernity and the stability of employment associated with it. As the linen factory was a usual place for school excursions and practical training for local students, many Smolensk residents still remember the factory workshops, its pungent smells and the moist air inside. Former factory-workers refused to visit the shopping mall, as it was unbearably painful for them to see the changes. I also heard that the head of the Smolensk eparchy urged adherents of the Orthodox Church to avoid shopping in *Galaktika*.

The controversies and debates surrounding the industrial heritage of the Soviet period provide a vantage point for illustrating a major shift from the regime of work citizenship, with its emphasis on work identity, to the regime of consumer citizenship, which prioritizes the sphere of market transactions and practices of consumption (Carrier 1997). In the case of Russia, this change has been precipitated by the market reforms of the 1990s. As the vignette hints, the process of turning workers into consumers did not go smoothly, since many residents of the Russian province were reluctant to unimagine the benefits of work citizenship and embrace new consumer identities.

The story of *Galaktika* illustrates one disturbing effect of the transition in Russia, namely the growing deindustrialization and expansion of 'the sphere of exchange at the expense of production', a condition that Burawoy famously called 'involutionary degradation' or 'transition without transformation' (2001: 270). After the liberal deregulation of the 1990s, Russia's policies during the period of Putin-Medvedev-Putin rule revealed controversial tendencies, since the further neoliberal restructurings and austerity measures of this period were interspersed with statist initiatives and protectionist policies aimed to preserve Russia's industrial base (Rutland 2016; Matveev 2019). In the wake of the Crimean crisis in 2014 and the ensuing Western sanctions against Russia, the Russian government announced a shift towards import-substitution in order to reduce Russia's dependence on Western technologies and ultimately develop competitive export-oriented industries (Matveev 2019: 40). Many political analysts call

---

²⁶ *Zhizn i smert Lnokombinata* (The life and death of the linen factory), 27.03.2013. Available online, http://www.rabochy-put.ru/society/42440-zhizn-i-smert-lnokombinata.html, accessed 14 March 2021.

into question the long-term prospects of the new policy measures, given that they were influenced by apparent political concerns (Rutland 2016). Meanwhile, during my stay in Smolensk in 2015-16 the talk about the 'revival' of linen cultivation and the textile industry repeatedly popped up in the media. However, it was not clear what was the practical outcome of such talk in urging the revival of an industry that mainly lay in ruins. It was reported that some big investors had already indicated their interest in linen-manufacture in the region.

This chapter focuses on production and looks at the ways in which local petty producers have experienced the larger shifts and transformations outlined above. Under marketization, regional garment manufacturing has undergone profound restructuring, but it has not been swept away in the same manner as the linen production. All three of the city's garment manufacturing giants of the Soviet era managed to stay afloat in the market economy, but they have gone through significant downsizing and have had several changes of owners. In the wake of post-Soviet market deregulation, a plethora of medium-sized and small-scale factories specializing in garment production have emerged. Being exposed to the pressures of global competition, a changing economic environment and a severe lack of capital, most regional petty producers have not proved particularly viable in the local market, and have turned to subcontracting for national or foreign suppliers instead.

Drawing upon a case study, I aim to understand what motivates local producers to stay in the garment industry and how they adapt their firms to the economic conditions of flexible accumulation and globalization that are being experienced worldwide. Why are local business-people opening garment manufacturing firms? Where does their capital come from? How are they responding to the competitive pressures that are chiefly related to the influx of cheap goods imported from Asian markets? To what extent are neoliberal conditions affecting production regimes and the positioning of labour within the settings of small-scale manufacturing?

To answer these questions, I conduct a close-up examination of Alpha, a small-scale production firm that employs around thirty workers and has, by local standards, a rather long history stretching back to the early stage of Russian privatization in the late 1980s. Its capital derives from the Soviet manufacturing sector, and in this sense Alpha may be called an heir to the context of Soviet production methods. With all its ups and downs, the firm has gone through significant restructurings by downsizing the workforce and reorienting the lion's share of its production towards subcontracting for Moscow-based clients. Drawing upon an analysis of Alpha history, its production and distribution strategies, and the patterns of its labour-capital relationships, I aim to elucidate the specific regimes of value that underlie and shape the agency of the multiple actors involved in its work. I will start by outlining the firm's history and the work biography of its founder.

Soviet-Era Developmental Hopes and Market Promises

Lidia Alekseevna (59 years), a founder of Alpha, is not a native of Smolensk. Born and raised in eastern Siberia, she ended up on the Western edge of Russia due to labour migration in Soviet times. In an impressive series of relocations throughout the Soviet Union in the late 1970s, Lidia primarily followed her husband, who had several changes of jobs before finally ending up in Smolensk. As an aircraft engineer, he was appointed to the position of constructor at the local aircraft factory. Lidia, also an aircraft engineer, got a job with the same enterprise but in a different department. She describes her work in the industry as extremely boring and frustrating since it lacked creativity, a concept she places at the heart of her narrative of work and self-fashioning. Her engineering duties had nothing to do with the creation of new models but boiled down to annoying re-workings of drawings and fixing mistakes made by the other aircraft specialists. She believes that the engineers made mistakes on purpose with the sole aim of being given a bonus for allegedly improving the initial drawings. Being stuck in this process of endlessly redoing other's work, she perceived her job as meaningless and repetitive. As a result, she quit.

Lidia says she could never stand 'routine duties' but always admired 'inventiveness' (*izobretatelnost*) and 'innovations' (*novshestva*). For the first time in her life, she tasted this sort of fulfilling career in her college years after joining Komsomol, the Party's youth organization. As a Komsomol leader, she supervised students' participation in the field of 'amateur art and performance', through which the Party aimed to 'introduce culture to the masses'. One of her duties was to recruit freshmen in various art and drama clubs and organize concerts with their involvement. Her biggest achievement in the field of cultural production was Borodin's opera *Prince Igor*, which she staged at her university, with several hundred students acting, singing, dancing and playing in the orchestra. The opera was a great success and was recognized at the top level of the university administration. To start a Komsomol was a typical career pattern among the class of Soviet *nomenklatura,* the party-state bureaucracy. Lidia was determined to get back to this path one day.

Having quit the aircraft factory, she was allocated to the local Palace of Culture and Technology, which was part of the social and cultural infrastructure of the city garment factory. Due to her credentials and technical expertise, this former aircraft specialist was put in charge of propaganda with responsibility for promoting technical knowledge among factory workers and improving or 'rationalizing' work processes.

In her nostalgic memories of factory work, Lidia mainly emphasized her positive input in cultivating a sense of solidarity among the factory's workforce, which comprised around four thousand employees in the 1980s. Thanks to the concerts, quizzes, technical clubs, lectures and guest talks that she organized at the factory, its workers were constantly reconnected to much larger social entities beyond their immediate work teams and households. By inviting renowned rationalizers from the largest academic centres to give a talk in this provincial city, she helped workers realize that 'they are much needed by their society' and thus bound the factory workforce to an imagined community of Soviet workers. In talking vividly about this stage of her career, she did not touch upon the issues of production targets, labour productivity or the degree of efficiency of Soviet enterprises.

In her capacity as a deputy director of the garment factory, Lidia entered the period of major restructurings of the Soviet economy, which began to gain momentum in the mid-1980s. When the first laws permitting the setting up of commercial enterprises (cooperatives) were passed in 1987-88, she decided to start a new firm on the premises of the garment factory. With her new enterprise she planned to produce rag dolls by utilizing production waste that the state-run manufacturing giant had left behind in quantity. In fact, the factory's by-products provided a quite substantial resource, since the factory had not economized on materials distributed by the state: in fact, whenever subtle mismatches in colour or quality between different fabrics were detected, the entire batch of fabric would be disposed of as defective. However, the new project of using waste to produce rag dolls did not take off because of the sudden dismissal of the factory director who had assisted in putting this idea into practice.

Nevertheless, eventually, some years later, Lidia set up a cooperative, but this time together with a partner. Their joint venture was the result of pure coincidence, as her associate had no relationship whatever with the apparel industry, but was looking for a specialist with knowledge of garment production to assist him in setting up a commercial enterprise. Factory managers advised him to talk to Lidia, who knew the basics of production, and she accepted his offer. The new cooperative took over one of the factory's sewing shops. In her account of the formative years of this new commercial enterprise, Lidia showcased her passion for innovation and creativity, despite having to cope with the rigidity and bureaucracy of the Soviet planned economy. First of all, the new cooperative started producing children's clothes out of the factory's waste, which was cost-free to the firm. At that time baby clothing was in huge demand, and the main concern was not to sell it but to obtain materials and produce more. The garment factory was littered with by-products, including large amounts of defective fabric, but after a while the cooperative exhausted this free source of materials. Thanks to her insider connections with factory management, Lidia was able to purchase fabric for her cooperative at low, state-regulated prices, but the shortage in materials was still high in the late 1980s. Permanent shortages pushed Lidia to be more 'creative' in designing new clothing. For example, cotton was hard to obtain even with access to *blat* connections, while the locally produced linen was still the most affordable type of fabric in the region. But unlike synthetic fabrics – highly appreciated by Soviet consumers for their durability and good-looking qualities – linen garments easily creased and required more careful treatment in general. Lidia responded to this predicament by creating linen apparels that featured creases as a major element of design. Similarly, they produced colourful garments if they could not obtain enough fabric of the same colour or tone. Lidia turned this practice of 'making do' into a key business strategy, which she called 'turning negatives into positives'. Rather than seeing external constraints as an obstacle, she preferred to stress their enabling qualities, saying that this motivated her to look for creative solutions and introduce innovations.

For several years, the cooperative had been on a roll due to the expansion of its manufacturing capacities and its take-over of more sewing shops in the state-owned factory. Its output tapped into the huge demand for consumer goods in the late Soviet Union. Moreover, the cooperative aimed to compensate for those products that the Smolensk garment factory did not produce, like children's clothes. The output was sold in Smolensk and also trafficked to Moscow wholesalers, and again the connections of the former propaganda director were utilized for marketing purposes. However, growing disagreements and mutual suspicion between Lidia and her partner led to their separation in the early 1990s. When her partner started to dismiss the firm's core employees, Lidia feared that she might become the next target of this policy. Anticipating an insidious move on the part of her partner, she initiated the separation, which resulted in a severe struggle for the company's assets.

Lidia was reluctant to go into details about how the property was eventually divided. Lighting up a cigarette at this point in our interview, she promised to write a book someday about this most 'adventurous' time of her life. What transpired from her reluctant remarks is that the property war was waged quite brutally. Lidia put up a fight by simply taking over the means of production from the cooperative, its equipment and 'basically everything I could remove'. She says it was important to intimidate her enemy and convey a message to him and to a wider group of economic agents scrambling for resources in general – 'that if anyone takes anything away from me, I will do everything possible and impossible to get it back'. In response, her partner filed a lawsuit, which ended up on terms advantageous to Lidia. At that point, her share in the cooperative amounted to 180,000 roubles, but she was persistent enough to get compensation for inflation and received over two million roubles in the end. With this capital, she purchased a huge amount of fabric, relying on her privileged access to low, state-regulated prices. In 1992, after the major disagreements had been settled, Lidia started her own limited liability company, which she called Alpha.

It is well documented in scholarship on the transition in Russia that the members of the party-state apparatus, especially Komsomol functionaries, greatly benefited from the initial attempts at economic reform that started in the mid-1980s. With the emergence of the so-called Komsomol economy, the state elites were allowed to engage in activities that were prohibited to others, such as obtaining soft loans, converting state assets into cash or engaging in property dealings. The outcome of this 'privatization before privatization' was 'a substantial move towards the conversion of power of the party-state nomenklatura into private property' (Kryshtanovskaya and White 1996: 721).

Lidia herself certainly belonged to this cohort of early Russian capitalists who profited from converting their privileges into private ownership. While her account is silent on the many ins and outs of her 'adventurous' experiences of early capital accumulation, it still hints at her privileged access to privatized state-owned property, probably purchased for just a nominal price, as was usually the case in that 'golden age' of Russian capitalism (ibid.: 719). Moreover, Lidia had secure access to advantageous prices fixed by the state that enabled her to amass a large inventory of fabrics and accessories. Last but not least, the new enterprise profited from its reliance on networks and connections that Lidia used as a form of social asset inherited from the past.

However, this trajectory 'from power to property', which was typical of the Soviet *nomenklatura*, seems not to have shattered Lidia's commitment to the moral ideals of the Soviet era. By evoking Soviet values, she asserts her commitment to the goals of the Soviet modernization project and conceives her involvement in private business as being driven by the same hopes and aspirations of development (to build a 'better future') that underpinned the Soviet state-building project:

> We were building communism. Everyone was building communism. Everyone believed in it, everyone believed in the better future. Where are we now? (laughs) I personally do everything for the better future to come, really (laughs).

Lidia says that, even after switching to the private sector, she remained a 'state' person and was reluctant to turn herself into a 'private' one. Under capitalism her 'state'-oriented commitments continued to dictate her hierarchy of social responsibilities, in which a high priority was granted to the broader goals of state development, while social reproduction and household duties played an inferior role. Lidia's two children rarely saw her at home, and their encounters mainly took place on the factory premises (her daughter, now a manager in Alpha, called herself 'a factory kid'). Lidia defends this set of priorities by mobilizing the communitarian ideals of Soviet modernity: 'You are alive so long as your society needs you'.

By reflecting on her reluctance to become a 'private' person, Lidia suggests that she must have inherited these attitudes from her father, who belonged to the ranks of the Soviet labour aristocracy. With this moral genealogy in mind, she portrays her father as a typical 'state' person who was ready to sacrifice his 'private' interests for 'a better future'. As a manager engaged in construction projects in the post-war years, he was eligible for a state-allocated apartment. All his family anticipated the day when they could finally move out of a wooden dwelling without plumbing into a newly built block of flats. However, this never happened, as Lidia's father refused his entitlement, saying that he would accept an apartment only after all the ordinary workers in his brigade had been given new accommodation and been moved out of their shabby, overpopulated barracks. Lidia's mother was angry and upset about his decision but could not convince her husband to change his mind. When Lidia visited her home town in Siberia in the 2010s, she noticed that some of the wooden barracks were still in use. 'So, we had no chances to get a new apartment', she chuckled.

The body of literature on post-Soviet transformations reveals the remarkable revival of the party-state bureaucracy and propaganda workers in the post-reform years and their prominence in remaking Soviet forms in the new Russia. Soviet cultural workers and propagandists actively participated in spurring religious activism in the postsocialist era (Luehrmann 2011). To explain why former Soviet atheists so easily shed their secular identities, Luehrmann examines their 'elective affinities', that is, their ongoing interactions and the similarities between the secular forms of state-driven atheist propaganda and post-Soviet methods of religious mobilization. Drawing on such parallels, she argues that some post-Soviet religious identities have been built upon the models and means of personal transformations promulgated by Soviet-era secular institutions. She stresses the dynamic nature of such interactions as an ongoing 'back-and-forth', when the drive to emulate and recreate secular forms, which she calls 'recycling', alternates with keeping a 'tension-ridden distance' from them.

Another case of the reincarnation of former party members and cultural workers has been documented in a completely different institutional setting, that of the oil corporation (Rogers 2015). In the new era of state-building that started in the 2000s, former factory-based party figures re-created themselves as cultural managers designing corporate social responsibility programmes for oil companies. These new players on the corporate side were valued for their ability to do ideological work and negotiate compromises with a wide range of people (ibid.: 182).

Just like the Soviet activists studied by Luehrmann, Lidia was inserted into Soviet educational networks that held out 'the promise of limitless transformations' (2011: 217). In her case, however, the focus on *creativity* and *innovation* speaks for ongoing interactions of the transformative and developmental promises of Soviet secular science and education with the market's promises of endless growth and affluence. In this sense, the reinvigoration of the Soviet discourse, the value of gift-giving and the denigration of utilitarian concerns emerges as a response to the new market conditions and the lack of state interventions that would provide a hedge against foreign capital for local producers at a time of global competition. In the next section, I will show how such developmental hopes, wrapped up with memories of the Soviet Union's glorious industrial past, fuel the workings of small enterprises in the new epoch of what Burawoy (2001) called 'involuntionary degeneration'.

Not Market but *Bazaar*

When it was set up in 1992, Alpha was striving to take off under the rather dire economic conditions brought about by the abrupt measures of economic liberalization, known as 'shock therapy'. Amidst galloping inflation[27], surplus value had rapidly vanished by the end of the production cycle, as the value of the final product was even lower than the costs of the raw materials involved in its production. In hindsight, Lidia could not believe that her enterprise had survived those trying times. What helped the firm mitigate the adverse consequences of hyperinflation was the large reserve of fabrics that

---

[27] The hyper-inflation skyrocketed in Russia over the first half of the 1990s, with annual inflation rates of the order of 150% in 1991, 1500% in 1992, 900% in 1993, 300% in 1994 and 150% in 1995 (Novokmet, Piketty, and Zucman 2018).

the owners had been able to exploit due to Lidia's access to low prices. In the 1990s, economic players in Russia typically responded to inflation by engaging in barter transactions and offsetting trade, which led to the demonetization of the whole economy (Woodruff 1999). Alpha also took that path by exchanging its output for textiles at the same garment factory that had employed Lidia in Soviet times. Her contacts and connections were another crucial factor contributing to the survival of the fledging firm. On the regional level, such contacts facilitated finding production facilities for rent at advantageous terms or getting new customers through her circle of friends and acquaintances. Her contacts in Moscow served to arrange the deals and sell the output to Moscow wholesalers.

Once the dust had settled by the mid-1990s, the firm had arrived at a relatively stable market position. This was achieved primarily due to its contracts with a couple of big customers, national representatives of Western pharmaceutical companies that ordered lab-coats from Alpha. It is worth giving an example of how Alpha made a deal with one such customer, since this provides a glimpse of the role of personal networks in business matters, as well as demonstrating the marketing approach as such. As the story goes, the director of the local concert hall, a friend of Lidia's, asked her to help him out in organizing a dinner for a group of visiting therapists who had rented a room in the concert hall for their corporate event. Driven by mutual obligations of long-standing friendship, Lidia helped her friend to arrange the dinner and, in exchange for this favour, was allowed to place some of her wares – samples of medical uniforms – for sale in the same room. One of her nylon lab-coats grabbed the attention of a future customer, who happened to be a representative of a German pharmaceutical company. He was thrilled to discover a nylon lab-coat, being aware of their life-long durability. 'He says... please give me this nylon lab coat..., I will wear it for the rest of my life'. He said he had been actively looking for a uniform made of nylon all over Europe, only to come across the desired product on the edge of Russia. After this memorable event, Alpha began producing white nylon coats for this new client. What is notable in this account is the minimal amount of effort involved in selling the product, which could basically speak for itself on the basis of its use-value. This was therefore a case not of a manufacturer looking for a client but of client actively hunting out a commodity and discovering it by chance on the periphery of the European garment industry. This incident was not just a happy coincidence, but rather implied that a high-quality commodity would always find a way to enter the market place without requiring any marketing or 'brand value'.

After its heyday in the early 2000s, the firm sank into crisis in 2008. Although this trajectory shadowed the global economic downturn, Alpha's slowdown was triggered by local conditions, especially changes to the national regulations for medical services. As the state attempted to do away with pharmaceutical companies that actively promoted their products among doctors and forced them to prescribe particular drugs, it outlawed any form of gift-giving between the two parties. For Alpha this ban put an end to its lucrative collaboration with the Western drugs firms, as it had given lab-coats to doctors in order to stimulate their loyalty to the brand. After losing two big clients, Alpha came close to shutting down. The only solution that let it stay afloat was to switch to subcontracting and assemble clothes for firms looking for cheap labour in provincial cities. The switch from own production to subcontracting was intended to be an emergency measure while waiting out the crisis, but as time passed it became clearer and clearer that subcontracting was the only viable option for this small apparel firm to survive the growing global competition and the new economic crunch.

That is not to say there were no attempts to end subcontracting and the dependence on bigger firms. Just before the economic crisis exploded at the end of 2014, Lidia set up a knitting workshop and hired four additional workers specializing in knitting operations. With this new unit, which she called an 'experimental shop', she planned to start producing school uniforms. However, when in 2014 the rouble lost almost half its value against the dollar and the cost of imported materials increased dramatically, it was decided to suspend the project. At the same time, Lidia set up a retail shop selling the lab-coats and other uniforms that the firm occasionally produced for its individual customers, usually local restaurants and industrial enterprises. Producing uniforms seemed to be the only viable option for the firm given that the local market had been flooded with cheap clothes imported from China. For Lidia, shopping was always a painful activity, as she was constantly reminded of global competition. One day she spotted a nicely decorated nightdress made in China on sale for only two hundred roubles or three euros. Shocked at how low the price was, she immediately calculated that to produce the same item at her firm would cost her a minimum of six hundred roubles or approximately eight euros.

As already mentioned, global competition was aggravated by the decline in the rouble's value in 2014. Since then, the prices of imported textiles have increased significantly, while the purchasing capacity of local customers has declined. To make uniforms, Alpha used fabrics imported from Turkey and Malaysia. Accordingly, fluctuations in national currencies immediately affected local garment producers. Attempts to engage with public procurement by submitting a bid proved pointless for a small firm that could not compete with big producers offering the lowest prices and thus winning the contracts. Like many other small firms in my sample, Alpha routinely sought to reduce its costs by manipulating its tax bill. The firm was registered as two independent companies, each with its own legal status and taxation scheme applied to different ends. This enabled the first firm to sell its products to the second one at artificially low prices and to record only a little profit or a loss, thus paying only a low profits tax. Reducing wages was the other firm's cost-cutting strategy. In early 2016, the firm announced its plan to reduce regular wages, justifying this measure with reference to the economic downturn and the decline in profits. Apart from the sewing workshop in Smolensk, Alpha ran a second workshop in the region surrounding the city, where the cost of labour was even lower than in the city.

In the wake of the currency crisis, there was a lot of uncertainty about the company's future. Lidia oscillated between showing discontent with the market and self-flagellation for being too 'lazy' to come up with a solution to escape her dependence on subcontracting. While she did not give up hope of overcoming the global competition by means of her creativity and savvy, her criticisms of the market prevailed. I will pause on this criticism, which revealed a disenchantment with the market and its value regime. According to Lidia, the market in Russia has never functioned in the way it was designed to do by the architects of the market transition. Instead, Russia has adopted the worst version of the market, one that Lidia called '*bazaar*', thus communicating the sense of disarray and backwardness that distinguished the Russian economy from Western, that is, civilized forms of market exchange. In everyday usage, the word *bazaar* refers to open-air markets and conjures up an image of cheap imported wares of low-quality, dirty surroundings and pungent smells, pickpockets, shuttlers and migrant labour – in other words, very primitive forms of exchange that were a far cry from the Western-inspired images of advanced capitalism.

With regard to the garment sector, *bazaar* stands for the poor quality of goods, but it is easily scaled up and coagulated into a regime of value in which considerations of taste, culture and morality no longer play a significant role. The predicaments Alpha faced illustrate how the logic of the *bazaar* economy clashes with Alpha's owner's hierarchy of values and imparts an image of disarray. The high quality of Alpha's wares, supposedly its main competitive advantage, paradoxically turned into a source of weakness that hindered the company's growth, since there was no need for its customers to purchase new garments as often as they would have to purchase poor-quality imported goods. As Lidia's daughter, a manager in Alpha, proudly reported, the average life-cycle of their lab coats was about ten years. In light of frequent changes in fashion and the mediocre quality of Chinese merchandise, Alpha just could not comply with the rhythms of a fast fashion industry: 'We make clothing of such high-quality that people do not need to exchange it hundred times. This is our main weakness'.

For her part, Lidia represented her way of doing business as a form of resistance to the pervasive patterns of production, accumulation and consumption that she described as the logic of the *bazaar* economy. She said she could purchase cheaper fabrics from Chinese suppliers and thus reduce the costs of her final product, but she would rather not to do so because she 'respected' her clients. She recalled one of her wealthy Moscow customers, who had placed a lucrative order that Lidia rejected since she considered his design to be in poor taste and decided not to risk her reputation by manufacturing such 'crap'. When diplomatic relations between Russia and Turkey turned sour in 2014, some customers started blaming Lidia for using Turkish fabrics in her production, which they equated with a lack of patriotism. To Lidia, all this proved just one thing – that the vast majority of urban consumers 'had been raised in the wrong way' and had failed to discern the 'deeper essences' of things. As a result, many people were easily seduced by appearances, whether brand names, fashion styles or superficial displays of patriotism.

It is easy to recognize this sort of criticism as echoing Soviet norms of consumption, with their imperatives of good taste and culturedness (Chernyshova 2013), but in a broader sense it evokes the 'language of depth' (Rogers 2015) as manifested, for instance, in the discourse of the Russian soul (Pesmen 2000). Many analyses of postsocialism demonstrate that the search for the deeper essences of things and denunciations of material concerns as shallow and superficial have been precipitated by the market reforms and have helped many Russians make sense of the growing deprivation, collapse of economic stability and loss of incomes that have occurred in the wake of economic liberalization (Lemon 1998; Ries 2002; Patico 2008). However, it is not only the victims of the Russian transition that have tapped into the language of depth. In his analysis of the rise of the Lukoil corporation, Rogers (2015) demonstrates how this oil company introduced a rhetoric of depth into the language of corporate social responsibility, drawing parallels between the geological depth of oil reserves and the depth of Russian culture. By evoking the authority of culture, Lukoil strove to shift the focus from the negative impact associated with oil extraction and refining – such as 'toxicity, convertibility into massive wealth, and inequalities of exclusion' – to the benefits for local communities associated with social projects and the revival of cultural production out of the post-Soviet ruins (ibid.: 232-4).

In the case of the small-garment business, the language of depth served to convey discontent and concerns about the growing global competition that was flooding over the national boundaries and driving local producers out of the market. We may expect that such criticism would call on the state to protect the nation's capital against the expansion of global accumulation; yet, the role of the state was insignificant and mainly missing from my conversations with Lidia and her daughter. For both of them, the state and its ruling cliques were represented as being so busy with the scramble for resources and asset-stripping that it would be naïve to expect them to serve public interests. Feeling that she had been abandoned by the state, Lidia regarded her resistance to global capitalist forces as a matter of individual responsibility and an inextricable moral choice. As the following excerpts from my fieldnotes show, she reflected at some length on this topic, showing how patriotic sentiments, hopes for development and the ethic of disinterestedness mutually reinforce each other and become coagulated in resisting the image of deindustrialized modernity:

[Lidia Alekseevna recounts a story she heard from a friend about a local garment producer who used to purchase fabric from China and one day decided to pay a visit his supplier in China.] He travelled to China himself to buy textiles. And there he was asked what he was going to do with this fabric. He says: 'I produce shirts' – 'But why do you do this if we have a lot of ready-made shirts?' And they led him to their storage and showed him a variety of shirts of different sorts. And they said: 'Three dollars each.' And he was shocked. He said: 'I pay my workers three dollars... in equivalent to local currency, of course... I pay three dollars to my workers to make one item, but there they offered me a ready-made garment for three dollars!' And I was shocked when I heard this story because... really, they will drive us out soon, manufacturers have already been pressed hard, and they are being pressed further.

[Then Lidia Alekseevna shared this story with a local business owner whose company sold bottled water.] So, we are chatting with him, and I say: 'But what's next? Am I supposed to travel to China, buy lab coats for three dollars, which cost here ten dollars (...) and just sell them here? But then I have to kick out my own workers from the company.' He says: 'So what?' I say: 'OK, I'll get rich. And the rest, who are as smart as I am, would go to China, do the same thing, and kick out everyone as I would have done.' And I ask: 'What's next?' He says: 'What do you mean? You will move to Austria, you'll amass money, you'll become rich and move to Austria.' I say: 'But I want to make Austria here!' He says: 'I don't believe you!' And I say: 'OK, I don't care.' After that we started chatting about the place where I was born [Lidia Alekseevna goes on to describe harsh Siberian conditions – D.T.]. And he says: 'Ah, now I believe you!' I ask: 'Why? What happened?' He says that once they travelled somewhere in the north and they got lost... or they lost someone. So, they were looking for someone, and they saw a hut. They walked into the hut and saw the wads of cash there. The money was just left there and nobody wanted it, nobody took it. I say: 'Well, people there use banknotes to light a fire. There is no other use for them (laughs).' He says: 'Now I believe you!' (laughs). Well... This is what life in Siberia is like. Really, it is such a good place... and people from Siberia they are quite different, I can say that for sure.

In these two excerpts, Lidia expressed her concerns and discontent with global competition as a matter of individual morality that had little to do with the state's responsibility to protect the interests of the nation's capital, as proclaimed in Russia's import-substitution policy. Her own moral ideals are a decisive factor holding her back in garment manufacturing and preventing her from switching into trade, where the margins are higher and accumulation is easier. In this sense, she presents engaging in production as a form of self-sacrifice inasmuch as small-scale manufacturing does not guarantee secure profits and seems to have no future. Her resistance to deindustrialized modernity is driven by exclusively personal sentiments, whose uniqueness, anomalous for the period of capitalism, is explained by virtue of being born in a pristine, remote place where money had no value. The geographical remoteness of her place of birth translates into a distance from the motivations and notorious lifestyles of the Russian nouveaux riches, who make fortunes by all available means and then move their capital abroad. All in all, this emphasis on individual responsibility and unique moral standing shifts the focus from questioning the presupposition of deindustrialization and renders the very moment of resistance a moral value in its own right.

As in many other global contexts of capitalist expansion, the workforce paid the bigger price when Alpha switched to subcontracting and aligned itself with the global division of labour. Since the transition, a dozen machine operators have started to assemble clothes that proudly state having been 'Designed in Paris' on their labels, but the cost of their operations dropped significantly and was measured in kopeks. Lidia told herself and her workers that this was just a temporary arrangement and that she hoped to make the business thrive again. In the next section, I will show how the retreat to the sphere of art and creative work as a space free from market constraints and uncertainties represented an affective response to stifling global conditions and enabled Lidia and her daughter to enjoy a level of job satisfaction that flew in the face of the precarious present of economic involution.

The Space of Creative Work and Market Value Suspended

One winter day the three of us, Lidia, her daughter Alina (29 years) and I, got together in the tiny office with the 'Director' sign on the door. As usual, the office was full of thick cigarette smoke, as Lidia smoked a lot. The factory occupied the ground floor in a block of flats located in a residential area that had been built in Soviet times to accommodate the workforce from the adjacent industrial enterprises. It was rather chilly inside since the central hitting barely functioned. Lidia offered us all a shot of cognac to warm ourselves up a bit and dispel any sad feelings provoked by the ongoing conversation. At that point we were chatting about religion. Lidia and her daughter both identified themselves as Orthodox believers, but, as is typical of many Russians, they did not trust religious institutions and avoided the guidance of religious specialists and other forms of religious belonging (Köllner 2012). In characteristic manner, they blamed Orthodoxy for being seduced by marketization and turning religious services into a commodity (cf. Caldwell 2010; Tocheva 2014). Alina objected to the price tags for religious services and the paraphernalia that were displayed in Orthodox churches, which she read as a message that 'Mercy is not to be deserved through your own spiritual efforts anymore, but can simply be purchased with money'. On the other hand, she regarded religious institutions as deeply detached from modern life, whose hectic rhythms were at odds with the slow pace of Orthodox rituals. At this point, she told the story of her memorable consultation with a priest who demanded that she attend a religious service that was starting at 10 am. Alina objected: she had to be at work at that time and could not afford to spend a couple of precious hours in the church. In his turn, the priest objected, advising her to be more relaxed about her job and giving her the Biblical example of birds and animals who did not have to work but were nevertheless generously fed by the Lord. Alina could not believe he was serious in telling her all this 'nonsense' about animals. She did not argue with him, but could not stop wondering whether the priest was aware that it was her taxes that enabled the state to function. Did not he know how much the state extracted from entrepreneurs? Or was he hinting that they should shut the factory down, move to countryside and switch to a subsistence economy? Or maybe he expected her to turn into an animal? None of this made sense to her and implied only involution and degradation. After this visit, Alina ceased to consult Orthodox priests altogether and changed to seeking assistance from magi. Her mother also consulted them, especially at times when her enterprise was not performing well. Moreover,

Lidia practised magic rituals herself and was good at folk medicine. Mother and daughter both attended Orthodox church irregularly, only when their 'souls' reminded them to do so.

While Alina was expressing her outrage against the church, her mother kept remarkably silent, although occasionally she nodded and grinned. Then Alina initiated a new round of complaining with a story that denounced the church authorities for replacing the famous icon of Smolensk's Virgin Mother with a copy, and what is more doing so without announcing it publicly. As a result, many visitors to Smolensk Cathedral, where the icon was kept, had been misled by this quiet replacement, but not Alina, who immediately detected the substitution. At this point, Lidia intervened. It did not matter, she said, whether the icon was original or not. After she had had a terrible accident in her car, she went to the Cathedral and spent hours crying in front of the icon. It did not matter to her whether the icon was original or not so long as she felt a connection with it in the form of some sort of '*energy*'. Her church visit coincided with a large religious feast, but she just completely ignored what she saw as a pompous religious service and the priests in their golden robes looming in front of her. Lidia concluded that ignoring 'bad things' was her ultimate rule in life. Drawing on this skill to render invisible the things she did not like, she could afford to save her time and energy and re-invest them in doing things she liked:

> I do not notice bad things just because I do not want to notice them (…), because if I notice them, I won't feel like doing something good, something beautiful. So, I prefer not to notice. I see things through rose-tinted spectacles (laughs). I put them on and go ahead. I turn on music really loud [in the car] and give it some gas. Otherwise it's so difficult to live in our country (laughs).

I see striking similarities between this principle and that described by Yurchak (2006) with regard to the style of living in late socialism, which he calls 'being *vney*', or outside. According to Yurchak, living *vnye* is better described as 'being simultaneously inside and outside of some context – such as, being within a context while remaining oblivious of it, imagining yourself elsewhere, or being inside your own mind. It may also mean being simultaneously a part of the system and yet not following certain of its parameters' (ibid.: 128). Yurchak argues that the principle of 'being *vney*' should not be equated with 'a form of opposition to the system' since it represents 'a central and widespread principle of living in that system' (ibid.). While some virtuosi mastered living a life of oblivion to an extreme extent, the majority of Soviet citizens, including Party and Komsomol leaders, oscillated between being uninterested in the Soviet system and drawing on the possibilities it offered. In this way, 'being *vney*' did not contradict being a good Soviet citizen.

In Lidia's case this familiar way of 'suspending' a context while still participating in it survived and retained its relevance after the Soviet-era normative discourse lost its authority. In the market epoch, she successfully recycled 'being *vnye*' as a crucial skill with which to manage the insecurities of the market economy. That is not to say that Lidia completely avoided being critical and expressing her discontent (her interview indicates that this was not the case), only to stress her capacity to dissociate herself from such constraints and to find satisfaction in realms she had carved out for herself as spaces of freedom and authenticity. This also seems to hold true for her Komsomol past and work in Soviet propaganda, as she mentioned the dark sides of these jobs in passing but preferred not to pay much attention to them. In the same vein, during her visit to the church, Lidia created her own personal space of religious authenticity, which was simultaneously outside the ritual context and yet within it. Moreover, her business strategy ('turn negatives into positives') stems from the same principle of not noticing 'bad things'. I also suggest that the Western idioms of 'positive thinking' that are successfully winning over the hearts of so many Russians have local cultural equivalents that are rooted in the Soviet practice of constructing imaginative distances from what were considered 'bad things', that is, externally imposed and inevitable things, akin to the Weberian life-order that seems to last 'forever', just as the collapse of socialism seemed unimaginable to its citizens. In the post-Soviet epoch, the 'iron cage' of the market came to represent a new set of constraints everyone had to deal with. Whereas post-Soviet actors admittedly developed different responses to market pressures, here I will elucidate one specific reaction that refers to the peculiar Soviet practice of being simultaneously inside and outside any particular context.

As I have already shown, running a small factory in a period of global competition and a lack of state protection was never an easy task for Lidia. In times of crisis, the prospect of having to close down was in the air, but Lidia persistently shrugged that off by looking for ways and resources to stay afloat. In severe cases, when, for example, her Moscow clients delayed payments for several months and her machine operators were ready to go on a strike, Lidia fell back on a family budget by asking her husband to lend her money from the savings he had made from his wages at the aircraft plant (military industry has been on the rise since the 2000s). In such situations, the garment firm turned into a liability for the family budget rather than being an asset. I outlined above the role of the moral values that motivated Lidia to run the firm and resist deindustrialization. In this section, I want to draw attention to yet another side of this situation that feeds Lidia's motivation to stay in the game, namely the factory as a place of creative work.

Earlier I pointed out the central role of creativity as a constitutive element of Lidia's work biography. Framed in the typical vocabulary of the Soviet technical intelligentsia as a love of innovation and invention, this aspect links the different stages of her career and instils a sense of continuity in the flipping of her work trajectory between labour and capital. In what follows, I will show to what extent the ideology of creative work has affected the process of decision-making and shaped the organization of work at the factory.

Given that the factory acts as a subcontractor for others and does not manufacture its own garments, the passion for creative work has been channelled in another direction. While industrial garment production was relegated to 'routine duties' and ultimately did not provide any work satisfaction, the field of creativity had its own spatiality: within the factory it was confined to the workings of the 'experimental' workshop and spilt over the factory walls in the form of active participation in fashion and trade shows. As mentioned earlier, the experimental unit was set up just before the rouble crashed in 2014 with the aim of producing knitted school uniforms. After the uniforms project had been put off until a better day, the unit continued to operate. The knitting team was mainly involved in making evening dresses for individual customers, usually well-off friends of the owner, craftwork (making accessories, home decorations, souvenirs, etc.) and producing complicated, hand-stitched apparel for fashion shows. The shows absorbed a lot of attention and work on the part of the owner and her daughter. As a rule, several months before a show started, the two women, accompanied by a designer from the 'experimental' team, immersed themselves in the preparations, discussing the items they would be presenting, creating new collections, selecting the music, contacting model agencies, etc. By participating in the trade shows that usually take place in the larger Russian cities, the company was attempting to sell its output, which was designed specifically for this sort of event. While preparations for the trade shows brought a great deal of satisfaction to Lidia and her daughter, it did not produce earnings as such. Their extravagantly costly dresses were rarely sold at fashion shows and trade fairs. Of the variety of such events, Lidia Alekseevna could recall only one held in St Petersburg where they had successfully sold a wedding dress to a Swedish customer for 350 euros. Upon returning from a trade show in Kazan in 2016, however, Alina admitted that they had brought back almost the whole batch of products they had offered for sale. The market has dropped, and people do not have enough money: that was the usual explanation for sluggish sales. It also transpired that the 'experimental' unit that served occasional individual customers but mainly assisted in preparations for new fashion shows was incurring losses covered by the income earned by the industrial workshop.

Ultimately, Alina's career path was moulded by the same passion for creativity. As a child Alina did not demonstrate any artistic talent whatsoever, and by the end of her school years she was preparing for medical school. However, her poor academic results in chemistry did not allow her to enter the prestigious Smolensk medical institute. At the time, her mother's friend, an artist and teacher at the local art college, suddenly discovered that Alina had a 'sense of colour'. Lidia was delighted to hear this and encouraged Alina to pursue a career in design. That was quite a challenge for a girl with no previous training in drawing, but after taking intensive private classes from the same artist, she was finally enrolled in one of Moscow's design institutes. Studying design and garment manufacture also posed a challenge for Alina due to her lack of extensive practice in drawing. Several times she was on the verge of dropping out, only to be saved by her mother, who intervened in a timely fashion and helped her resolve her arguments with her teachers. Even so, Alina successfully defended her diploma, despite being in the last months of her pregnancy, and then moved back to Smolensk to raise her child and assist her mother in the factory. At the end of the day, her degree in design proved to be more of symbolic value, since she has never utilized her design skills, apart from spontaneous participation at fashion shows. Design tasks at the factory were regularly performed by two other employees: Inessa, a former Soviet model and a tailor from the 'experimental' unit who accompanied Alina to fashion shows; and Anna Albertovna, a specialist with a university degree in garment manufacturing whose professional advice Alina often sought in relation to her own experiments in design. Despite having professional training, Alina considered herself an 'amateur' who had missed a lot of technical knowledge about design during her studies (the boring part) but could compensate for this lack with her practical knowledge and imagination (that is, her creativity).

Lidia was very proud of her daughter's achievements in clothes design. She cherished Alina's diploma project, and we spent much time in her office going through Alina's drawings and discussing the peculiarities of her artistic vision. When I first saw Alina's sketches, I was struck by the violence of her fantasy, as all the drawings featured people in bizarre costumes, adorned with geometrical ornaments and the elements of industrial design, and more suitable as an illustration for a science-fiction novel than for mass market production. I asked Lidia whether they had made any use of Alina's student works. The answer was no, although some rare elements of design have been utilized in the items prepared for fashion shows. Lidia showed me some photos from the shows, pointing to the garments that had won first prize, such as a linen skirt covered with handmade fluorescent paintings. Finally, she explained why she was so willing to invest her time, energy and money in fashion shows:

> The thing is that all this routine work… I do not like it… this [industrial] workshop… it is routine. And sometimes I want, so to say, to distract myself.

I argue that such occasional retreats from industrial production into the realm of creative work enabled Lidia and her daughter to carve out spaces where they could finally realize their creative selves and acquire a sense of agency in their work against a backdrop that placed substantial limits on it. This realm of creativity ultimately existed outside of market rationality and its regime of value. Or, to be more precise, through their creative work mother and daughter have both striven to suspend market imperatives by rendering them invisible for a while. Creative work did not generate a profit as such, and from the market perspective it was considered a liability, but precisely as a result it allowed them to enjoy an alternative regime of value in which considerations of taste and job satisfaction came to the fore. The extent to which the realm of creative work turned out to be detached from any market value was made evident by the sarcastic remarks that Anna Albertovna, the technical designer, continually made about the 'experimental' unit's output. Based on her experience of working in big garment factories, she saw the extravagant dresses that Alina produced as being hopelessly outdated, stuck in the fashions of the 1990s, and merely unprofessional ('*domoroshchennyi*' design, as she put it derogatorily). On several occasions, she advised Alina to check out the nearest shopping mall and alter the design of what she produced to suit what was currently in demand in the market. Alina just made fun of such comments and shrugged them off. After all, she could afford the luxury of not paying attention to crazy changes in fashion design and could rely exclusively on her own aesthetic values and considerations of taste.

However, in being detached from market value spatially, temporally and aesthetically, creative work was simultaneously deeply interwoven into the realm of the market. The market was an ever-present reality in the talk of Lidia and her daughter, but its criteria were constantly changing, oscillating between the oblivion of market value and its mobilization. When asked about their involvement in fashion and trade shows, both mother and daughter pointed out their material interest and considerations of profit, as they expected their output to be sold entirely during such events. But even though trade shows provided a place for market exchange, both women were perfectly aware of their low chances of generating a profit due to the high costs of participating in this sort of event. Not only did they have to pay their travel expenses (mainly petrol, as they usually travelled in their own car), but also a rent for a pitch in the market, which was quite expensive for a small business. In the previous decade, these costs had partly been covered by the local Chamber of Industry and Commerce, which encouraged Smolensk's manufacturers to present their products at big textile exhibitions, but this support dried up after 2008. For Alpha's owners, the opportunity to present their local brand at trade fairs and fashion shows to a wider audience of visitors – not necessarily prospective customers – proved to be no less important than the phantom possibilities of market exchange. Given this tension between the high symbolic value of shows and their low returns, I see a profit-seeking motive as a legitimizing exercise that justified material investments in trade shows and fairs, which would otherwise be seen as wasteful and extravagant in the face of increasing local and global economic constraints.

Yet, despite these little tricks, which allowed the firm's management to ease the economic pressures and unleash their creative selves, in the end it was local and global market forces that dictated the realm of possibilities and put a limit on this fragile space of creativity. Since the possibilities for creative work were predicated upon surplus value generated by industrial production, such work was inevitably paid for out of the labour power of the firm's industrial workers. For them creativity meant something different, being reformulated by the firm's management in terms of flexible skill. Moreover, the kind of distraction from 'routine duties' that Lidia and her daughter sought in creative work affected the rhythms of production and time discipline in a peculiar way that reinforced flexible forms of exploitation.

Creativity for Workers: Flexible Skills and Arbitrary Control

Much like her mother, Alina admired creative work, but her take on creativity had additional layers that led her to understand creativity in the context of managerial control. For her, creative attitudes to a job implied the flexibilization of skill and the ability to perform multiple tasks. Alina saw herself as a perfect example of the embodiment of this principle: from a young age she had performed a variety of tasks in the family business, working as a night watchman, a packer, a book-keeper, a cutter and a manager. In her official capacity as a deputy director, Alina coordinated the overall work processes at the factory, but in case of need she could substitute for any skilled worker. She did not reflect upon her intermediate position between capital and labour, an ambiguity that provided her with moral arguments to demand the same flexibility from the workers. For Alina herself this flexibility made part of her work beneficial, since she could switch back and forth between different tasks and avoid tedium: as soon as she got bored with the task in hand, she just dropped it and turned to something else, like chatting with other workers or making phone calls. When their regular clients dropped by, Alina led them to the director's office and spent an hour or so discussing things and drinking tea, then slowly walked them to the entrance, and then chatted a bit more outside before saying a final goodbye. That sort of flexibility was an enjoyable part of her job, but hardly affordable for the rest of workforce.

Moreover, Alina never did the sewing, claiming that she would only destroy expensive machinery, and then the cost of her labour would be exceeded by the damage she had caused. Thus, she defined a number of tasks she was ready to perform if the need arose to fill in for an absent worker. Given labour turnover and unexpected sick-leave, it was crucial for a small enterprise to ensure a smooth workflow in order to meet a deadline and deliver output to the client in due time. Sewing aside, Alina claimed she could easily replace any other skilled worker. Indeed, when the firm was looking for a new cutter to work on individual tailoring orders, Alina took on this job for a couple of months while the position was vacant. Any time a new candidate showed up at the factory and Alina introduced her to a job, she stressed the creative aspect of the worker's cutting responsibilities. By evoking creativity, she aimed to spark an interest in the candidate, hoping to see 'a gleam in her eyes' in return. However, for Alina creativity was also a euphemism referring to a variety of skills involved in the work process, as well as a flexible schedule and the need to work longer hours to meet a deadline without extra pay. The firm had been searching for a good candidate for several months, but none of them had the required skill levels. In the end, Alina chose Elena (45 years) who had previously cut fabric in the big garment industry. With a university diploma in accounting, Elena had never dealt with tailoring before. As a result, she had no experience in taking measurements or cutting fabric manually, since her previous duties involved only industrial cutting. It was not creativity as such that attracted her to a new job but the fact that it was less physically demanding than her previous place of work, and the salary in Alpha was not significantly lower (200 euros per month as against 240 in the larger enterprise). Other than that, in taking up a new job, she expected to acquire new skills and thus acquire a competitive edge in the labour market.

Plate 3. The cutter fulfilling individual orders in Alpha.

With her usual enthusiasm, Alina started to train the new worker from scratch, dusting off her university textbooks and giving Elena some extended lectures on designing and tailoring clothing. In a week, when her zeal had worn off, Alina lost any interest in teaching and became absorbed in the preparations for an upcoming trade show. In the end, the task of training the new worker was transferred to Anna Albertovna, the designer, who shared the same shop floor with Elena and hoped to shift some of her responsibilities on to the new worker. Anna spent several months teaching her apprentice when there was any spare time in working hours. She became very upset when Elena quit six months later as a result of a conflict with her employer. The conflict erupted when Elena found out that all this time she had been working informally in Alpha, although the employer had agreed to give her formal status from the very beginning (it was common practice in Alpha to negotiate one's employment status). In fact the employer just took her labour book and never registered Elena officially. Anna fully supported Elena in her claims, despite deeply regretting losing a specialist whom she 'had trained from scratch'. Being one of the critical voices among the workforce, Anna did not hide her moral outrage against the firm's owner and expressed it directly after Elena had left, saying to her boss that 'one can tolerate low wages and wage arrears, but one cannot tolerate being fooled!'

Thus, however hard the manager tried to disguise the precarious working conditions or compensate for them with the allure of creativity, it never worked well. The employees at the factory were not really convinced of Alina's ability to perform multiple tasks. Instead, they saw her work as a perfect example of lousy work discipline and began to question her authority. Anna was perfectly aware that Alina could handle a sewing machine, as she had seen her stitching bedclothes for her child with her own eyes. To her it was obvious that Alina avoided sewing because she was 'lazy' and not capable of focusing on 'routine tasks' and getting things done, not because she lacked the skill. What Alina regarded as a manifestation of her creative self was actually evidence of her lack of self-discipline and self-control in the eyes of her employees. Lacking these qualities, her managerial power and attempts to convince others to work more intensively were constantly questioned and ignored by the workers on the shop floor. That was evident in remarks they made behind her back. Once Alina told two industrial cutters, who were about to start cutting fabric for outerwear for dogs, to 'economize' on the materials, urging them to reduce the space between the pieces to a minimum and thus save more textiles from being wasted. 'Economize!' shouted one of the cutters as soon as Alina left, mimicking her order. 'What's next? We are not paid for that! She herself has been cutting hats for a month while we were trying to economize'. Indeed, what irritated the workers more than the low wages was this tension between the manager's attempts to increase their productivity and the relaxed working conditions that Alena was able to enjoy herself. How could she demand that they work more intensively if she could not achieve the same level of work productivity herself? And given that she constantly failed to measure up to the standards of labour discipline, why was she eligible to receive guaranteed wages and they were not?

To persuade garment workers to work more intensively in order to meet a deadline was particularly hard in the workshop. Eleven operators, packers, pressers and ironworkers were paid on a piece-work basis. Depending on the number of orders, their monthly wages fluctuated between thirty and two hundred euros. Part of the workforce was registered with the firm (as a rule, the most skilled operators), while the other part (all pensioners and low-skilled workers) worked unofficially. In an effort to persuade the sewing team to work faster, the forewoman, Ksenya Ivanovna (52 years), appealed to the model of the 'entrepreneurial worker', with its impetus to redirect the source of work discipline and control from employer to employee (Voss and Pongratz 2003). She kept telling the operators that they could easily earn more if they worked more efficiently and faster and not in their usual 'goose-stepping' manner (*v razvalochku*). 'I just want you to earn more!' was her usual way of justifying the strict time discipline on the shop floor. Apart from these attempts to increase labour productivity in working hours, the operators were welcome to stay longer at the workplace or to come into the factory at weekends and on holidays. Almost none of them responded to such urging. The material incentives were too meagre to motivate them to work longer hours. Instead, they preferred to invest their off-hours in cultivating their own plots, doing domestic work or spending time with their children and grandchildren.

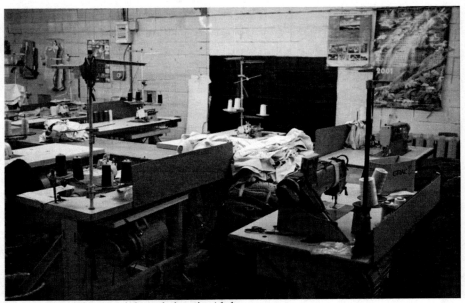

Plate 4. Part of industrial workshop in Alpha.

Moreover, some operators rejected the model of the entrepreneurial worker. Instead of assuming that their low wages resulted from their poor work discipline, they blamed the forewoman for that. Vika (35 years), an operator and another critical voice in the factory, was a big opponent of Ksenya Ivanovna. According to Vika, a good forewoman should align with the interests of the workforce and fight against reductions to their wages, as their previous forewoman did before she was sacked. Vika despised people in power like Ksenya Ivanovna, who, instead of protecting labour from capital, turned their backs on labour and chose to secure themselves the profits of capital instead. When Ksenya Ivanovna had just started to work in Alpha, Vika tried to teach her how to be a good forewoman, but her attempts to publicly shame their new forewoman came to nought and typically ended in the two women shouting and swearing at each other intensively. In the end, Vika had had to step back, since these exchanges of hatred were badly affecting her own health, and she had started taking sedatives (rumours had it that Ksenya also worked under sedation). But even when holding back her anger and keeping her silence, Vika ignored the calls to work more intensively, proceeded to sew at her usual speed and took regular breaks. As a high-skilled operator, Vika, who had worked for Alpha for eight years, acquired a high level of authority among both workers and management, which entitled her to have a degree of autonomy at work.

Not all the operators supported Vika in her quarrels with the forewoman. Some defended Ksenya, arguing that Vika was acting too harshly to a person who simply represented labour and mediated the wage policies imposed on them by the owner. Yet, what unified the workforce against the attempts to increase productivity was the arbitrary nature of the control of labour in the factory, when, in the brief period before a deadline, the management raised the production norms. The closer the deadline, the more sharply the norms were raised. If a deadline was well ahead, the norms were not even an issue. As mentioned earlier, Lidia, as the owner, sought to 'distract' herself from industrial production, which she considered 'routine' and boring. As a result, she rarely showed up on the shop floor, instead putting her daughter in charge to supervise the production. However, although Alina definitely spent more time in the sewing workshop than her mother, she was more preoccupied with trade and fashion shows than with labour discipline and control. Accordingly, at certain moments when her bosses were paying more attention to creative parts of the work process, Ksenya was the only source of managerial control on the shop floor. Some workers used this irregularity of managerial control to their advantage by asking the forewoman for a day off, usually citing their maternal needs (roughly half the operators were the mothers of school-age children, while the other half were grandmothers). As a rule, the managers responded positively to the maternal needs of the workforce, which contributed to the lack of dissent in the workplace.

The pattern of labour control changed dramatically when a deadline was close and missing it was a possibility. Time-thrift became the main issue, and new production norms were announced to the workers every day. The norm could be set up at thirty items per day and then be increased to fifty items a couple of days later. Workers resented the arbitrariness of such measures and demanded that the norms be based on careful calculations of the target time needed for each operation. They therefore appealed to Taylorist principles in order to protect themselves from the arbitrariness of the flexible labour regime. The management could not provide reasonable explanations for how they arrived at the norms other than making a reference to an indeterminate past when operators had allegedly produced greater outputs, despite making much more complicated garments. This did not make much sense to the workers, who also argued that the management did not take into account the time they had to spend making a piece of fabric good when it had been cut badly. The workers were supposed to solve such dilemmas on the fly, and the managers took that for granted. Alina argued that making such repairs was the only creative task in a generally dull process of industrial production. In saying this, she complained that the operators lacked a creative attitude to work and performed their sewing tasks automatically, without making any intellectual effort. As for the owner, she had a very simple understanding of why the operators could not raise their productivity levels – they were simply lazy. On any day when the production norms had not been reached, which was usually the case, an ultimate despotic measure was brought to bear: Lidia herself showed up on the shop floor and started to shout at the workers in her deep, booming voice. Swearing at them and scolding them for being lazy, she argued that their poor discipline was the only reason for their low wages and the delays in payment. In response, though behind her back, the workers blamed Lidia for poor management and her complete withdrawal from production, which they attributed to her poor knowledge of industrial manufacturing. All in all, after tightening control, productivity usually increased and the firm managed to ship the goods out on time. But then the same fluctuating regime of labour control, similar to the notorious patterns of Soviet-time 'shock work', were repeated when new orders came in.

Conclusion

In this chapter, I have delved into the workings of a small garment firm in order to identify the different regimes of value that are intertwined in different aspects of the firm's functioning. I opted not to see privatization solely as a process of former Soviet enterprises being grabbed by their cynical managers, as in one typically analysis of privatization in Russia. Instead, I have tried to reveal the parallels between the language of Soviet modernity and the promises of marketization, both of which are rooted in the developmental hopes of the Soviet modernization project. I am not claiming that such attitudes reflect the general pattern of privatization, but this additional view provides a more nuanced picture of processes of accumulation in Russia and the multiple moralities that different economic agents give voice to.

I also argue that these ideals of development have been mobilized in the face of the increased global competition in the garment industry and the lack of state interventions in or protection for national industry, especially in the small-scale sector. In Alpha's case, the developmental zeal of the garment producer, accentuated by the ethics of disinterestedness, motivates the firm's owner in her attempts to keep her head above water, despite the firm's low level of profitability and its bleak prospects for any improvement in the future. But rather than questioning presuppositions about Russia's deindustrialization, Lidia, the owner, reiterates the trope of disinterestedness and denies that material interest is her ultimate business goal. In practice, the desire to suspend market value and turn away from the market's demands encourages a retreat to the sphere of creativity as the only space in which authenticity and agency are possible. This is mainly achieved by focusing on the production of unique clothing items and demonstrating them to the wider public during fashion and trade shows.

Finally, I have shown how the search for creativity and job satisfaction had the effect of strengthening the exploitation of labour, which is relegated to doing the most 'dull' and uncreative tasks in industrial production. By denigrating the input of labour, it becomes easier for capital to justify strict discipline, its demand for flexibility and the introduction of arbitrary and despotic forms of control.

Chapter 7
'I Will Never Let You Down': Personal Dependencies and Informal Assistance at Work

The type of economic system that has emerged in Russia since the transition is characterized by the pervasiveness of non-market mechanisms and stimuli such as social networks and informal institutions, which came to compensate for the lack of institutional development and political stability in post-reform Russia. Political economists have coined terms such as 'network capitalism' (Puffer and McCarthy 2007) and 'patrimonialism' (Szelenyi 2016; Becker and Vasileva 2017) to explain this situation, stressing the importance of 'clans' and networks in the Russian economy and showing the failure of Russian policy-makers to introduce capitalist institutions and ensure their proper functioning.

In her critique of the tendency to conceptualize (post)socialism as a capitalist 'other', Thelen (2011) urges us to move away from normative approaches that have been influenced by neo-institutional theory and instead to use the potential of anthropological knowledge to produce alternative explanations of postsocialist societies and economies. More specifically, she argues that a detailed ethnographic study of work-related ties would enrich our understanding of informality, making us more attentive to local specifics and understandings of public and private.

I take inspiration from Thelen's criticism in exploring the multiplexity of relationships at work by unpacking the mixture of everyday concerns, values and affections involved in relationships between labour and capital in the private sector. These relationships unfold within small-scale private firms and exist beyond formal regulation, since firms hire labour informally based on verbal agreements between employer and employee. These informal arrangements enable an array of personal dependences and power structures that fit the patron-client type of relationship, characterized by unequal exchanges and the vulnerable position of the client, who is dependent on the whims of a patron. While the lack of formal labour protection certainly encourages more authoritarian and exploitative policies in the workplace, I would rather focus on those enabling aspects of paternalistic authority that induce workers to seek out employment in the private sector in which informal arrangements prevail (Clarke and Borisov 1999). In what follows, I will show that some workers seek more personal relations of dependence with their employers, as this entitles them to special treatment and allows them to negotiate individual terms of employment, such as flexible working hours or specific payment systems – a prerogative which is less likely to be found in those sectors and branches of the economy where labour relations are more subject to formal rules and regulations. The possibility to negotiate individual terms of employment enables less advantaged workers to cope with everyday emergencies in their lives, and at this point it outweighs the system of social and welfare benefits they are entitled to with formal labour contracts.

The idea that full-time waged employment constitutes a 'normative' status has been increasingly challenged by a number of ethnographic works demonstrating the analytical limitations of the dichotomy between formal and informal, particularly in contexts where stable, full-time waged employment has never been the norm, unlike in Europe and North America (Hart 1973; Millar 2014). With regard to the Russian labour market, Morris pushes against the 'marginality' thesis of informal employment and points out that 'diverse (informal) economic practices in some cases are important ways of "hedging" against precarity in formal work' (Morris 2011: 621). Stressing the socially embedded nature of work, Morris traces how blue-collar workers in provincial Russia move between formal and informal employment by relying on their social networks and work-related identities. Echoing Morris's argument, this chapter demonstrates why informal employment in Russia may be a deliberate choice rather than a forced necessity.

Much like the dichotomy between formal and informal, understandings of patron-client forms of dependence have been challenged by those anthropologists who question its anti-modern and anti-rational connotations. In the body of literature on socialism, the paternalistic expectations of Soviet citizens and the image of a paternal-like state have commonly been evoked to describe the deficiencies of state socialism. Proponents of this view argue that the Soviet state systematically strengthened patronage by turning its citizens into supplicants, who were fully dependent on a system of social welfare that in practice operated on a personal and discretionary basis (Ashwin 1999). Accordingly, many mainstream analysts have read the resistance to paternalistic expectations since the demise of socialism as subverting the logic of the purely commoditized purchasing of labour power (Becker and Vasileva 2017). A few ethnographic works examining forms of social membership and regimes of work under socialism, as well as what came next, offer an alternative framework for thinking about paternalism as a form of social belonging. Humphrey (1983) argues that social distinctions within Soviet society reflected a complex system of citizenship rights based on belonging to officially recognized categories of workers. Being more than just a system of statuses, those rights guaranteed certain civic entitlements, such as state-allocated housing, wages, pensions and access to education. However uneven and hierarchical the civic infrastructure of socialism was, its rapid demise infused a sense of the loss of and exclusion from collective entitlements that had been dismantled and replaced by the logic of the market, while consumer identities had replaced earlier forms of social membership centred on waged labour (Anderson 1996; Humphrey 1999).

The notion of civic entitlements as the key feature of the Soviet order resonates with Ferguson's (2013) observations on paternalism in contemporary South Africa. Observing how impoverished Africans voluntarily pursue subordination and dependence on others, Ferguson describes such 'declarations of dependence' as inherent in indigenous conception of personhood. He argues that the social value of dependence has been strengthened under a regime of 'work membership' where the state guarantees a full social position to waged labour. The dramatic decline of the system of work membership that ensued has strengthened the desire of the labouring poor to retain meaningful forms of belonging, attachment and care in a new era of mass unemployment. Ferguson provocatively contradicts liberal common sense by arguing that relations of dependence do not preclude agency but in fact enable the urban poor to embrace a level of social inclusion, protection and recognition.

Taking my lead from Ferguson here, I argue that voluntary dependence may become desirable to the postsocialist working poor who are facing the demise of waged work and a deterioration in their living standards. When the socialist system of social wages collapsed in the wake of the market reforms, it was informal forms of assistance – 'bottom-up welfare provision' – that came to complement or even replace public arrangements (Polese et al. 2014). In the spatially marginalized places of postsocialist Russia, it was the informal sector that opened up possibilities for survival and that offered a way out of the insecurity of formal employment (Morris 2012, 2016). In what follows, I will flesh out how the reciprocal dynamics and relations of dependence between employer and employee provide the labouring poor with alternative means of social protection. This is not to deny the exploitative and unequal nature of paternalistic control, but to stress that informal negotiations within a paternalistic framework may protect those actors who find themselves on the margins of survival. While Morris focuses on horizontal networks of assistance, I will elaborate on the vertical relations of authority that structure the mutual dependence of labour and capital and that embrace social inequalities and the class dimension.

Clientelism as a form of social protection has been extensively examined by anthropologists in relation to Mediterranean communities. Davis (1977: 134-5) demonstrates that an act of submission to a powerful magnate can provide access to resources for his clients, enabling them to impose a series of checks on their patron's use of power, that is, provide them with bargaining power. The enormous bargaining power of Soviet industrial workers has been well documented in studies of socialism (Burawoy and Lukács 1992; Filtzer 2002a). In postsocialism, memories of the relative autonomy of Soviet workers continue to inform working identities as 'mnemonic resources' that facilitate resistance to the demands of close supervision and self-discipline on the shop floor (Morris 2012: 230). Consequently, the dependence incurred by patron-client relations allows some workers to mitigate in-work poverty and manage job and income insecurity.

However, patron-client negotiations are not only about making instrumental and rational choices. In his study of political clientelism in Argentina, Auyero (2000) describes how clients' rational motivations and calculations coexist with a sense of moral obligation towards their patrons, who are usually perceived as friends or even fictive kin.

Drawing upon the literature on patronage and clientelism from distant spatial and historical contexts, I will explore the changing role of personal dependence in post-Soviet Russia and answer the following questions: What is actually at stake in the exchange of favours between labour and capital? To what extent do personal loyalties in the workplace enable business-owners to make labour power more flexible and adjust it to the demands of capitalism? What kinds of moral values and sensibilities underpin relations of dependence at work? To what extent does the struggle for resources to seek personal loyalty affect social relationships among co-workers and threaten their solidarity? To what extent do class and gender shape the dynamics of power relations of this sort?

Oksana's Work Biography: Trying to Become her Own 'Master'

Before introducing the stamp firm where the ethnographic part of this research took place, I will start by describing the work biography of Oksana (45 years), an employee at the stamp firm and the hostel receptionist described right at the start of the introductory chapter. Here I will trace her previous experience of work, as it explains many of her attitudes and expectations I observed during fieldwork.

Unlike other employees in the firm, Oksana is not originally from Smolensk. She was born and raised in Ukraine in a family with a military background. She married a flight lieutenant and moved with him to the Arctic region, where her husband was sent in 1991. In this new place, Oksana was trained in how to decipher aerial images and did military service along with her husband for the next seven years. In 1998, her husband was relocated again to a military base in Smolensk. As soon as the family arrived in this new place, they were informed that the local military base was to be dismantled due to ongoing restructurings in the military. At that time Oksana had two small daughters. Fortunately, her husband managed to take advantage of his entitlement to free housing allocated to military personnel in his unit. While in post-reform Russia the whole structure of civic entitlements has largely been eroded (Anderson 1996; Humphrey 1999), Oksana's husband seized the opportunity to make use of the rapidly shrinking system of state redistribution.[28] After buying a spacious new apartment at the state's expense, the couple had to achieve another arduous task – to find a job 'on civvy street'.

The transition to civilian life was not easy for either of them. They not only lacked the skills and education that limited their options in finding a job in the local labour market. Oksana felt that their habits and personalities fell short of the demands of the new market society. As she put it, while working at the military base 'they did not belong to themselves', by which she meant that they were just the passive objects of the will of their superiors and therefore dependent subjects. Beyond the military base they encountered the opposite logic of value: 'everyone was his own master (*khoziain*)'. At that time Oksana was 26 and had just given birth to her second child. Feeling lost and disappointed, she was nevertheless determined to 'catch up' (*ukhvatitsa*) and reinvent herself in accordance with the demands of Russia's rapidly marketizing society. While her husband, a former pilot, could not find anything more rewarding than physical labour on a construction side, Oksana invested all her energy in a small venture, setting up a kiosk to buy used glass bottles. Personal networks played a key role in starting this

---

[28] That was not an easy task but rather a game of chance. When one morning the announcement about allocated housing was made, Oksana's husband got only several hours till the end of the working day to collect a whole package of required documents. Only because he just moved to a new place and the same documents had been already prepared for his relocation, he succeeded in getting the certificate that entitled him to buy an apartment in Smolensk on state's expense. The family purchased the apartment in the summer of 1998, shortly before the economic crisis sprang up. The couple was lucky again buying the 3-room flat three days before the crisis broke out and the rouble lost its value.

business up with minimal investment: Oksana's former co-workers from her days in the military offered her premises and charged her a very low rent for them. However, the bottle venture proved to be unprofitable because of its high taxation and modest returns. Oksana closed it down within a year but started up a new business in petty trade in the early 2000s.

Unlike shuttlers involved in long-distance trade with foreign countries, Oksana travelled to Moscow to buy goods which she sold at a higher price in Smolensk. Relations of trust were key in this type of trade, which was largely unprotected by the state (Humphrey 1999; Holzlehner 2014). For Oksana, it was ties of kinship that encouraged her to enter trade: some distant relatives ran a garment factory in Moscow and offered her the opportunity to sell their output in Smolensk. The shuttle trade proved to be more lucrative than the previous endeavour, but nevertheless Oksana eventually had to close it down. By the time of its closure she had done pretty well, developing a network of individual sellers to distribute the cloth at open-air markets; in addition, she also rented an outlet in the shopping centre, where she sold the cloth herself. However, the more her trade expanded the more investments she had to make in inputs of both capital and time. Due to the lack of free assets, the financial pressures became more urgent. But more than that, it was the pressures associated with her maternal duties that urged her to give up this petty trade.

Oksana said she was torn between household and trade. Spending most of her time doing domestic work, managing the shop and commuting between Smolensk and Moscow, she felt that she was neglecting her duties as a mother. Oksana's husband supported her with neither her domestic duties nor her business. Because of employment problems he gave up the role of primary breadwinner, which was his major role in the family, as in many Russian families in general (Ashwin and Lytkina 2004). Apart from her husband, Oksana did not have any other relatives in the city to rely on. She hoped to find a solution to her precarious situation by summoning her mother to move to Smolensk from Ukraine and take over some of her domestic work and childcare. Despite her efforts this did not work out, and Oksana felt even more devastated. She could commute in Moscow only at night when her children were in bed. One night she was dragging a cart loaded with new bales of cloth along a Moscow street when her heel suddenly collapsed and she could not move any further. Feeling miserable and wretched, Oksana burst into tears, and a stranger in the street tried to calm her down, urging to give up her precarious job. All Oksana could do was to break off another heel and drag the cart further to catch the night train to Smolensk. This incident became a turning point and convinced her to withdraw from trade. She then put her aspirations for upward mobility on hold but hoped to accomplish them later, if not for herself then 'through the children'. More than a decade has passed since Oksana gave up trading, but she still religiously kept the documents related to her endeavours as an entrepreneur and still could not help thinking that she'd missed a big chance to succeed. At the same time, she had no doubts that she had made the right choice in prioritizing her maternal duties over earning a good livelihood. As she said, 'I want my children to know that I did not swap them for something else'. Oksana's dilemma resembles what Morris calls 'the double-bind of ultra-flexible femininity' in referring to the contradictory messages underlying the Russian version of neoliberal feminine subjectivity (Morris 2016: 139). One the one hand current constructions of femininity encourage women to remake themselves as autonomous and self-sufficient subjects, while on the other hand these new conceptions of femininity do not weaken the traditional female identity of the care-giver. However strong Oksana's desire to remake herself as a successful entrepreneur and enter the space of opportunities offered by commerce, she gave up this path when she failed to reconcile this desire with the moral obligation to care for her children. At that point, she rearticulated her main priority as the provision of maternal care. However, her commitment to reproduction has not completely deterred her from pursuing her project of self-improvement, which she came to realize by consuming self-help literature and absorbing the neoliberal ideologies of successful femininity. Accordingly, she worked actively not only on her own personality but also on those of her growing daughters as well. Oksana turned her aspirations for social mobility into a long-standing family project and a task her children were to accomplish if she did not.

After her withdrawal from the shuttle trade, Oksana made another attempt at upward mobility. While still involved with trade, she underwent vocational training as an interior designer. By that time, she already had been trained in cooking and public catering, but she scrupulously avoided this blue-collar job, which she reckoned was both precarious and physically demanding. Nevertheless, the day came when she was forced to fall back on her early credentials out of the dire need she regularly experienced after taking over the role of her family's primary breadwinner. She easily found a part-time job as a cook in a restaurant, but soon quit after being attacked and robbed on her way home after the late-night shift.

With her new diploma in interior design, Oksana could finally obtain a coveted white-collar job as a furniture-maker at a medium-size furniture manufacturer. She felt excited finally to be able to deploy her mental skills in making calculations to assemble the furniture, a job she proudly called 'brain gymnastics'. However, the precarious nature of her new employment was hidden in the harsh conditions of work. Under a tacit arrangement, the firm's employees were supposed to avoid taking sick leave, as this would threaten production process. Oksana had followed this rule patiently for three years until the moment came when her maternal responsibilities again became a challenge. Her daughter had to undergo a medical examination before entering a public school. Oksana asked her employer to let her off during the lunch break to accompany her daughter to the clinic. However, this was not allowed. After extended negotiations with the factory management, Oksana was finally given permission to leave for one hour on condition that she would inform each of the sixty factory workers beforehand about her brief absence.

Oksana saw this as humiliating and resolutely quit the job, otherwise she could not adjust her work schedule to her daughter's school schedule, since someone had to pick up the seven-year-old child from school. Paid childcare was a luxury she could not afford. As in many other contexts worldwide, there are grandmothers who voluntarily take on a share of the housework and childcare for their working daughters (Utrata 2008). In contrast to those local urbanites who were able to tap into their horizontal networks of kin, Oksana found herself in a more precarious situation, as she was deprived of any support from within the family and was forced to cope with her duties as a mother on her own. At that time too, she divorced her unemployed husband. The status of a single mother entitled her to some additional welfare benefits, though they were rather meagre. Being separated from her safety network, she was forced to become self-reliant. However, rather than praising her self-reliance as a virtue, she viewed her autonomy in this respect as something unnatural and hoped to overcome it as soon as her children became financially independent. Given her own detachment from networks of care among her kin, Oksana encouraged her children to nourish their ties as siblings and assume mutual responsibilities for each other (*derzhatsa drug za druga*) as the most reliable way of coping with future uncertainties.

Without any other source of support than her wages, Oksana tended to rely more and more on interpersonal connections in the workplace, expecting that her status as a single mother would entitle her to special consideration from her superiors. It was not surveillance and control as such that had made her feel humiliated at her previous place of work, but the fact that the manager had disregarded her status and special needs. She wanted to be acknowledged not only as a worker but as a single mother who was forced to juggle her home and work responsibilities, but the manager questioned the legitimacy of her maternal needs in a work context. Dunn (2004) describes similar attitudes and 'embedded' work identities that she encountered in postsocialist Poland. Dunn observed that working mothers demanded that others acknowledge their multiple social identities and respective needs based on them. She traces such claims back to memories of socialist gender policies and the system of maternal welfare that continued to feed expectations among the blue-collar female workforce in the Alima factory (ibid: 146-7). Oksana failed to force the company to meet her needs as a mother, and that led her to quit her job. Soon afterwards she joined another furniture manufacturer, where she managed to negotiate her maternal needs successfully and was allowed to leave the company at lunch time, a concession that enabled her to pick her daughter up from school. But apart from settled agreements about her absences from work, she also requested time off more spontaneously to deal with everyday emergencies, and this gradually increased the tensions between herself and her employer and led to disagreements between them. In the end, she left this job as well. After a spiral of other casual work experiences, Oksana met Vadim, the owner of the stamp firm.

In 2007, Vadim employed twice the number of workers he had in 2016, but he still needed extra help due to the growing number of orders. He offered Oksana a job making plastic signboards and door-plates in his firm. The new tasks involved cutting plastic plates and then arranging plastic letters on them. The stamp firm has a small workshop in a gloomy basement where other workers cut and painted plastic signboards, but Oksana was allowed to do her work at home. This flexibility enabled her to fulfil her childcare needs and spend more time at home. Even though her new manual job was a definite throwback to the blue-collar past, Oksana was satisfied with it due to the overall flexibility of her new working arrangements. Having set up a workshop in her home kitchen, Oksana rapidly become allergic to the toxic fumes of the glue used in the production of signboards. However, this did not prevent her from working with Vadim, nor did it undermine her feelings of deep gratitude to him for 'his support', which she considered a generous response to her personal needs and an acknowledgment of her status as a mother.

When Oksana became pregnant again, she and her ex-husband faced new risks and uncertainties. Her pregnancy was a surprise but, as an Orthodox Christian, she never considered abortion as an option, being encouraged by the local priest to live by Orthodox standards of virtue, which had been recently reinforced by the rise of anti-abortion activism within the Church (Luehrmann 2017). However, Oksana's ex-husband was against their having another child. Oksana never mentioned whether the newly introduced 'maternal capital' – a substantial allowance paid when a second, third, etc. child was born – had encouraged her reproductive choice. Anyway, with her certificate for 'maternal capital' (worth approximately four thousand euros) she could partly cover her daughter's university tuition fees ten years later. Before a new child was born, the ex-spouses, who still shared the same apartment, sorted out the housing issue on terms favourable to Oksana's situation: she took over the apartment, while her ex-husband moved into a rented flat. In return for his cooperation over the housing situation, Oksana never claimed alimony for the new-born child. Indeed, she and her adolescent daughters were relieved that he had finally moved out.

As a single mother of three, Oksana was entitled to special child benefits allocated to large families. However, it was not the maternal welfare package but Oksana's wages that provided a major part of her household budget. From the very moment she moved to Smolensk, Oksana had been struggling to escape poverty and provide a decent life for her children. It was important for her not only to supply them with food and clothing, but also to enable them to attend dancing and swimming classes, take private lessons to improve their school performance, and spend a month in the summer in Ukraine or elsewhere. In her daily struggles for subsistence, Oksana became accustomed to leading an abstemious life, saving every kopek and keeping track of her daily expenditure to be sure that she would not run out of money before payday.

To survive the market transition of the 1990s, many working-class families in Russia intensified household production in order to rely more on self-provisioning and kinship networks. Burawoy, Krotov and Lytkina (2000: 48) define the retreat to a primitive domestic economy as a 'defensive strategy' – 'the defense against destitution is to spread risk by diversifying productive activities and sharing resources across households'. Compared to typical defensive responses, far fewer households dared to exploit market opportunities by deploying extremely risky 'entrepreneurial strategies'. The fact that Oksana did not have an extensive network of kin in the city, nor a dacha, a car or a plot in a rural area, made her more insecure and limited her self-provisioning capacities compared to her neighbours, who could typically rely on their extended horizontal networks of friends and relatives. Among the resources available to Oksana's household was an apartment received from the state and a number of 'citizenship assets' (ibid.: 47), that is, a range of social benefits and entitlements, very modest to get by on alone in the postsocialist era. Oksana turned to an entrepreneurial strategy out of necessity in order to survive after the birth of her second child. At that time she could rely on a diversified family budget, including her husband's earnings of an army pension and wages from construction work, which reduced her risks as an entrepreneur. But apart from her material and citizenship-related assets, Oksana made use of her 'social assets' as well – a circle of friends and relatives, to whom she resorted in order to mitigate the lack of resources and state protection. With hindsight, she regretted not trying to make the most out of her personal networks before she quit trading. In saying this, Oksana was referring to some of her weak ties, assuming that she might have utilized them and stayed in business. After her exit from petty trading, Oksana continued to increase her social assets by forging new relationships and expanding weak ties and connections, which she considered to be a crucial source to fall back on, given that other assets were scarce or difficult to obtain.

Paternal Care, Reciprocity and Control

When I met Oksana, she had been working in Vadim's stamp firm for over ten years. Since the early 1990s, when the firm was set up, it has specialized primarily in stamp production, becoming the first licensed stamp-maker in the city. Using ready-made stamp equipment from a large Austrian supplier, the firm produces its own rubber stamps in a small workshop managed by one operator. Other than stamps, the capacities of a laser engraver are used to produce supplementary output such as engraved door-plates and stickers. Although marketing is generally neglected, the manufacturing rarely stands idle. This is due to the lack of other licensed stamp producers in the city, as well as ongoing reforms in administrative law that oblige businesses and administrative bodies to introduce occasional changes to their legal documents and hence to update their stamps. The local municipality, large industrial enterprises and small private firms make up the majority of Vadim's clientele. Along with stamps, the firm also makes business cards and plastic signboards, relying on rather outdated technologies that have not been upgraded since the 1990s.

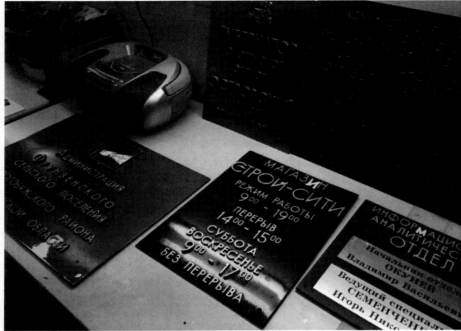

Plate 5. The signboards produced by the stamp firm.

As already mentioned, Oksana joined the firm to assist in the production of plastic signboards. Her enthusiasm for this work was related to the fact that she could arrange her working hours on the basis of her own needs. At the time, she was employed formally, which allowed her to claim the whole package of maternal benefits when she fell pregnant with her third child. For Vadim, the flexibility of these working arrangements was equally advantageous, as it opened up ways to adapt Oksana's labour power to the firm's specific requirements. When Oksana took maternity leave, he hired a new worker in her stead. However, as soon as her maternity leave was over, Vadim informed her that he did not see any reason to sack the temporary worker, who had done an excellent job. Instead he suggested that Oksana start making business cards and replace another employee who had fallen seriously ill, otherwise Oksana would have to quit. Without hesitation she took up her new duties while keeping the same flexible schedule. Although she did not have any previous experience in making business cards, she was expected to acquire the new skills on spot after Vadim briefly showed her how to handle a hot foil-stamping machine. Luckily, she was fast enough to 'seize' the process and 'feel' the machine's moods, which required fine adjustment. However, making business cards was so poorly paid that Oksana was forced to do multiple jobs, taking a supplementary job as a cashier in a grocery store. Only some years later, when her former position in Vadim's firm became vacant again, was she able to take it back and leave the side job. Thus, by relying on Oksana's flexible labour power, Vadim could fill the gaps in his labour requirements involving blue-collar work in his firm.

Other than that, the flexibility in working hours implied that Oksana was expected to undertake 'shock' work in order to meet a deadline. If an urgent order came along, she was supposed to work at weekends or during the holidays as well. When the city administration placed a lucrative order at short notice for a number of memorial signboards for a Victory Day celebration, Oksana put her home life on hold for a week. During ten days of the May holidays, she cut plastic sheets, arranged plastic letters in the long lines of texts, glued them to the base and then painting the signboards. Her working hours extended late into night, being punctuated by short breaks for sleep in between shifts. As usual in such situations, Oksana called upon her teenage daughters to assist her in the production process. After a deadline, Oksana – physically exhausted, with hands shaking and back pain – requested a week off, which she spent in bed recovering from the 'shock' assignment.

Oksana never complained that her work was hard or exploitative; on the contrary, she considered herself lucky to be employed in Vadim's firm. Given a typical workload, she started work at around 2 pm and left the workshop at 6 pm, whereas the normal working hours in the firm were from 9 am till 6 pm. As before, Oksana requested special treatment on the basis of her needs as a mother. She informed Vadim that she needed free morning hours to take care of her ten-year-old son so she could help him with his school assignments or take him to the school or sports activities. On the same grounds, Oksana negotiated salary advances whenever she ran out of cash before payday. Even though this did not always work out and occasionally Vadim rejected her requests, Oksana appreciated the fact that many aspects of her work were generally negotiable.

Furthermore, when Vadim set up a hostel as a second business, he offered Oksana the position of receptionist, relying on her ability to juggle her duties in the stamp firm with round-the-clock shifts in the hostel. Oksana took up the offer. When I asked Vadim why he had chosen Oksana for this job, his reply echoed Oksana's explanation and pointed to her specific needs: 'Because she has a lazy husband[29] and three kids', he explained to me. Vadim did not dismiss Oksana's needs as a mother but accepted the role of a 'problem solver' who was willing to protect a 'problem holder' against the

---

[29] Oksana kept her divorce a secret and preferred not to discuss her marital status at work.

risks of everyday life (Auyero 2000). It is important to note that Vadim also had a military background, like Oksana and her ex-husband. In the 1980s, he graduated from the local military academy and joined the Soviet forces in the GDR. After a year he resigned from the service for reasons he preferred to conceal. Whatever they were, his military identity was his biggest source of pride, one that had not waned even thirty years after he had left military service. This shared military background contributed to a sense of solidarity and trust that strengthened the bonds between employer and employee. Again, for the new job in the hostel Oksana's skills were largely irrelevant. Taking up a position that required her to use specific software to make hotel bookings, Oksana had no knowledge whatsoever of how to use a computer. As usual, she was expected to catch up quickly.

Plate 6. Working two jobs: Oksana making signboards during her shift at the hostel.

As mentioned above, Oksana felt that her needs as a mother entitled her to special consideration from her employer. As long as Vadim acknowledged these needs, she felt obliged to reciprocate his favours in the form of flexible working hours, salary advances or a second job. Working overtime was her usual way of reciprocating. In fact, it was not easy to calculate how much time she actually spent in the workplace because of her flexible working hours and Vadim's occasional demands for 'shock' work. But whenever an urgent order came in, Oksana expressed her willingness to work extra hours and prove to Vadim that she 'will never let him down'. Her personal loyalty to her boss was striking. I never heard her gossiping about him with the other workers, nor was she willing to reveal the details of his business career or personal life when we chatted.

All Vadim's businesses moved into the informal economy in the aftermath of his divorce and the division of property between the former spouses. But the withdrawal from a formal contract does not seem to have affected the exchange of favours between Oksana and her boss: indeed, each for their own reasons, they both saw the transition to informal employment as more beneficial than formal work. For Oksana, the increase in real wages became a significant perk from the point that registered employment entailed significant tax deductions. Upon my inquiry whether she had any worries in relation to her informal work status, Oksana assured me that she did not:

> One has to live in the present moment. And at the moment my number one priority is to raise my children, feed and clothe them. Now. What comes next? Well, you know, I do not worry about the future, to tell the truth. If the Lord grants me good health, we will keep working, that's it. But now I have to raise my children. And if my circumstances are such that I met this man (Vadim – D.T.) on my way who gave me a job, that is, money... well, to be sure, I take the offer. And I do not have any worries. Any worries.

One might see certain religious connotations in Oksana's reply. Not worrying about one's future, which is primarily God's concern, invokes one of the powerful tenets of Orthodox teachings. Oksana did identify herself as an Orthodox believer. She used to be actively involved in the life of her parish, having spent a year singing in the church choir. No longer a regular churchgoer, she resorted to the Church only in critical moments in her life. However, in her engagement with spirituality, she was open to a wide range of ideas and practices, embracing exoteric spirituality, yoga, Orthodox teachings and its vernacular forms. As a result, she drew on the multiple sources of spirituality that were available to her: she believed that Orthodox icons guarded the well-being of her family, that her prophetic dreams prevented future misfortunes, that a *feng shui* 'money tree' brought good luck in career, and that scarlet wooded strings would ward off misfortune and the evil eye from her children. Oksana's biggest dream was to travel to Tibet and learn meditation there. Apparently, she did not adhere to the majority of strict Orthodox rules and regulations, seeing her main virtues stemming from her maternal duties. The need to raise three children alone plunged her into a spiral of hardships, self-denial and sacrifice, but in the end she was rewarded with the job she deserved. In her account, Vadim appeared as a helping hand reaching out to her in her moment of need. To have a patron like him enabled her to fulfil the requirements of social reproduction and to invest her labour in her children's future. Like many other interlocutors of mine, Oksana was sceptical of state-allocated support and tended to rely more on her networks and family than on the state. The early career achievements of her daughters, now aged 25 and 19, made her believe in the secure future she envisaged as a collective effort of the whole family. At the same time, she was concerned with her ten-year-old son because of his poor school performance. While his teachers generally neglected him and regarded him as a hopeless case, Oksana did not give up and continually consulted doctors, private teachers and psychologists to find out how she could improve his academic record. With her second job at the hostel she could afford to pay for medical examinations and private tutors for her son. Thus it was her own children rather than state support that she expected to provide for her after her own earning capacity was reduced or ended altogether.

The discussions of workplace paternalism that exist in modern capitalist societies tend to foreground the mechanisms of oppression and ideological control that allow paternal employers to impose their own definitions of reality on their workers (Abercrombie and Hill 1976; Newby 1977). Evidently, Oksana was subjected to Vadim's control, which resulted in her self-exploitation and personal dependence. Oksana explained her dependence in gendered terms, acknowledging in Vadim the role of 'the master' (*khozjain*), the traditionally the role of the head of the household, a patriarch.

Yet, it was clear to everyone in the firm that Vadim hardly satisfied the image of a prudent and efficient *khozjain*. His drinking habits, blatant cynicism and vulgar jokes confused many of his clients and irritated his workers. Usually, after the working day in the stamp firm was over, Vadim headed to the hostel, his second business. This was the site of his leisure activities, where he socialized with friends or random guests on the spot. Over the years his evening ritual had remained the same: in the hostel, or the 'club', as Vadim christened it, he occupied a tiny kitchen, drank alcohol for a couple of hours while persuading the guests to join him, and then started to sing songs or declaim poems, enjoying the sound of his loud voice. It was the task of the hostel receptionist to get rid of her drunken boss before the guests started complaining.

Apart from his drinking habits, the ambiguities surrounding Vadim's managerial skills were evident in many other aspects of how he organized his business. In the autumn Oksana run out of the Scotch tape she needed to fix the plate inside the stamping machine when making business cards. This very specific type of heat-resistant Scotch tape was not available in the local market and was usually ordered from Moscow. At that time, Vadim was frequently travelling to Moscow to participate in court proceedings over the division of property between himself and his ex-wife. Vadim promised Oksana that he would fetch the Scotch tape himself during his next trip to Moscow. However, that did not happen, and Oksana was kept patiently waiting. When she gently reminded her boss about the item she needed, Vadim suggested she find an alternative solution to fixing the plate in the machine. To this end, Oksana started experimenting with various types of glue and Scotch tape. Whenever an experiment failed, she became profoundly anxious, as it meant she had 'let Vadim down'. Oksana kept reminding her boss to buy the tape by pointing to the waiting orders, but without any effect. It took Oksana a month of experimenting and wasting materials before Vadim eventually supplied her with the required tape. As a result, they lost all the orders for business cards for a whole month. While Vadim dismissed this loss as insignificant, Oksana felt relieved at being able to stop her experiments and get back to normal work.

While Vadim's authority was constantly questioned by the other employees, Oksana's loyalty to her boss remained unshakable. She never complained, expressed resentment or even discussed how Vadim was managing the firm. Her usual response to his drinking habits was to turn a blind eye to it. 'This is his life, and I do not want to interfere', was her usual reply whenever I asked her opinion about Vadim. It was evident that Oksana was not just subject to Vadim's control but actively performed the role of submissive subject as long as her boss fulfilled the role of her 'problem solver'. But her loyalty and consent were shaken when Vadim breached their tacit agreement. In summer Oksana took on a few extra shifts in the hostel to fill in for two other receptionists who were on leave. She expected that she would be remunerated for this extra job, as had been the case with other receptionists previously. However, on payday Vadim refused to pay her for the extra work, as he regarded her working overtime as just another favour that Oksana was expected to do for free. Oksana tried to object. She felt humiliated and tried to negotiate payment by stressing her needs as a mother, as she had done before. But this time it did not work, and Vadim turned her down again. Moreover, after this incident Vadim seemed to avoid showing up at the hostel while she was on duty there. For Oksana this detachment was a clear signal that their special relationship had come to an end. Her personal loyalty to Vadim rapidly vanished thereafter, and for the first time she became openly critical about her working conditions, and she secretly started searching for a new job.

Thus, Oksana was not a mere object of paternalistic control but intensively participated in extracting favours from her boss, which allowed her to impose a series of checks on his behaviour. To extract these favours and maintain their flow, Oksana tapped into her social skills, particularly her talent to negotiate and solve problems. Any time she was determined to ask for some of her salary in advance, Oksana would first chat with a secretary, trying to assess the amount of cash available, and then gauge Vadim's mood. She was astute in getting a sense of when was the right moment to approach him, and she would wait for days if necessary. Describing herself as 'a non-conflict person', she believed that any problem should be solved through negotiations instead of open conflict. In this sense, she is a good example of a 'smooth operator', of those 'who socialize easily and nurture relationships with everyone because one day they might be needed' (Ledeneva 2008: 121).

Nonetheless the cultivation of personal connections was not a talent with which Oksana had been naturally endowed, nor was it a source of pride and self-esteem to her. She recalled that in the early years of her marriage her mother-in-law used to scold her for being too naïve and simple-hearted (*beskhitrostnaya*). With hindsight, Oksana agreed that this was an accurate description of her personality at the time, although she herself would put it rather differently, saying that she used to be 'a kind person' who had never pursued self-interest (*koryst*). But later on, being dragged into daily struggles to make a living, she had to admit that being just 'a kind person' would never lead to a good life in the sense of material well-being (*dostatok*). Eventually, Oksana put aside her moral reservations and took her mother-in-law as a role model. She admired the successful trajectory of upward mobility that her mother-in-law had been able to achieve in Soviet times by moving from a Ukrainian village to the city. Her modern two-room apartment was stuffed with carpets and cut-glass. To achieve this level of material progress, her mother-in-law had actively used her *blat* connections to acquire access to material goods. Gradually Oksana adopted the same strategy in order to build her social capital, which she saw as the only avenue of social mobility open to her. The self-help literature she actively consumed encouraged networking practices and fuelled Oksana's determination to make the most out of her social capital. Her reliance on vertical ties with a powerful 'problem-solver' was the most reliable way to secure her position, though it was also morally questionable. While Oksana's bargaining tactics proved to be rewarding in the short-term, they simultaneously affected her social relationships within the work group. The existence of informal alliances in the workplace did not go unnoticed among her fellow workers, often causing conflicts and protests in the workplace.

Contested Values and a Disunited Collective

In Soviet times, workers were organized and managed through a system of labour collectives (*trudovoi kollektiv*). As an ideological construct, the collective represented the ideals of solidarity and unity in labour. In a practical sense their role was more contradictory, as work collectives served simultaneously as a locus of social integration and control: 'the labour collective was the point at which the individual's integration into Soviet society was monitored and regulated, but it was also a focus of sociability where workers spent half of their lives together' (Ashwin 1999: 14). In the transition era, labour collectives shed many of their functions, but some workers retained a strong identification with their work groups, which continued to function as vital networks of support and mutual solidarity (Clarke 1995; Ashwin 1999; Morris 2016).

The employees in the stamp firm routinely applied the term 'collective' to their tiny work group of five. Apart from Oksana, the collective consisted of a secretary, Nadya (24 years), a designer, Sveta (45 years), an operator of the laser engraver, Kostya (31 years), and an accountant and deputy director, Zina (37 years). The firm's units were dispersed throughout a spacious building that had been built in the late Soviet era to accommodate the Centre for Scientific and Technical Information. Since the 1990s, the public office has shrunk to occupy just a small corner of the huge building, the other facilities being rented out to private businesses. In the stamp firm, the white-collar employees occupied the neat office space, split into several cubicles for individual workers. The workshops for manual tasks were located in remoter parts of the building, one in the basement, the other at the back of the building.

Much as was usual in Soviet enterprises, worker's birthdays and major public holidays never go unnoticed in the stamp firm. To buy the gifts, all employees contribute the money in equal shares, while Vadim was expected to make a major contribution. Oksana had enthusiastically volunteered to collect money and buy gifts, which required all her social skills, mediating capacities and excellent knowledge of local retail. She recalled that in previous years, when the firm prospered, each workers' child received a 'high-quality' New Year's present from Vadim. In these golden times, they used to celebrate public holidays collectively in restaurants and entertain themselves with fireworks supplied for such occasions by Vadim. When the stamp business was going through hard times, Vadim introduced some austerity measures and start to throw parties right in the office. Even so, he always covered all the costs of food and drink and repeatedly invited his crowd of friends from the city administration and elsewhere to join the party.

Plate 7. The production process in the signboard workshop.

When Oksana described the quality of their small labour collective, she pointed out the conflicts and tensions that strained social ties within the work group: 'Our collective is very unfriendly (*nedruzhnyi*)'. In saying this, she was referring above all to Sveta, the designer, who openly expressed her criticism of Vadim's management and privileged workers like Oksana. Sveta has worked in the firm for over twenty years, longer than any other employee. She joined the firm soon after graduating from the local university, where she earned a degree in computer engineering. With no experience of work whatsoever, she started her career as the operator of the laser engraver. This type of manual job carried with it a lot of health hazards (then, as now, there was no proper air conditioning on the shop floor), and it was physically demanding. Sveta attempted to exchange her blue-collar responsibilities for a job in the office. In order to do so she had to learn the design software and started to prepare layouts for the engraving machine. For the next several years, she combined her manual job with making designs, but later on she switched entirely to design duties. Like Oksana, Sveta was a single mother raising a nineteen-year-old son, a student at the same engineering university where she had studied in the 1990s.

Unlike Oksana, Sveta voiced sharp criticism of Vadim and his managerial style. Like everyone else in the firm, Sveta was well aware of the critical financial situation that resulted from Vadim's indebtedness. His total debt amounted to millions of roubles comprised of outstanding alimony payments and money he had borrowed from a friend to set up the hostel. But it was not only his indebtedness that put the stamp firm's future at risk, according to Sveta. She claimed that the hostel, Vadim's second business, was growing at the expense of the stamp firm's resources. Instead of developing and modernizing stamp production, she said, Vadim had abandoned his first firm and channelled its surplus value into the hostel business. Accordingly, Sveta's labour power was being exploited and alienated by being transformed into investments in the second business, one she had no identification with. Even the plastic New Year tree that Vadim had taken away from the stamp firm to adorn the empty hall in the hostel had turned into a symbol of such alienation for Sveta. Last but not least, she could not tolerate his drinking habits, especially when Vadim threw parties in their office in work time. Like all the other employees Sveta was invited to join the party, but she never accepted these invitations and resolutely left the office to wait until the party had finished, 'under the cypress trees'. In his usual assertive manner, Vadim persuaded all his employees to drink collectively, and only a few dared to defy him. When Vadim started his hostel in 2014, he relocated his drinking activities there, much to the relief of the stamp firm's workers. For Sveta, to stand 'under the cypress trees' became a symbol of her personal resistance and of the humiliation she suffered at work.

Eventually Sveta quit her job, which she could no longer bear. However, the printing house where she took on new employment soon went bankrupt. At this moment, Vadim showed up again and offered to take her back into the stamp firm. He convinced Oksana that, with his new laser engraver, he would be able to increase production and raise their salaries. As things turned out later, Sveta said sadly, 'he promised me the earth', but at the time she took up his offer and returned to the same position a second time.

What is striking in Sveta's account is her affective relationship with the stamp firm, which was reminiscent of the identification and emotional attachment to a place of work of the Soviet period (Alasheev 1995). In Sveta's case, her emotional connection with the stamp firm and its owner was imbued with a feeling of betrayal – a feeling that she conveyed in openly gendered terms. She expressed gradual dissatisfaction with her boss through the metaphor of romantic relationships, in which moral commitments come to the fore and overshadow the contractual obligations between labour and capital. In her emotional account of the early years of the firm's life, Sveta stressed her initial enthusiasm for the job and her hopes that the firm would steadily grow and develop, just as Vadim had promised her. As she said, in the formative years of the firm's life his female employees all adored Vadim and were inspired by his enthusiasm. When he was taken to hospital after a fight with his wife's lover, it was his employees, not his wife, who regularly visited him and supplied him with *kefir*. When his wife threw his possessions out of their house after the fight, it was again his employees who picked everything up and gave it back to him. In other words, they cared for him and expected that he would care for them in return.

But he betrayed us, says Sveta. He turned into a 'tyrant', sacked the good workers, enforced work discipline and violated workers' privacy by searching their office computers and desks. All these measures Sveta attributed to the perturbations in Vadim's personal life ('he just took it out on us'), and she refused to see any rationale for his behaviour. She was shocked to see Vadim's furious reaction when one of his workers had asked him to make a stamp for her husband's business at the firm's expense. It was normal to Sveta that workers should be entitled to use the resources of 'their own firm' (*svoya kontora*) for their private benefit. She did not approve of Vadim's reaction either from the ethical standpoint or rationally – after all, the stamp in question was tiny in size, whereas the operator wasted far more materials every day, which went unnoticed. What Vadim regarded as stealing and cheating and tried to eradicate through surveillance at work, his workers viewed as a part of their normal exchange relations and of the mutual obligations of care that employees and employer owed each other.

In Sveta's view, Vadim betrayed his commitments many times over. Most importantly, he promised to develop the stamp business but instead abandoned it, switching to his new hostel project and risking their futures by recklessly borrowing money. On the other hand, she also felt a little sorry for Vadim. In the end, she saw him not only as a manager but as someone who had gone through a divorce and separation from his children and who had become stuck in legal disputes over property issues with his ex-wife. In her view, Vadim had already been punished by his greedy ex-spouse and thus deserved a bit of sympathy (*on khlebaet lozhkoi za eto vse... Znaesh, eto otdacha*). Sveta assumed that their own incompatibility stemmed from their different personalities: being a 'bad boy', Vadim just could not stand 'good girls' like Sveta. By switching to the language of psychology, Sveta basically justified Vadim's behaviour and reconciled herself to the fact of his betrayal.

Sveta's uneasy relationship with the firm echoes the trope of 'difficult love' that Morris (2016: 124) described in the story of Galina, a post-Soviet worker whose affective attachment and feeling of responsibility toward her industrial enterprise remained 'unrequited' in the postsocialist period. In the case of Sveta, her 'difficult love' for the firm where she had worked for most of her adult life was aggravated by the fact that she did not see any other employment alternatives. Like Oksana, Sveta was a single mother and the only provider in her household consisting of her son and her retired mother.

Although Sveta could justify her boss's behaviour, what she could not tolerate is how her co-worker Oksana secured her own interests at work. Sveta viewed Oksana's bargaining power as resting on her strategic manipulation of her maternal status. Although a single mother herself, Sveta had never claimed to be evaluated on the basis of her needs as a mother. For her, it was efficiency at work that was relevant. She did not regard Oksana as a valuable worker but saw her rather as a skilful manipulator trying to compensate for her lack of work-related skills by demonstrating unquestioning loyalty to her boss. Observing how Oksana paid respectful and grateful deference to Vadim while neglecting her fellow workers, especially those in inferior positions, like the cleaning lady, was a source of everyday frustration to Sveta. To express her resentment of Oksana, Sveta resorted to ethnic stereotypes, dismissing the way Oksana behaved at work as a typical Ukrainian trait. Seeing her as a threat to group solidarity, Sveta called Oksana a '*banderovka*', referring to Ukrainian fascists and therefore echoing the anti-Ukrainian discourse that has been activated in Russia by mainstream mass-media in the aftermath of the Ukrainian crisis. For her part, Oksana tried to minimize her contacts with Sveta to business-related issues and carefully avoided open conflict. Nevertheless, one such conflict flared up one day, and Oksana admitted that all her diplomatic abilities and social skills were useless in the face of Sveta's 'troublesome' personality.

This disagreement was not just a matter of individual hostility but had broader social, cultural and class implications. By pointing her stinging criticism at a co-worker, Sveta was arguing against the whole social system whereby a person's worth was determined by her proximity to someone else's power. While Oksana was just a single illustration of this social order, Sveta observed plenty of other situations at work when her co-workers measured each other's worth on the same basis. Outraged, she recounted the cases when former workers who had been dismissed from the stamp firm had readily been forgotten by their former colleagues. According to Sveta, the stamp firm's employees would never greet former co-workers if they happened to meet them somewhere else. She thought that this hostility stemmed from the fear of losing one's job for socializing with someone

Vadim openly disliked. In order to oppose this logic of value, Sveta deliberately kept in touch with some former colleagues and openly visited a friend in a neighbouring office who used to work for the firm. In the same manner, Sveta criticized Vadim's circle of friends, which consisted of people of higher status and authority. Frequent guests at the stamp firm's parties, they treated Vadim's employees as if they were 'servants' who were there to set up the table and clean the dishes. If Sveta should meet them one day in the street, they would pretend they had never known her.

Sveta tried to resist this corrupt logic of value, which she regularly observed in her place of work but easily found everywhere. In opposing it, she reduced her relationships with her co-workers to the minimum: she did not attend any corporate events, nor did she ever take a meal or tea with her fellow workers. Unlike Oksana, Sveta has never asked for a salary advance, which she regards as humiliating. In the same way, she has never demanded flexible working hours, even though she was often left idle when there were no orders. Whenever she had any spare time at work, she spent it on her two major hobbies – learning Polish and watching movies. As she said, she started learning Polish for just one reason: because her work bored her to death. When talking about her 'strange' hobby, Sveta stressed that this was 'just a cultural thing' which had nothing to do with religion (she was a devout atheist), ethnicity (she was Russian) or politics (she said she had no sympathy with Polish nationalism). Whereas no one in the stamp firm knew about her hobby, Sveta has spent many working hours watching Polish movies or reading Polish books on her computer. By attending a free Polish language course, she got to know people with the same interests – something she missed at work. Other than learning a language, Sveta claimed a broad interest in high culture, whether independent films, which she also consumed mainly at her workplace, or the local chamber theatre, where she would go after work.

In post-Soviet Russia, the concept of culturedness (*kulturnost'*) has played an important role in asserting the moral worth of those social groups for whom marketization resulted in the devaluation of their statuses and identities. In her study of consumption in contemporary Russia, Jennifer Patico (2008: 99) demonstrates how Russian teachers construe their own value – their moral and personal worth – through the concept of culturedness, which helps them differentiate themselves from 'uncultured' New Russian nouveaux riches, whom they consider 'materially rich and morally bankrupt'. Drawing on the same dichotomy, Sveta asserted her personal worth through the moral attributes of culturedness and professionalism, which enabled her to preserve her self-esteem and dignity in a morally corrupt place. For Sveta, one's status at work should depend primarily on one's professional skills. When she was finally fired as a result of a long-term conflict with an accountant – her other big opponent in the firm – she managed to get her job back, as Vadim had failed to find a replacement for her.

Meanwhile the lack of professionalism was evident to Sveta in many aspects of others' performance at work. She complained that their machine operator ignored defects when producing stamps, though clients rarely complained and accepted defective products. Sveta explained clients' willingness to tolerate the poor quality of the products because of their general social apathy and their inability to stick up for themselves. She contrasted the apathy of their Russian clients with a demanding client from Poland who placed a difficult and time-consuming order with the firm. The Polish customer actively intervened in the production process: he carefully examined the quality of the layout prepared by Sveta before approving its printing and literally checked 'each feather' on the Polish national emblem. For Sveta, it was one of those rare moments when her skills and professionalism had been acknowledged.

Like Oksana, Sveta did not express any concerns regarding her informal labour status. As her formal employment history covered more than fifteen years, this entitled her to a minimum pension. But she resented the fact that a reversion to formal employment was still negotiable for some privileged employees in the firm. When their accountant Zina became pregnant, Vadim arranged a formal contract for her so that she could claim a maternal welfare package. Needless to say, that was not an easy task given his strategies of concealment. As he could not provide official employment at his own firm, Vadim tapped into his social networks and temporarily registered Zina at his friend's legal firm, which was based in the same premises. This exchange of favours between two entrepreneurs had a long history and varied in size and substance, ranging from the flow of office supplies or legal advice to more substantial help when the lawyer became the legal owner of Vadim's firm for a while. It was clear to everyone in the stamp firm that official employment was a prerogative available only to privileged workers. Zina, who was not only an accountant but also the firm's deputy director, asked Vadim for a new favour when her husband faced a problem with his employment. Referring to the difficult financial situation in her household, Zina asked her boss to give her a side job at the hostel. Vadim agreed, though this meant that he had to make one of his three receptionists redundant. After some consideration, his choice fell on a retired woman in her fifties. Vadim regarded his decision as a fair solution given that this woman received a substantial pension and thus enjoyed a more secure economic position than the other receptionists. The only delicacy involved was that the worker he was going to dismiss was a close friend of Vadim's friend. Initially Vadim did not have the heart to tell her the sad news, as this would definitely affect his long-term friendship. After some days of hesitation, however, he finally did precisely that and employed his bookkeeper in the hostel in the woman's stead.

Conclusion

This chapter has discussed paternalistic relations of dependence at work. It has argued that subjection to the whim of a paternalistic employer may be a voluntary choice on the part of an employee, as it benefits the labouring poor by increasing their possibilities for survival. This is especially the case for those workers who find themselves in the most precarious situations, being cut off from horizontal networks of assistance and/or having no option for a subsistence existence – the commonest coping strategies in post-reform Russia. Cultivating personal relations with her boss enabled Oksana, the main protagonist of this chapter, to balance waged work with childcare. She considered her earlier entrepreneurial strategy to be a better alternative to waged work but had to quit her involvement in petty trade when it challenged her identity as a mother and hindered her social reproduction. She continued pursuing her aspirations to upward mobility through education and a white-collar job, only to come up against the same dilemma. Reflecting on the structural limitations in her class position that she had to overcome, Oksana regarded her retreat to a blue-collar job as a temporary halt on her way to middle-class security, a break she had taken so as not to compromise her maternal responsibilities, to which she attached great value. Her dependence on a powerful 'problem-solver' at work came as a solution to her precarious present and was a way to manage her lack of security. For her boss, Oksana's voluntary compliance provided her with an opportunity to demand flexibility at work. But however beneficial it was for her to sustain informal networks of survival with her employer, it raised irredeemable moral concerns and tensions in the workplace.

First, the cultivation of personal relations of dependence has an aspect of moral ambiguity that is characteristic of *blat* transactions (Ledeneva 2008). In the stamp firm, personal relations of dependence split the tiny work collective into an 'inner circle' permeated by dense and intense interactions and an 'outer circle' in which ties had a sparser and more intermittent quality (Auyero 2000). Regardless of her blue-collar position, Oksana put a great deal of effort into entering the 'inner circle' of privileged employees. Sveta, a designer, did not belong to this inner group, nor did she indicate any desire to join it. On the contrary, she consciously opposed such alliances, which cultivated personal loyalty to her employer and instead upheld an alternative logic of value that linked dignity in labour and personal worth to work-related skills and professionalism. Thus, personal dependence in the workplace secured the positions of some actors while dividing workers among themselves, thus contributing to the larger process of growing labour fragmentation and atomization. The major conflicts and tensions I witnessed in the stamp firm occurred among the workers themselves and rarely affected relations between labour and capital, as even Sveta, Vadim's most vocal critic, accepted his managerial control and turn her outrage towards her co-workers.

Second, Oksana's 'declaration of dependence' is better understood through the lens of class relationships and her aspirations to upward mobility. According to Morris (2016), the major hurdle to upward mobility for working-class women is their lack of social capital beyond their immediate horizontal class links. Without established social networks, such women rarely succeed in white-collar work and simply end up becoming more marginalized (ibid.: 136). Oksana falls into the category of 'the most marginalized' working-class women studied by Morris. Such women 'had undertaken a rigorous remaking of themselves in neoliberalism's image, but had failed to "pass", in a number of senses' (ibid.: 136). Oksana tried to mould herself in the image of successful femininity, but failed to enter the middle-class and after several such failures became increasingly sceptical of her ability to exit blue-collar work. She passed this arduous task of upward mobility to her daughters, whom she equipped with higher education and the motivation to strive for a 'good life'. Oksana kept trying to increase her social capital by forging connections with people of higher status but did so rather ineffectively, given that she could not avoid disagreements with her boss and eventually decided to quit both jobs.

I am not arguing that this strategy reveals much in the sense of the openly instrumental exploitation of social capital. However pragmatic Oksana's desire to sustain her relations of dependence with her patron, she simultaneously felt grateful to Vadim for recognizing the value of her reproductive labour. As a single mother of three and a responsible worker, she believed that she was a legitimate and deserving dependent, and her pledge not to let Vadim down was a grateful response to his recognition of her maternal needs and precarious situation.

Chapter 8
Conclusion: Neoliberalism and Flexible Capitalism in Postsocialist Conditions

This book has explored the moral dimension of the Russian economy and the social reproduction of capital through an ethnographic investigation of small-scale family-based private enterprises in the city of Smolensk in the far west of the country. I situate the moral frameworks of Russian entrepreneurs within the broader dynamics of local and global politico-economic restructurings. In contrast to the body of literature that focuses primarily on the symbolic and discursive aspects of capitalist morality, my research locates values in material processes and examines how changing ideas of personhood, understandings of moral responsibilities and obligations, and conceptions of work and labour are entangled in circuits of production and struggles for reproduction in present-day Russia.

The book is theoretically anchored in approaches to the moral economy elaborated by E.P. Thompson and James Scott. I strive to avoid depicting morality as necessarily opposed to economic interest; rather, values are approached as forces that may well justify and strengthen the principles of economic rationality by endowing them with greater moral legitimacy. Ultimately, I argue that the moral frameworks of Russian entrepreneurs incorporate multiple, discrete and conflicting values such that egalitarian ideals, reciprocity, family obligations and the nostalgia for 'socialist' order overlap with values associated with the new order (though they were by no means unknown in the past), namely self-interest, competition and commodification.

The diverse topics I address in the book converge on a larger question, namely how the symbolic hegemony of capitalism is reproduced in postsocialism. Marxist-oriented analyses assume that this can only be attributable to the 'false consciousness' that lies at the core of the social reproduction of capital. In other words, capitalism naturalizes its domination by obscuring the conditions of its own existence and producing 'the gap between experience and reality for all who enter a specific set of social relations' (Burawoy 2012: 191). According to Marxist approaches, mystifications or misrecognitions are the key mechanisms sustaining the symbolic domination of capital.

By contrast, the moral economy approach opens up more nuanced and complex articulations of economic behaviour that are attentive to individual agency and voices 'from below'. Ordinary actors participating in circuits of production and reproduction are viewed not just as participants in the misrecognition of domination but as engaging in everyday struggles to relate to the world and 'make life worth living' (Narotzky and Besnier 2014: S5). The focus on subjective meanings and individuals' sense-making struggles helps us to understand how people can find meaning in the interests of capital, or, conversely, strive to distance themselves from market values. My study reveals the complex and contradictory motivations and values that guide the economic behaviour of ordinary actors and account for their everyday struggles to 'make life worth living'. The question remains how actors' motivations and their entanglement in diverse logics of value are articulated with the social reproduction of capital. And what, if anything, is specifically postsocialist about the local dynamics of value in Smolensk, which constitute the moral economies of small businesses in Russia and distinguish them from comparable businesses in other spatial and historical conjunctures?

Numerous analysts of eastern and central Europe concur in stating that references to socialism have persistently been employed by the winners of the post-1991 transition to buttress neoliberal policies and new inequalities (Dunn 2004; Kürti and Skalník 2009; Makovicky 2014). For example, Chelcea and Druță (2016) argue that the experience of socialism has prompted a more radical embracing of capitalism in Central and Eastern Europe than it has occurred in countries with a longer capitalist tradition. Chelcea and Druță coined the metaphor of 'zombie socialism' to capture how the socialist past is constantly being resurrected in public discourse in order to sustain 'neoliberal monoglossia' and disguise a range of neoliberal policies that keep wages low and reduce social spending. In the same vein, Simonica (2012: 238) argues that a hegemonic anti-communist discourse is reinforcing capitalism in Romania by creating a normative space 'that defines what can be uttered in a legitimate way and what will be sanctioned as a heresy'. The 'dogma of anticommunism' acts as a tool to neutralize and silence social criticism. Simonica unpacks how the 'ghost of socialism' has persistently been evoked to discipline the workforce: employees who do not demonstrate the desired attitudes to work but who long for job security, stability or more free time are easily accused of being nostalgic for communism or of having a 'faulty mentality' inherited from the stigmatized socialist past. The crude demonizing of communism enables social claims for justice to be dismissed. As a result, the CEE region provides a pool of cheap and educated but docile workers for the core capitalist countries. Simonica concludes that in postsocialist Romania 'the anti-communist discourse constitutes the most overarching framework for reality, setting the yardsticks against which all action, at all levels and undertaken by all actors is to be measured' (ibid.: 237-8).

The 'unmaking of Soviet life' in Russia has been more controversial and less straightforward than in the CEE region. In recent decades, representations of Soviet socialism in media and political discourses have become somewhat more positive, reflecting the unevenness of state policies and the hybrid social formations created under Putin's rule (Hemment 2009; Matveev 2019). Anti-communist rhetoric has lost its hegemony in society, though it remains strong in academic knowledge production. As ambiguities multiply, it becomes possible to ask whether positive memories of socialism may have emancipatory potential for ordinary actors entangled in the circuits of production and reproduction. If some socialist ideas are attractive, do they create possibilities for criticizing capitalism?

In this book, I have shown that some entrepreneurs do mobilize memories of socialism in formulating such criticisms. In particular, Lidia Alekseevna, owner of Alpha and a former *nomenklatura* worker in a Soviet factory (see Chapter 6), was openly critical of market morality and supportive of the communist project and its moral imperatives. Expressing her discontent, Lidia formulated a typical 'reformist critique', that is, a critical judgment that does not question the whole system but pinpoints a particular institution or situation needing to be changed (Boltanski 2011). She criticized the Russian variant of the market economy – which she dismissed as a bazaar economy – as being at odds with the high Western standards of capitalism that allegedly rest upon a different regime of value. Her reformist critique centred on the precarious positionality of small garment-producers within the global circuits of capital. At the same time, her sense of justice and dissatisfaction with the market did not have practical consequences for the way she treated her employees. When it came to the organization of labour in her factory, Lidia acted like any other manager in the age of flexible accumulation, invoking the notion of the entrepreneurial employee to discipline her workers and adapt their labour power to the flexible regime of production she required.

The relationship between capital and labour was also an object of social criticism for Polina, the owner of the advertising agency (see Chapter 5). Her attempts to redefine social relationships with her workers in a more horizontal manner were fuelled by her imaginations of enterprise collectivism in the Soviet epoch. However, this image of a labour collective consisting of like-minded individuals coexisted with the neoliberal ideals of personhood and self-regulation that Polina learned about from Western success manuals. Being in her mid-thirties, Polina did not have any significant experience of life and work under socialism, but nevertheless she shared a feeling of nostalgia for the socialist project and upheld its moral imperatives. With her distaste for social inequalities and exclusion, she strove to reformulate intra-firm relations by mobilizing an idiom of kinship that captured reciprocal obligations of care and stressed the affective dimension of social bonds. Yet Polina too followed the logic of reformist criticism by not questioning the justice of the capitalist system as a whole, but merely seeking to remedy its flaws in particular domains, like the quality of social relations at work. However, her attempt to impart a family feeling to the company generated new inequalities by creating lines of exclusion between those who were more affected by the language of *svoi* morality and those who did not belong to the circle of *svoi* people or only occupied its margins. Paradoxically, her reformist criticism of social inequalities reproduced the major ideologies and the regime of production that are intrinsic to flexible forms of accumulation but expressed them in the language of *svoi* morality.

Thus, nostalgia for socialism produces highly contradictory outcomes. This type of critical engagement can hardly be conceptualized as resistance, given that capitalism's moral hegemony still goes unquestioned. Yet the effects of this critical engagement are highly controversial and dubious. As demonstrated above, memories of socialism tend to strengthen more embedded, personalistic and reciprocal ties between capital and labour, articulated within the framework of shared moral responsibilities and obligations. This framework may benefit individual workers and grant them additional perks, whether symbolic or material, and thus make their working lives in capitalism relatively more secure, stable and enjoyable. In Chapter 7, I described how some workers actively appealed to the framework of moral obligations and sought to create reciprocal ties with their employers in order to secure transfers of 'favours' and informal support at work.

However, as Narotzky (2015) reminds us, reciprocity and embeddedness, when subordinated to the logic of market value, are far from representing benevolent forms of sociality but rather facilitate the expansion and accumulation of capital. Contrary to the simplistic interpretations of Karl Polanyi, the dominance of market exchange does not lead to a 'disembedding' of the economy from other social relations. On the contrary, even the most extreme forms of neoliberal capitalism are sustained by entangling social values with material interests, as ethnographies of local economies in many global contexts demonstrate (Humphrey 2002; Mollona 2009; Weiss 2011; Makovicky 2014; Narotzky 2015; Kofti 2016; Morris 2016). When small businesses in this Russian province echo the personalized patron-client world of socialist enterprises, rather than opposing 'capitalist realism' or challenging its legitimacy (Fisher 2009), they are subjected to new forms of capitalist discipline. Ultimately, this book provides more ethnographic evidence that ideological labels such as 'liberal' or 'socialist' do not correspond to diametrically opposed regimes of value and that their conceptual worth for empirical research is highly dubious.

Bibliography

Abercrombie, N., and S. Hill. 1976. Paternalism and Patronage. *The British Journal of Sociology* 27 (4): 413–429.
Agadjanian, A. 2003a. Breakthrough to Modernity, Apologia for Traditionalism: the Russian Orthodox View of Society and Culture in Comparative Perspective. *Religion, State and Society* 31 (4): 327–346.
——. 2003b. The Social Vision of Russian Orthodoxy: Balancing Between Identity and Relevance. In J. Sutton, and W. van den Bercken (eds.), *Orthodox Christianity and Contemporary Europe*, pp. 163–182. Leuven: Peeters.
Alasheev, S. 1995. On a Particular Kind of Love and the Specificity of Soviet Production. In S. Clarke (ed.), *Management and Industry in Russia: Formal and Informal Relations in the Period of Transition*, pp. 69–98. Aldershot: Edward Elgar.
Anderson, D. 1996. Bringing Civil Society to an Uncivilised Place. In C. Hann, and E. Dunn (eds.), *Civil Society: Challenging Western Models*, pp. 99–120. London: Routledge.
Angé, O., and D. Berliner (eds.). 2014. *Anthropology and Nostalgia*. Oxford: Berghahn Books.
Ashwin, S. 1999. *Russian Workers: The Anatomy of Patience*. Manchester: Manchester University Press.
—— (ed.). 2006. *Adapting to Russia's New Labour Market: Gender and Employment Behaviour*. Abingdon: Routledge.
Ashwin, S., and E. Bowers. 1997. Do Russian Women Want to Work? In M. Buckley (ed.), *Post-Soviet Women: From the Baltic to Central Asia*, pp. 21–37. Cambridge: Cambridge University Press.
Ashwin, S. and T. Lytkina. 2004. Men in Crisis in Russia: The Role of Domestic Marginalization. *Gender & Society* 18 (2): 189–206.
Åslund, A. 1992. *Post-Communist Economic Revolutions: How Big a Bang?* Washington: Center for Strategic and International Studies.
——. 2007. *Russia's Capitalist Revolution: Why Market Reform Succeeded and Democracy Failed*. Washington: Peterson Institute for International Economics.
Auyero, J. 2000. The Logic of Clientelism in Argentina: An Ethnographic Account. *Latin American Research Review* 35 (3): 55–81.
Barker, H. 2016. *Family and Business During the Industrial Revolution*. Oxford: Oxford University Press.
Bauman, Z. 2005. *Work, Consumerism and the New Poor*. Berkshire: Open University Press.

Becker, U., and A. Vasileva. 2017. Russia's Political Economy Re-Conceptualized: A Changing Hybrid of Liberalism, Statism and Patrimonialism. *Journal of Eurasian Studies* 8 (1): 83–96.

Berglöf, E., A. Kunov, J. Shvets, and K. Yudaeva, (eds.) 2003. *The New Political Economy of Russia*. Cambridge: MIT Press.

Bergman, J. 1992. Soviet Dissidents on the Russian Intelligentsia, 1956-1985: The Search for a Usable Past. *The Russian Review* 51 (1): 16–35.

Bloch, M. 1973. The Long Term and the Short Term: The Economic and Political Significance of the Morality of Kinship. In J. Goody (ed.), *The Character of Kinship*, pp. 75–87. Cambridge: Cambridge University Press.

Boltanski, L. 2011. *On Critique: A Sociology of Emancipation*. Cambridge: Polity.

Boyer, D., and A. Yurchak. 2008. Postsocialist Studies, Cultures of Parody and American Stiob. *Anthropology News* 49 (8): 9–10.

Breslauer, G. W. 1978. On the Adaptability of Soviet Welfare-State Authoritarianism. In K. Ryavec (ed.), *Soviet Society and the Communist Party*, pp. 3–25. Amherst: University of Massachusetts.

Bridger, S., and F. Pine (eds.). 1998. *Surviving Post-Socialism: Local Strategies and Regional Responses in Eastern Europe and the Former Soviet Union*. London and New York: Routledge.

Buchowski, M. 1997. *Reluctant Capitalists: Class and Culture in a Local Community in Western Poland*. Berlin: Center Marc Bloch.

Burawoy, M. 2001. Transition Without Transformation: Russia's Involutionary Road to Capitalism. *East European Politics and Societies* 15 (2): 269–290.

———. 2012. The Roots of Domination: Beyond Bourdieu and Gramsci. *Sociology* 46 (2): 187–206.

Burawoy, M., P. Krotov, and T. Lytkina. 2000. Involution and Destitution in Capitalist Russia. *Ethnography* 1 (1): 43–65.

Burawoy, M., and J. Lukács. 1992. *The Radiant Past: Ideology and Reality in Hungary's Road to Capitalism*. Chicago and London: The University of Chicago Press.

Burawoy, M., and K. Verdery (eds.). 1999. *Uncertain Transition: Ethnographies of Change in the Postsocialist World*. Oxford: Rowman and Littlefield.

Buss, A. 2003. *The Russian-Orthodox Tradition and Modernity*. Leiden: Brill.

Caldwell, M. L. 2004. *Not by Bread Alone: Social Support in the New Russia*. Berkeley: University of California Press.

——. 2010. The Russian Orthodox Church, the Provision of Social Welfare, and Changing Ethics of Benevolence. In C. Hann, and H. Goltz (eds.), *Eastern Christians in Anthropological Perspective*, pp. 329–350. Berkeley: University of California Press.

——. 2011. The Politics of Rightness: Social Justice Among Russia's Christian Communities. In J. Zigon (ed.), *Multiple Moralities and Religions in Post-Soviet Russia*, pp. 48–66. New York: Berghahn Books.

Carrier, J. 1997. Introduction. In J. Carrier (ed.), *Meanings of the Market: The Free Market in Western Culture*, pp. 1–67. Oxford: Berg.

——. 2018. Moral Economy: What's in a Name. *Anthropological Theory* 18 (1): 18–35.

Chari, S., and K. Verdery. 2009. Thinking Between the Posts: Postcolonialism, Post-socialism, and Ethnography After the Cold War. *Comparative Studies in Society and History* 51 (1): 6–34.

Chelcea, L., and O. Druţă. 2016. Zombie Socialism and the Rise of Neoliberalism in Post-Socialist Central and Eastern Europe. *Eurasian Geography and Economics* 57 (4-5): 521–544.

Chernyshova, N. 2013. *Soviet Consumer Culture in the Brezhnev Era*. London: Routledge.

Clarke, S. 1993a. The Contradictions of 'State Socialism'. In S. Clarke, P. Fairbrother, M. Burawoy, and P. Krotov (eds.), *What About the Workers? Workers and the Transition to Capitalism in Russia*, pp. 5–29. New York: Verso.

——. 1993b. Privatisation and the Development of Capitalism in Russia. In S. Clarke, P. Fairbrother, M. Burawoy, and P. Krotov (eds.), *What About the Workers? Workers and the Transition to Capitalism in Russia*, pp. 199–241. New York: Verso.

—— (ed.). 1995. *Management and Industry in Russia: Formal and Informal Relations in the Period of Transition*. Aldershot: Edward Elgar.

——. 1999. *The Formation of a Labour Market in Russia*. Warwick: Edward Elgar.

Clarke, S., and V. Borisov. 1999. New Forms of Labour Contract and Labour Flexibility in Russia. *Economics of Transition* 7 (3): 593–614.

Clarke, S., P. Fairbrother, M. Burawoy, and P. Krotov (eds.). 1993. *What About the Workers? Workers and the Transition to Capitalism in Russia*. New York: Verso.

Cohen, S. 2013. Image of a Secretary: A Metapragmatic Morality for Post-Soviet Capitalism. *Anthropological Quarterly* 86 (3): 725–758.

Collins, J. L. 2009. *Threads: Gender, Labor, and Power in the Global Apparel Industry*. Chicago and London: The University of Chicago Press.

Cook, L. J. 1993. *The Soviet Social Contract and Why it Failed: Welfare Policy and Workers' Politics from Brezhnev to Yeltsin*. Cambridge: Harvard University Press.

Crisp, O. 1976. *Studies in the Russian Economy Before 1914*. London: The Macmillan Press

Davies, R. W. 1998. *Soviet Economic Development from Lenin to Khrushchev*. New York: Cambridge University Press.

Davis, J. 1977. *People of the Mediterranean: An Essay in Comparative Social Anthropology*. London: Routledge and Kegan Paul.

Donahoe, B., and J. O. Habeck (eds.). 2011. *Reconstructing the House of Culture: Community, Self, and the Makings of Culture in Russia and Beyond*. New York: Berghahn Books.

Dunham, V. 1990. *In Stalin's Time: Middleclass Values in Soviet Fiction*. Durham: Duke University Press.

Dunn, E. 2004. *Privatizing Poland: Baby Food, Big Business, and the Remaking of Labor*. Ithaca: Cornell University Press.

Edelman, M. 2005. Bringing the Moral Economy Back in... to the Study of 21st Century Transnational Peasant Movements. *American Anthropologist* 107 (3): 331–345.

Ertman, T. (ed.). 2017. *Max Weber's Economic Ethic of the World Religions: An Analysis*. Cambridge: Cambridge University Press.

Fainsod, M. 1958. *Smolensk under Soviet Rule*. Cambridge: Harvard University Press.

Ferguson, J. 2013. Declarations of Dependence: Labour, Personhood, and Welfare in Southern Africa. *Journal of the Royal Anthropological Institute* 19 (2): 223–242.

Field, D. A. 1998. Irreconcilable Differences: Divorce and Conceptions of Private Life in the Khrushchev Era. *The Russian Review* 57 (4): 599–613.

Filtzer, D. 1996. Labor Discipline, the Use of Work Time, and the Decline of the Soviet System, 1928–1991. *International Labor and Working-Class History* 50: 9–28.

——. 2002a. *Soviet Workers and De-Stalinization: The Consolidation of the Modern System of Soviet Production Relations 1953-1964*. Cambridge: Cambridge University Press.

——. 2002b. *Soviet Workers and Late Stalinism: Labour and the Restoration of the Stalinist System after World War II*. Cambridge: Cambridge University Press.

———. 2006. From Mobilized to Free Labour: De-Stalinization and the Changing Legal Status of Workers. In J. Polly (ed.), *The Dilemmas of De-Stalinization: Negotiating Cultural and Social Change in the Khrushchev Era*, pp. 168–184. London: Routledge.
Firsov, B. 2008. *Raznomyslie v SSSR, 1940-1960-e gody* (Dissent in the USSR, 1940s-1960s). St Petersburg: European University at St Petersburg Press.
Fisher, M. 2009. *Capitalist Realism: Is There no Alternative?* Ropley: John Hunt Publishing.
Fitzpatrick, S. 1992. *The Cultural Front: Power and Culture in Revolutionary Russia*. Ithaca: Cornell University Press.
———. 1994. *Stalin's Peasants: Resistance and Survival in the Russian Village after Collectivization*. New York: Oxford University Press.
———. 2000. Ascribing Class: The Construction of Social Identity in Soviet Russia. In S. Fitzpatrick (ed.), *Stalinism: New Directions*, pp. 20–46. London: Routledge.
———. 2002. *Education and Social Mobility in the Soviet Union 1921-1934*. Cambridge: Cambridge University Press.
Freeland, C. 2000. *Sale of the Century: Russia's Wild Ride from Communism to Capitalism*. New York: Crown Business.
Friedrich, C., and Z. Brzezinski. 1956. *Totalitarian Dictatorship and Autocracy*. Cambridge: Harvard University Press.
Gaddy, C., and B. W. Ickes. 2002. *Russia's Virtual Economy*. Washington: Brookings Institution Press.
Gal, S., and G. Kligman. 2012. *The Politics of Gender After Socialism: A Comparative-Historical Essay*. Princeton: Princeton University Press.
Gapova, E. 2002. On Nation, Gender, and Class Formation in Belarus ... and Elsewhere in the Post-Soviet World. *Nationalities Papers* 30 (4): 639–662.
Gatrell, P. 1982. Industrial Expansion in Tsarist Russia, 1908-14. *Economic History Review* 35 (1): 99–110.
Gerschenkron, A. 1962. *Economic Backwardness in Historical Perspective: A Book of Essays*. Cambridge: Belknap Press of Harvard University Press
Gohberg, L. (ed.). 2017. *Ranking of Innovative Regions of Russia* 5. Moscow: Higher School of Economics Press.
Golichev, V. D., I. E. Alfimov, N. D. Golicheva, O. M. Gusarova, L. T. Kiashchenko, P. I. Komarov, V. M. Kondrashev, O. A. Lapshova, I. E. Nozdreva, V. V. Popova, S. J. Sivakova, and M. V. Shelomentseva. 2013. *Zemlja Smolenskaja i ee naselenie: istoriko-*

statisticheskij obzor v cifrah i faktah [The Smolensk land and its population: historical and statistical review in figures and facts]. Smolensk: Smolenskaya Gorodskaya Tipographia.
Golovshinskii, K., S. Parkhomenko, V. Rimskii, and G. Satarov. 2004. *Business and Corruption: How to Combat Business Participation in Corruption. Final Report.* Moscow: INDEM.
Graeber, D. 2001. *Toward an Anthropological Theory of Value: The False Coin of Our Own Dreams.* New York: Springer.
Gregory, C. A. 2015 [1989]. *Gifts and Commodities (2nd edition).* Chicago: HAU Books.
Gronow, J. 2003. *Caviar with Champagne: Common Luxury and the Ideals of Good Life in Stalin's Russia.* Oxford: Berg.
Gurova, O. 2006. Ideology of Consumption in Soviet Union: From Asceticism to the Legitimating of Consumer Goods. *Anthropology of East Europe Review* 24 (2): 91–98.
——. 2012. 'We are Not Rich Enough to Buy Cheap Things': Clothing Consumption of the St. Petersburg Middle Class. In S. Salmenniemi (ed.), *Rethinking Class in Russia*, pp. 149–166. Surrey: Aschgate.
Haimson, L. H. 1988. The Problem of Social Identities in Early Twentieth Century Russia. *Slavic Review* 47 (1): 1–20.
Hall, C., and L. Davidoff. 2002. *Family Fortunes: Men and Women of the English Middle Class 1780-1850.* London: Routledge.
Hann, C. 2002. Farewell to the Socialist "Other". In C. Hann (ed.), *Postsocialism: Ideals, Ideologies and Practices in Eurasia*, pp. 1–11. London: Routledge.
——. 2007. A New Double Movement? Anthropological Perspectives on Property in the Age of Neoliberalism. *Socio-Economic Review* 5 (2): 287–318.
——. 2011. Eastern Christianity and Western Social Theory. *Erfurter Vorträge zur Kulturgeschichte des Orthodoxen Christentums* 10. Erfurt: Universität Erfurt, Lehrstuhl für Religionswissenschaft.
——. 2018. Moral(ity and) Economy: Work, Workfare, and Fairness in Provincial Hungary. *Archives Européennes de Sociologie* 59 (2): 225–254.
Hann, C., and E. Dunn (eds.). 1996. *Civil Society: Challenging Western Models.* London: Routledge.
Hann, C., C. Humphrey, and K. Verdery. 2002. Introduction: Post-socialism as a Topic of Anthropological Investigation. In C. Hann (ed.), *Postsocialism: Ideals, Ideologies and Practices in Eurasia*, pp. 1–28. London: Routledge.

Hann, C., and J. Parry (eds.). 2018. *Industrial Labor on the Margins of Capitalism: Precarity, Class, and the Neoliberal Subject*. New York: Berghahn Books.
Hart, K. 1973. Informal Income Opportunities and Urban Employment in Ghana. *Journal of Modern African Studies* 11 (1): 61–89.
Harvey, D. 1989. *The Condition of Postmodernity: An Enquiry into the Origins of Cultural Change.* Cambridge MA: Blackwell.
Hauslohner, P. 1987. Gorbachev's Social Contract. *Soviet Economy* 3 (1): 54–89.
Hedlund, S. 1999. *Russia's 'Market Economy': A Bad Case of Predatory Capitalism.* London: University College London.
——. 2005. *Russian Path Dependence: A People With a Troubled History.* London and New York: Routledge.
Heintz, M. 2009. Introduction: Why There Should Be an Anthropology of Moralities. In M. Heintz (ed.), *The Anthropology of Moralities*, pp. 1–19. New York: Berghahn Books.
Hellman, J., G. Jones, and D. Kaufmann. 2003. Seize the State, Seize the Day: State Capture and Influence in Transition Economies. *Journal of Comparative Economics* 31 (4): 751–773.
Hellman, J., and M. Schankerman. 2000. Intervention, Corruption and Capture: The Nexus Between Enterprises and the State. *Economics of Transition* 8 (3): 545–576.
Hemment, J. 2009. Soviet-Style Neoliberalism? Nashi, Youth Voluntarism, and the Restructuring of Social Welfare in Russia. *Problems of Post-Communism* 56 (6): 36–50.
Hessler, J. 2000. Cultured Trade: The Stalinist Turn Towards Consumerism. In S. Fitzpatrick (ed.), *Stalinism: New Directions*, pp. 182–209. London: Routledge.
Ho, K. 2009. *Liquidated: An Ethnography of Wall Street.* Durham: Duke University Press.
Holzlehner, T. 2014. *Shadow Networks: Border Economies, Informal Markets and Organized Crime in the Russian Far East*. Berlin: Lit Verlag.
Humphrey, C. 1983. *Karl Marx Collective: Economy, Society and Religion in a Siberian Collective Farm.* Cambridge: Cambridge University Press.
——. 1999. Traders, 'Disorder', and Citizenship Regimes in Provincial Russia. In M. Burawoy, and K. Verdery (eds.), *Uncertain Transition: Ethnographies of Change in the Postsocialist World*, pp. 19–52. Lanham: Rowman & Littlefield.

———. 2002. *The Unmaking of Soviet Life: Everyday Economies After Socialism*. Ithaca: Cornell University Press.
Ikonen, H.-M. 2013. Precarious Work, Entrepreneurial Mindset and Sense of Place: Female Strategies in Insecure Labour Markets. *Global Discourse* 3 (3-4): 467–481.
Kalb, D. 2011. Introduction. In D. Kalb, and G. Halmai (eds.), *Headlines of Nation, Subtexts of Class: Working-Class Populism and the Return of the Repressed in Neoliberal Europe*, pp. 1–36. New York: Berghahn Books.
———. 2014. Afterword: Elias Talks to Hayek (and Learns from Marx and Foucault): Reflections on Neoliberalism, Post-socialism and Personhood. In N. Makovicky (ed.), *Neoliberalism, Personhood, and Postsocialism: Enterprising Selves in Changing Economies*, pp. 187–202. Surrey: Ashgate Farnham.
Kelly, C., and V. Volkov. 1998. Directed Desires: Kul'turnost' and Consumption. In C. Kelly, and D. Shepherd (eds.), *Constructing Russian Culture in the Age of Revolution: 1881-1940*, pp. 291–313. Oxford: Oxford University Press.
Kenworthy, S. M. 2008. To Save the World or to Renounce it: Modes of Moral Action in Russian Orthodoxy. In M. Steinberg, and C. Wanner (eds.), *Religion, Morality, and Community in Post-Soviet Societies*, pp. 21–54. Washington: Woodrow Wilson Center Press.
———. 2010. *The Heart of Russia: Trinity-Sergius, Monasticism, and Society after 1825*. Oxford: Oxford University Press.
Keskūla, E. 2014. Disembedding the Company from Kinship: Unethical Families and Atomized Labor in an Estonian Mine. *Laboratorium* 6 (2): 58–76.
———. 2015. Reverse, Restore, Repeat! Class, Ethnicity, and the Russian-Speaking Miners of Estonia. *Focaal* 72: 95–108.
Kharkhordin, O. 1999. *The Collective and the Individual in Russia: A Study of Practices*. Berkley: University of California Press.
Kideckel, D. A. 2002. The Unmaking of an East-Central European Working Class. In C. Hann (ed.), *Postsocialism: Ideas, Ideologies and Practices in Eurasia*, pp. 114–132. London: Routledge.
Kjaerulff, J. (ed.). 2015. *Flexible Capitalism: Exchange and Ambiguity at Work*. New York: Berghahn.
Klimenko, I. 2001. *Dumy o bylom* (Thoughts about the Past). Smolensk: Oblastnaja zhurnalistskaja organizacija.
Koellner, T. 2012. *Practising Without Belonging? Entrepreneurship, Morality, and Religion in Contemporary Russia*. Münster: LIT Verlag.

Kofti, D. 2016. Moral Economy of Flexible Production: Fabricating Precarity Between the Conveyor Belt and the Household. *Anthropological Theory* 16 (4): 433–453.
Komaromi, A. 2012. Samizdat and Soviet Dissident Publics. *Slavic Review* 71 (1): 70–90.
Kondo, D. K. 2009. *Crafting Selves: Power, Gender, and Discourses of Identity in a Japanese Workplace*. Chicago: The University of Chicago Press.
Kormina, J. 2015. Recenzija: Aleksej Jurchak: Jeto bylo navsegda, poka ne konchilos' Poslednee sovetskoe pokolenie. (Review: Alexei Yurchak: Everything was forever, until it was no more. The Last Soviet Generation). *Antropologicheskij forum* (Forum for Anthropology and Culture) 26: 209–221.
Kormina, J., and S. Shtyrkov. 2015. 'Jeto nashe, iskonno russkoe, i nikuda nam ot jetogo ne det'sja': predystorija postsovetskoj desekuljarizacii.' ('This is our, primordially Russian, and we can't avoid it': the prehistory of post-Soviet desecularization). In J. Kormina, A. Panchenko, and S. Styrkov (eds.), *Izobretenie religii: desekuljarizacija v postsovetskom kontekste* (The Invention of Religion: Desecularization in the Post-Soviet Context), pp. 7–45. St Peterburg: European University at St Petersburg Press.
Kornai, J. 1980. *Economics of Shortage*. Amsterdam: North-Holland.
Kotkin, S. 1997. *Magnetic Mountain: Stalinism as a Civilization*. Berkeley: University of California Press.
Kozina, I., and E. Zhidkova. 2006. Sex Segregation and Discrimination in the new Russian Labour Market. In S. Ashwin (ed.), *Adapting to Russia's New Labour Market: Gender and Employment Behaviour*, pp. 57–87. New York: Routledge.
Kryshtanovskaya, O., and S. White. 1996. From Soviet Nomenklatura to Russian Elite. *Europe-Asia Studies* 48 (5): 711–733.
Kürti, L., and P. Skalník (eds.). 2009. *Postsocialist Europe: Anthropological Perspectives from Home*. New York: Berghahn Books.
Laidlaw, J. 2002. For an Anthropology of Ethics and Freedom. *Journal of the Royal Anthropological Institute* 8 (2): 311–332.
Lane, C. 1981. *The Rites of Rulers: Ritual in Industrial Society - the Soviet Case*. Cambridge: Cambridge University Press.
Ledeneva, A. 1998. *Russia's Economy of Favours: Blat, Networking and Informal Exchange*. Cambridge: Cambridge University Press.
——. 2006. *How Russia Really Works: The Informal Practices That Shaped Post-Soviet Politics and Business*. Ithaca: Cornell University Press.

———. 2008. *Blat* and *Guanxi*: Informal Practices in Russia and China. *Comparative Studies in Society and History* 50 (1): 118–144.

———. 2011. Open Secrets and Knowing Smiles. *East European Politics and Societies* 25 (4): 720–736.

———. 2017. The Ambivalence of Favour: Paradoxes of Russia's Economy of Favours. In D. Henig, and N. Makovicky (eds.), *Economies of Favour After Socialism*, pp. 21–49. Oxford: Oxford University Press.

Lemon, A. 1998. "Your Eyes Are Green like Dollars": Counterfeit Cash, National Substance, and Currency Apartheid in 1990s Russia. *Cultural Anthropology* 13 (1): 22–55.

Levada, J. A. 2003. Homo Post-Sovieticus. *Russian Social Science Review* 44 (1): 32–67.

Lima, P. de. 2000. Is Blood Thicker Than Economic Interest in Familial Enterprises? In P. Schweitzer (ed.), *Dividends of Kinship: Meanings and Uses of Social Relatedness*, pp. 153–178. London: Routledge.

Luehrmann, S. 2011. *Secularism Soviet Style: Teaching Atheism and Religion in a Volga Republic*. Bloomington: Indiana University Press.

———. 2017. Innocence and Demographic Crisis: Transposing Post-Abortion Syndrome into a Russian Orthodox Key. In S. De Zordo, J. Mishtal, and L. Anton (eds.), *A Fragmented Landscape: Abortion Governance and Protest Logics in Postwar Europe,* pp. 102–122. New York: Berghahn Books.

Lunyakova, L. 2004. 'Chem muzhika kormit', luchshe rebenka vospityvat' odnoj': social'nyj portret materinskih semej. ('Rather than feed a man, it is a better to raise a child alone': the social profile of single mothers). In S. Oushakine (ed.), *Semejnye uzy: modeli dlja sborki. Kniga 2.* (Family ties: The model kits. Vol. 2), pp. 60–82. Moskva: Novoe Literaturnoe Obozrenie.

Makovicky, N. (ed.). 2014. *Neoliberalism, Personhood, and Postsocialism: Enterprising Selves in Changing Economies*. Surrey: Ashgate.

Makrides, V. 2005. Orthodox Christianity, Rationalization, Modernization: A Reassessment. In V. Roudometof, A. Agadjanian, and J. Pankhurst (eds.), *Eastern Orthodoxy in a Global Age. Tradition Faces the Twenty-first Century*, pp. 179–209. Walnut: Altamira Press.

Mars, G. 1994. *Cheats at Work: An Anthropology of Workplace Crime*. Aldershot: Dartmouth.

Matveev, I. 2019. State, Capital, and the Transformation of the Neoliberal Policy Paradigm in Putin's Russia. *International Review of Modern Sociology* 44 (1): 27–48.

Matza, T. 2009. Moscow's Echo: Technologies of the Self, Publics, and Politics on the Russian Talk Show. *Cultural Anthropology* 24 (3): 489–522.

McKay, J. P. 1970. *Pioneers for Profit: Foreign Entrepreneurship and Russian Industrialization 1885-1913*. Chicago: The University of Chicago Press.

Millar, J. R. 1985. The Little Deal: Brezhnev's Contribution to Acquisitive Socialism. *Slavic Review* 44 (4): 694–706.

Millar, K. 2014. The Precarious Present: Wageless Labor and Disrupted Life in Rio de Janeiro, Brazil. *Cultural Anthropology* 29 (1): 32–53.

Mollona, M. 2009. *Made in Sheffield: An Ethnography of Industrial Work and Politics*. New York: Berghahn Books.

Morris, J. 2011. Socially Embedded Workers at the Nexus of Diverse Work in Russia: An Ethnography of Blue-Collar Informalization. *International Journal of Sociology and Social Policy* 31 (11/12): 619–631.

———. 2012. Unruly Entrepreneurs: Russian Worker Responses to Insecure Formal Employment. *Global Labour Journal* 3 (2): 217–236.

———. 2013. Precarious Work, Entrepreneurial Mindset and Sense of Place. Female Strategies in Insecure Labour Markets: A Response to Hanna-Mari Ikonen. *Global Discourse* 3 (3-4): 482–485.

———. 2016. *Everyday Post-Socialism: Working-Class Communities in the Russian Margins* London: Palgrave Macmillan.

———. 2017. Cheesed off, but not because of sanctions: Russians adapt to immiseration as global capital increases its grip. *Focaalblog*, November 16, https://www.focaalblog.com/2017/11/16/jeremy-morris-cheesed-off-but-not-because-of-sanctions/. Available online, accessed 14 March 2021.

———. 2019. The Informal Economy and Post-Socialism: Imbricated Perspectives on Labor, the State, and Social Embeddedness. *Demokratizatsiya: The Journal of Post-Soviet Democratization* 27 (1): 9–30.

Müller, M. 2019. Goodbye, Postsocialism! *Europe-Asia Studies* 71 (4): 1–18.

Munn, N. D. 1992. *The Fame of Gawa: A Symbolic Study of Value Transformation in a Massim (Papua New Guinea) Society*. Durham: Duke University Press.

Narotzky, S. 2015. The Payoff of Love and the Traffic of Favours. In J. Kjaerulff (ed.), *Flexible Capitalism: Exchange and Ambiguity at Work*, pp. 173–206. New York: Berghahn Books.

Narotzky, S., and N. Besnier. 2014. Crisis, Value, and Hope: Rethinking the Economy. *Current Anthropology* 55 (S9): S4–S16.

Nathans, B. 2007. The Dictatorship of Reason: Aleksandr Vol'pin and the Idea of Rights under 'Developed Socialism'. *Slavic Review* 66 (4): 630–663.

Neve, G. de. 2008. 'We are all Sondukarar (Relatives)!' Kinship and its Morality in an Urban Industry of Tamilnadu, South India. *Modern Asian Studies* 42 (1): 211–246.

Newby, H. 1977. Paternalism and Capitalism. In R. Scase (ed.), *Industrial Society: Class, Cleavage and Control*, pp. 59–73. New York: St. Martin's Press.

Nikula, J., and I. Tchalakov. 2013. *Innovations and Entrepreneurs in Socialist and Post-Socialist Societies*. Newcastle: Cambridge Scholars Press.

Novokmet, F., T. Piketty, and G. Zucman. 2018. 'From Soviets to Oligarchs: Inequality and Property in Russia 1905-2016'. *The Journal of Economic Inequality* 16 (2): 189–223.

Ong, A. 2010. *Spirits of Resistance and Capitalist Discipline: Factory Women in Malaysia*. New York: SUNY Press.

Osipian, A. 2012. 'Predatory Raiding in Russia: Institutions and Property Rights after the Crisis'. *Journal of Economic Issues* 46 (2): 469–480.

Oushakine, S. 2000. 'The Quantity of Style: Imaginary Consumption in the New Russia'. *Theory, Culture & Society* 17 (5): 97–120.

Pallot, J. 1999. *Land Reform in Russia, 1906-1917: Peasant Responses to Stolypin's Project of Rural Transformation*. Oxford: Clarendon Press.

Palomera, J., and T. Vetta. 2016. Moral Economy: Rethinking a Radical Concept. *Anthropological Theory* 16 (4): 413–432.

Paneyakh, E. 2008. *Pravila igry dlja russkogo predprinimatelja* (The rules of the game for a Russian entrepreneur). Moscow: Kolibri.

Parry, J., and M. Bloch. 1989. *Money and the Morality of Exchange*. Cambridge: Cambridge University Press.

Patico, J. 2008. *Consumption and Social Change in a Post-Soviet Middle Class*. Stanford: Stanford University Press.

Pesmen, D. 2000. *Russia and Soul: An Exploration*. Ithaca: Cornell University Press.

Petrovici, N. 2015. Framing Criticism and Knowledge Production in Semi-Peripheries: Post-Socialism Unpacked. *Intersections: East European Journal of Society and Politics* 1 (2): 80–102.

Pine, F. 2002. Retreat to the Household? Gendered Domains in Postsocialist Poland. In C. Hann (ed.), *Postsocialism: Ideals, Ideologies and Practices in Eurasia*, pp. 95–113. London: Routledge.

Platt, K., and B. Nathans. 2011. Socialist in Form, Indeterminate in Content: The Ins and Outs of Late Soviet Culture. *Ab imperio* 2011 (2): 301–324.

Polese, A., J. Morris, B. Kovács, and I. Harboe. 2014. 'Welfare States' and Social Policies in Eastern Europe and the Former USSR: Where Informality Fits In? *Journal of Contemporary European Studies* 22 (2): 184–198.

Polterovich, V. 2001. Institutional Traps. In L. Klein, and M. Pomer (eds.), *The New Russia: Transition Gone Awry*, pp. 93–116. Stanford: Stanford University Press.

Pomer, M. 2001. Introduction. In L. Klein, and M. Pomer (eds.), *The New Russia: Transition Gone Awry*, pp. 1–20. Stanford: Stanford University Press.

Puffer, S., and D. McCarthy. 2007. Can Russia's State-Managed, Network Capitalism be Competitive? Institutional Pull Versus Institutional Push. *Journal of World Business* 42 (1): 1–13.

Randall, L. M. 2001. *Reluctant Capitalists: Russia's Journey Through Market Transition*. New York: Routledge.

Ratilainen, S. 2012. Business for Pleasure: Elite Women in the Russian Popular Media. In S. Salmenniemi (ed.), *Rethinking Class in Russia*, pp. 45–66. Surrey: Ashgate.

Ries, N. 1997. *Russian Talk: Culture and Conversation During Perestroika*. Ithaca: Cornell University Press.

———. 2002. 'Honest Bandits' and 'Warped People': Russian Narratives about Money, Corruption, and Political Decay. In C. Lewin, R. Gordon, E. Mertz, K. Warren, and C. Greenhouse (eds.), *Ethnography in Unstable Places: Everyday Lives in Contexts of Dramatic Political Change*, pp. 276–315. Durham: Duke University Press.

Rivkin-Fish, M. 2009. Tracing Landscapes of the Past in Class Subjectivity: Practices of Memory and Distinction in Marketizing Russia. *American Ethnologist* 36 (1): 79–95.

Robbins, J. 2009. Morality, Value, and Radical Cultural Change. In M. Heintz (ed.), *The Anthropology of Moralities*, pp. 62–80. New York: Berghahn Books.

Rochlitz, M. 2014. Corporate Raiding and the Role of the State in Russia. *Post-Soviet Affairs* 30 (2-3): 89–114.
Rogers, D. 2010. Postsocialisms Unbound: Connections, Critiques, Comparisons. *Slavic Review* 69 (1): 1–15.
——. 2015. *The Depths of Russia: Oil, Power, and Culture After Socialism*. Ithaca: Cornell University Press.
Rose, N. 1992. Governing the Enterprising Self. In P. Heelas, and P. Morris (eds.), *The Values of the Enterprise Culture: The Moral Debate*, pp. 141–164. London: Routledge.
Rutland, P. 2001. Introduction: Business and the State in Russia. In P. Rutland (ed.), *Business and State in Contemporary Russia*, pp. 1–33. New York: Westview Press.
——. 2008. Putin's Economic Record: Is the Oil Boom Sustainable? *Europe-Asia Studies* 60 (6): 1051–1072.
——. 2016. The Place of Economics in Russian National Identity Debates: Imperialism, Ethnicity and Authoritarianism 2000–2015. In P. Kolstø, and H. Blakkisrud (eds.), *The New Russian Nationalism*, pp. 336–361. Edinburgh: Edinburgh University Press.
Sakwa, R. 2008. *Russian Politics and Society*. London: Routledge.
——. 2011. Raiding in Russia. *Russian Analytical Digest* 105 (5): 9–13.
Salmenniemi, S. 2012a. 'Post-Soviet Khoziain: Class, Self and Morality in Russian Self-Help Literature'. In S. Salmenniemi (ed.), *Rethinking Class in Russia*, 67–84. Farnham: Ashgate.
—— (ed.). 2012b. *Rethinking Class in Russia*. Farnham: Ashgate.
Sampson, S. 1994. Money Without Culture, Culture Without Money: Eastern Europe's Nouveaux Riches. *Anthropological Journal on European Cultures* 1 (3): 7–30.
Scott, J. C. 1976. *The Moral Economy of the Peasant: Subsistence and Rebellion in Southeast Asia*. New Haven: Yale University Press.
Sennet, R. 1998. *The Corrosion of Character: The Personal Consequences of Work in the New Capitalism*. New York: W. W. Norton.
Shanin, T. 1985. *Russia as a 'Developing Society': Roots of Otherness – Russia's Turn of Century*. London: Macmillan.
Shatz, M. 1980. *Soviet Dissent in Historical Perspective*. New York: Cambridge University Press.
Shevchenko, O. 2002. 'Between the Holes': Emerging Identities and Hybrid Patterns of Consumption in Post-Socialist Russia'. *Europe-Asia Studies* 54 (6): 841–866.
Shlapentokh, V. 2006. Trust in Public Institutions in Russia: The Lowest in the World. *Communist and Post-Communist Studies* 39 (2): 153–174.

Shunin, V. (ed.). 2015. *Smolenskaja oblast' v cifrah 2015. Kratkij statisticheskij sbornik* (Smolensk oblast in numbers, 2015 Statistic Digest). Smolensk: Smolenskstat.

Simonica, A. 2012. *Critical Engagements With and Within Capitalism: Romania's Middle Managers after Socialism*. Unpublished PhD Thesis. Central European University, Budapest.

Smirnov, I. 1968. *Biografija muzhestva: Iz istorii komsomola Smolenshhiny* (The biography of courage: from the history of the Komsomol of the Smolensk region). Moskva: Moskovskyi Rabochyi.

Smolkin, V. 2009. '*Sviato mesto pusto ne byvaet': Ateisticheskoe vospitanie v Sovetskom Soiuze, 1964–1968*'. ('A holy place is never empty': atheistic education in the Soviet Union). *Neprikosnovennyi zapas* (Emergency Reserve) 3 (65): 36–52.

Standing, G. 2011. *The Precariat: The New Dangerous Class*. London: Bloomsbury Academic.

Stark, D. 1996. Recombinant Property in East European Capitalism. *American Journal of Sociology* 101 (4): 993–1027.

Stephenson, S. 2015. *Gangs of Russia: From the Streets to the Corridors of Power*. Ithaca: Cornell University Press.

Stiglitz, J. 2001. Preface. In L. Klein, and M. Pomer (ed.), *The new Russia: Transition Gone Awry*, pp. xvii–xxiii. Stanford: Stanford University Press.

Stites, R. 1991. *Revolutionary Dreams: Utopian Vision and Experimental Life in the Russian Revolution*. New York and Oxford: Oxford University Press.

Szelenyi, I. 1988. *Socialist Entrepreneurs: Embourgeoisement in Rural Hungary*. Cambridge: Polity Press.

———. 2016. Weber's Theory of Domination and Post-Communist Capitalisms. *Theory and Society* 45 (1): 1–24.

Terpe, S. 2016. Max Weber's 'Spheres of Life': A Tool for Microsociological Analysis. *Working Paper* 179. Halle (Saale): Max Planck Institute for Social Anthropology.

Thelen, T. 2005. The Loss of Trust: Changing Social Relations in the Workplace in Eastern Germany. *Working Paper* 78. Halle (Saale): Max Planck Institute for Social Anthropology.

———. 2011. Shortage, Fuzzy Property and Other Dead Ends in the Anthropological Analysis of (Post)socialism. *Critique of Anthropology* 31 (1): 43–61.

Thompson, E. P. 1971. The Moral Economy of the English Crowd in the Eighteenth Century. *Past & Present* 50 (1): 76–136.

——. 1991. *Customs in Common: Studies in Traditional Popular Culture*. London: Penguin Books.

Tlostanova, M. 2015. Can the Post-Soviet Think? On Coloniality of Knowledge, External Imperial and Double Colonial Difference. *Intersections: East European Journal of Society and Politics* 1 (2): 38–58.

Tocheva, D. 2011. Ot vosstanovlenija hrama k sozdaniju obshhiny: samoogranichenie i material'nye trudnosti kak istochniki prihodskoj identichnosti. (From church restoration to community building: self-restraint and material hardship as sources of parish identity). In A. Agadjanian, and K. Russele (eds.), *Prihod i obshhina v sovremennom pravoslavii: kornevaja sistema rossijskoj religioznosti* (The parish and community in modern Orthodoxy: the roots of Russian religiosity), pp. 277–297. Moskva: Ves Mir.

——. 2014. The Economy of the Temples of God in the Turmoil of Changing Russia. *European Journal of Sociology/Archives Européennes de Sociologie* 55 (1): 1–24.

——. 2017. *Intimate Divisions: Street-Level Orthodoxy in Post-Soviet Russia*. Berlin: Lit Verlag.

Todorova, M., and Z. Gille (eds.). 2010. *Post-Communist Nostalgia*. New York: Berghahn Books.

Tolkachev, S., and A. Teplyakov. 2018. Import Substitution in Russia: The Need for a System-Strategic Approach. *Problems of Economic Transition* 60 (7): 545–577.

Tompson, W. 2005. Putin and the 'Oligarchs': A Two-Sided Commitment Problem? In A. Pravda (ed.), *Leading Russia: Putin in Perspective: Essays in Honour of Archie Brown*, pp. 179–203. Oxford: Oxford University Press.

Turbine, V. 2007. *Women's Perceptions of Human Rights and Rightsbased Approaches in Everyday Life: A Case Study from Provincial Russia*. Unpublished PhD Thesis, University of Glasgow.

——. 2012. Women's Use of Legal Advice and Claims in Contemporary Russia: The Impact of Gender and Class. In S. Salmenniemi (ed.), *Rethinking Class in Russia*, pp. 167–184. Farnham: Ashgate.

Ulianova, G. 2015. *Female Entrepreneurs in Nineteenth-Century Russia*. London: Pickering & Chatto.

Unfried, B. 2001. Review: Oleg Kharkhordin, The Collective and the Individual in Russia: A Study of Practices. *Journal of Modern History* 73 (3): 716–719.

Utrata, J. 2008. *Babushki as Surrogate Wives: How Single Mothers and Grandmothers Negotiate the Division of Labor in Russia*. Program in Eurasian and East European Studies, Working Paper Series. Berkley: Institute of Slavic, Eastern European, and Eurasian Studies.

Vanke, A., and E. Polukhina. 2018. Territorial'naja identichnost' v industrial'nyh rajonah: kul'turnye praktiki zavodskih rabochih i dejatelej sovremennogo iskusstva. (Territorial Identity in Industrial Areas: The Cultural Practices of Factory Workers and Contemporary Artists). *Laboratorium: Russian Review of Social Research* 10 (3): 4–34.

Vasileva, A. 2014. Continuity and Change in Russian Capitalism. In U. Becker (ed.), *The BRICs and Emerging Economies in Comparative Perspective: Political Economy, Liberalization and Institutional Change*, pp. 100–122. Abingdon: Routledge.

Verdery, K. 1991. Theorizing Socialism: A Prologue to the 'Transition'. *American Ethnologist* 18 (3): 419–439.

——. 1996. *What Was Socialism, and What Comes Next?* Princeton: Princeton University Press.

——. 2003. *The Vanishing Hectare: Property and Value in Postsocialist Transylvania*. Ithaca: Cornell University Press.

Vihavainen, T., and E. Bogdanova. 2015. *Communism and Consumerism: The Soviet Alternative to the Affluent Society*. Leiden: Brill.

Visser, O., and D. Kalb. 2010. Financialised Capitalism Soviet Style? Varieties of State Capture and Crisis. *European Journal of Sociology/Archives Européennes de Sociologie* 51 (2): 171–194.

Vladimirova, V. 2006. *Just Labor: Labor Ethic in a Post-Soviet Reindeer Herding Community*. Uppsala: Uppsala Universitet.

Volkov, V. 2002. *Violent Entrepreneurs: The Use of Force in the Making of Russian Capitalism*. Ithaca: Cornell University Press.

Voß, G., and H. Pongratz. 2003. From Employee to Entreployee: On the Way to a New Entrepreneurial Labour Power. *Concepts and Transformation* 8 (3): 239–254.

Walker, C. 2012. Re-Inventing Themselves? Gender, Employment and Subjective Well-Being Amongst Young Working Class Russians. In S. Salmenniemi (ed.), *Rethinking Class in Russia*, pp. 221–240. Farnham: Ashgate.

Walkowitz, D. J. 1995. 'Normal Life' in the New Ukraine: The Crisis of Identity Among Donetsk's Miners. In L. Siegelbaum, and D. Walkowitz (eds.), *Workers of the Donbass Speak: Survival and Identity in the New Ukraine, 1989-1992*, pp. 159–184. New York: SUNY Press.

Wanner, C. 2005. Money, Morality and New Forms of Exchange in Postsocialist Ukraine. *Ethnos* 70 (4): 515–537.

Weber, M. 2004. Introduction to the Economic Ethics of the World Religions. In S. Whimster (ed.), *The Essential Weber: A Reader*, pp. 55–80. London: Routledge.
———. 2009. *The Protestant Ethic and the Spirit of Capitalism with Other Writings on the Rise of the West*. New York: Oxford University Press.
Weiss, H. 2011. On Value and Values in a West Bank Settlement. *American Ethnologist* 38 (1): 36–46.
West, J., and J. Petrov (eds.). 2014. *Merchant Moscow: Images of Russia's Vanished Bourgeoisie*. Princeton: Princeton University Press.
White, J. 2000. Kinship, Reciprocity and the World Market. In P. Schweitzer (ed.), *Dividends of Kinship: Meanings and Uses of Social Relatedness*, pp. 125–152. London: Routledge.
Woodruff, D. 1999. *Money Unmade: Barter and the Fate of Russian Capitalism*. Ithaca: Cornell University Press.
Yakovlev, A. 2006. The Evolution of Business-State Interaction in Russia: From State Capture to Business Capture? *Europe-Asia Studies* 58 (7): 1033–1056.
Yanagisako, S. 2002. *Producing Culture and Capital: Family Firms in Italy*. Princeton: Princeton University Press.
———. 2018. Reconfiguring Labour Value and the Capital/Labour Relation in Italian Global Fashion. *Journal of the Royal Anthropological Institute* 24 (S1): 47–60.
Yurchak, A. 2002. Muzhskaja jekonomika: 'Ne do glupostej, kogda kar'eru kuesh'. (Male economy: 'Don't be silly when you're forging a career'). In S. Oushakine (ed.), *O muzhe(N)stvennosti* (About masculinity), pp. 245–267. Moscow: Novoe Literaturnoe Obozrenie.
———. 2006. *Everything Was Forever, Until It Was No More: The Last Soviet Generation.* Princeton: Princeton University Press.
Yusupova, M. 2016. *Shifting Masculine Terrains: Russian Men in Russia and the UK*. Unpublished PhD Thesis, University of Manchester.
Zdravomyslova, E., A. Rotkirkh, and A. Temkina (eds.). 2009. *Novyi byt v sovremennoi Rossii: gendernye issledovaniia povsednevnosti* (New lifestyles in modern Russia: gender studies of everyday life). St Petersburg: European University at St Petersburg Press.
Zigon, J. 2011. Multiple Moralities: Discourses, Practices, and Breakdowns in Post-Soviet Russia. In J. Zigon (ed.), *Multiple Moralities and Religions in Post-Soviet Russia*, pp. 3–15. Oxford: Berghahn Books.

Index

advertising agency 70, 79, 97-8, 100, 105, 169
alienation 159
alternative enforcement 96, 108
authority 29-30, 36, 58, 76, 92, 102, 121, 126, 133, 135, 142, 155, 162; paternalistic 140
autonomy 37, 50-3, 81, 107, 146; at work 135; of workers 96, 142

bandits 66
bankruptcy 32, 98
bargaining power 142, 161
Bases of the Social Concept of the Russian Orthodox Church 46
bazaar economy 120-1, 169
betrayal 49, 99-100, 159-60
blat 30, 100, 114, 156, 164
bookkeeping 90, 97, 101
bribes 72-3; bribe-giving 35
Burawoy, M. 13, 110, 117, 148
business 1-5, 12-5, 17-20, 33-6, 47, 57, 61, 65-7, 69-70, 72-3, 76-7, 79-91, 93-100, 103-8, 111, 114-5, 118, 121-3, 126, 130, 137, 142, 144, 149-51, 153-5, 157, 159-61; ombudsmen 18; partners 86, 88, 98
Business Club 17-8, 85, 88, 105

Caldwell, M. 39, 47
care 8, 26, 66, 78, 89, 90, 92-3, 106-7, 141, 145-6, 149, 151, 160; childcare 79, 89-90, 144-7, 164
civic entitlements 38-9, 141, 143
Clarke, S. 29, 32
class 6-9, 14, 24-7, 37, 40-1, 44, 49-50, 53-4, 56-9, 62, 72, 83, 87, 97, 102, 106, 112, 142, 148, 161, 164-5; new elite 58
collectivism 50, 170

contract 3, 61, 66, 77, 96, 118-9, 140, 153, 159, 163; contractual rights 3, 33, 35; social 27, 51, 106
control 2, 7-8, 23, 29-30, 34-7, 50, 52, 56, 65, 66, 69, 74, 76-7, 89, 92, 94-5, 101-2, 106, 108, 133, 135-7, 149, 154, 157; arbitrary 130; managerial 32, 88, 95-7, 101, 130, 135, 165; paternalistic 141, 156; self control 133
cooperative 31, 68n, 113-5
creative work 109, 123-4, 127, 129-30
culturedness 14, 17, 41, 49, 58, 121, 162

debt; indebtedness 9, 32, 93, 108, 159
dependence 3, 34, 36-7, 71, 97, 110, 119-10, 140-2, 154, 164-5; personal 139, 142, 154, 165
development 7, 12-3, 18, 23, 34, 36, 42, 44-6, 59, 61, 71, 79, 84, 88, 109, 112, 115-7, 122, 136-7; economic 45, 61, 79; institutional 3, 139
discipline 11, 28, 74, 77-8, 108, 133, 136-7, 168-9, 171; self-discipline 9, 86, 133, 142; time 130, 134; work 28, 77-8, 80, 103, 108, 133-5, 160
domestic economy 148

embeddedness 4, 6, 47-8, 73, 82-3, 170
employment; formal 40, 75-6, 78, 140-1, 163; full 26-7, 140; informal 75-7, 140, 153
entrepreneurialism; entrepreneurial worker 133-4; socialist entrepreneurs 12; spirit of 8-9, 41, 105, 107
ethic 77, 82-3, 122

exploitation 9-10, 53, 89, 93, 106, 108, 130, 137, 165; self-exploitation 8-9, 154

family 7, 9, 37-8, 49, 51, 57, 83, 85-8, 90-1, 96-7, 99-103, 105, 107, 116, 143-6, 153-4, 170; budget 126, 148; business 15, 82, 84, 89, 106, 108, 130; family-based enterprise 5, 20, 81-2, 87, 89, 92, 106, 108, 167; flexible family labour 93, 108; mutuality 92; obligations 4, 20, 92-3, 167, *see also* kinship
favours 5, 73, 100-1, 142, 152-3, 156, 163, 170
Filtzer, D. 27
Fitzpatrick, S. 25-6
flexibility; flexible accumulation 2, 14, 21, 111, 169; flexible capitalism 5, 7, 9, 106, 167; flexible labour power 151; flexible labour regime 135; flexible regime of production 169; flexible schedule 131, 150; flexible skill 130; of working arrangements 147, 150
friendship 19, 73, 82, 118, 164

garment manufacturing 14-6, 19, 79, 90, 92, 109, 111, 123, 128
gender; femininity 57, 101, 145, 165; masculinity 57, 102
gift-giving 89, 117, 119
global competition 13, 63, 111, 117, 119-20, 123, 126, 136

hegemony 8-9, 21, 59, 106, 167, 169-70
household; economy 29, 107
Humphrey, C. 26, 28-9, 38, 141

Ikonen, H.-M. 8
import-substitution policy 123
industry 16-7, 24, 26-7, 30, 40, 61, 63, 71, 80, 87, 90, 92, 111-3, 118, 121, 126, 130-1, 136-7
informality 19, 30, 40, 72-3, 75-7, 80, 139, *see also* employment
involution 37, 124

job satisfaction 105, 129, 137
justice 2, 6, 46, 56, 66, 169-70

kinship; fictive kinship 102; morality 2, 14, 20, 83, 85, 93, 100-2, 108; networks 37-8, 91, 96, 107, 148; solidarity 14, 96
Kofti, D. 7
kolkhoz 26, 28-9, 64, 94, 109
Köllner, T. 47
Komsomol 31, 53-4, 105, 112, 115, 125-6
Kormina, J. 53, 55

labour; books 77; collective 38, 104, 157-8, 170; dignity in 165; female 93; flexible 88-9, 93, 135, 151; informality of 40; labour-capital relationships 111; shortages 27-8
Laidlaw, J. 43
Ledeneva, A. 30, 94
leisure 17, 25, 27, 105, 109, 154
limited liability company 68n, 115
loyalty 25, 27, 83, 85, 93, 99-100, 102, 108, 119, 142, 153, 155, 161, 164

market; dissatisfaction with 169; labour 20, 38, 57, 73, 75, 79, 90-2, 108, 131, 140, 143; open-air 65, 74, 97, 109
migrants 73-4, 78

mobility; aspirations for 89, 107, 144-5; upward 89, 107, 144-5, 156, 164-5
modernity; deindustrialized 122-3; Soviet 13, 116, 136
money borrowing 69, 160
morality; capitalist 2-3, 167; kinship 14, 20, 101-2; long-term 56, 100, 108; moral economy 2, 5-7, 14, 44, 48, 167-8; moral framework 20, 67; religious 5, 47-8; Soviet 13, 48-50
Morris, J. 8, 40, 140, 142, 145, 161, 165
Moscow 39, 62, 71, 74-5, 79, 89-91, 104, 109, 111, 114, 118, 121, 126, 128, 144, 155
motherhood; maternal benefits 98, 150; maternal needs 135, 146-7; single mother 98-9, 108, 146, 148, 158, 161, 165

Narotzky, S. 9, 106-7, 170
neoliberalism; neoliberal policies 36, 168; Soviet-style 39
networks; horizontal 142, 146, 148, 164; of survival 164
nomenklatura 12, 25, 32, 112, 115, 169

occupational crime; fiddling 93, 96, 98; misreporting 95-6, 108; theft 51, 77, 93-4, 96, 108
oligarchs 33, 35
Orthodox Church; in Soviet times 45, 59, 62; Orthodox morality 45, 47; other-worldly orientations 45, 47; religious revival 53, 55; religious service 124-5

paperwork 69-70, 72
party-state 27, 112, 115-6
paternalism; paternal care 149

patron; patronage 72-3, 140, 142; patron-client 21, 36, 139-40, 142, 171
pay system; salary advance 162
planned economy 11, 20, 28-31, 36, 41, 113
Polanyi, K. 6, 170
postsocialism 10-2, 21, 30, 36, 41, 43, 57, 83, 108, 121, 142, 167
precarity 7, 10, 40, 93, 105, 109, 140
privatization 15, 32-5, 39-40, 90, 94, 111, 115, 136
production; norms 135-6; regimes 111; rhythms of 130
professionalism 162-3, 165
property; division of property 153, 155; private 3, 36, 94, 108, 115; privatization 115; protection 35; rights 33, 39, 94
Putin, V. 34-6, 39, 66-7, 110, 169

reciprocity 4, 9, 72-3, 82-3, 88-9, 100-1, 103, 106, 108, 149, 167, 170
resistance 4, 7, 13-4, 21, 27, 39, 59, 121-3, 140, 142, 159, 170
retail 16, 51, 71, 80, 101, 119, 157
risk 11, 37, 67, 93-4, 97, 103-4, 121, 147-8, 152, 159-60
rituals 53-4, 79, 102, 104, 124-5; workplace 79
Robbins, J. 43-4
Rogers, D. 40, 121

self-interest 4, 7, 46, 156, 167
service sector 16, 71, 80
shuttlers 64, 80, 120, 144
skill; deskilling 16; flexible 130; social 156-7, 161; unskilled 16, 77
small businesses; license 70, 149; subsidy programme for 70; taxation 19, 33, 35, 68n., 120, 144

Smolensk 15, 17-8, 20, 66, 77-9, 81, 84, 89, 93, 97, 104, 109-11, 114, 120, 125, 128, 130, 144, 167-8; associations of businessmen in 17; economic profile 61, 73-5, 75n; geographical location 61, 71; history 61-2, 64-6, 69-71
social reproduction 5, 7, 82, 108, 116, 154, 164; of capital 167-8
social welfare 39, 140
socialism 10-4, 20-1, 24, 28-31, 37, 39-41, 46, 51-3, 55-6, 59, 83, 94, 105, 126, 139-42, 168-70; late 30, 50-3, 125; nostalgia for 4, 12, 170
spirituality 153
stamp firm 94, 142, 147, 149-51, 154, 157, 159, 161-5
subcontracting 16, 111, 119-20, 123
subjectivity; neoliberal 145; personal transformation 107; self-cultivation 3
subsistence economy 37, 77-8, 124
surveillance 50, 80, 146, 160; horizontal 50
svoi 14n, 100-1, 104, 106, 108, 170

tacit agreement 49, 51, 73, 155
taste 49, 58, 120-1, 129
tax 3, 19, 23, 31-5, 72, 75-6, 97, 120, 153; avoidance 35, 97; evasion 34-5, 96; regulations 34, 97
technical intelligentsia 53, 127
Thelen, T. 3, 11, 30, 38, 83, 105, 139
Thompson, E. P. 6, 167
Tocheva, D. 47
trade 16, 24, 26, 32, 61, 64-5, 68-9, 74, 118, 123, 135, 144-5; petty 12, 20, 37, 64-5, 80, 95, 144, 164
transition 7, 10, 13, 30-1, 34, 36, 50, 55-6, 58-9, 63, 79-80, 82, 105, 110, 115, 120-1, 123, 139, 143, 148, 153, 157, 168
trust 13, 37-8, 72, 83, 93, 95-8, 100, 102, 108, 124, 144, 152

value 5-6, 9-10, 14, 20, 28-9, 31-2, 40-4, 48-9, 52, 81, 83-4, 94, 99-100, 102, 106-8, 117-9, 123-4, 128, 130, 141, 143n, 159, 162, 164-5, 168; conflicting values 4, 9, 44, 167; exchange 4; local dynamics of 168; logic of 8, 143, 162, 165; market 14, 29, 129, 137, 170; regime of 7, 40, 57, 59, 106, 112, 120, 129, 136, 169, 171; spheres 6, 9, 107
Verdery, K. 13, 29, 39, 94

Weber, M. 9, 36, 44-5, 47
woman/women 8, 15, 37-8, 57-8, 78, 84, 90, 92-3, 101, 127, 129; businesswoman 77; female employees 102, 160
workers 3, 7, 17, 21, 24-9, 32, 37, 38, 40, 49, 54, 62, 74-7, 79, 83, 92-7, 100, 102-6, 108, 110-1, 113, 116-7, 119, 122-3, 130-1, 133, 135-6, 140-2, 146-7, 153-4, 156-7, 159-62, 164-5, 169-70; blue-collar 101, 106, 140; family 96; female 38, 77; industrial 7, 26, 40, 130, 142; male 100, 101, 103, 106; privileged 158, 163; Soviet 27, 113, 142; white-collar 25-6, 106

Yurchak, A. 2, 52-3, 125

Halle Studies in the Anthropology of Eurasia

1 Hann, Chris, and the "Property Relations" Group, 2003: *The Postsocialist Agrarian Question. Property Relations and the Rural Condition.*

2 Grandits, Hannes, and Patrick Heady (eds.), 2004: *Distinct Inheritances. Property, Family and Community in a Changing Europe.*

3 Torsello, David, 2004: *Trust, Property and Social Change in a Southern Slovakian Village.*

4 Pine, Frances, Deema Kaneff, and Haldis Haukanes (eds.), 2004: *Memory, Politics and Religion. The Past Meets the Present in Europe.*

5 Habeck, Joachim Otto, 2005: *What it Means to be a Herdsman. The Practice and Image of Reindeer Husbandry among the Komi of Northern Russia.*

6 Stammler, Florian, 2009: *Reindeer Nomads Meet the Market. Culture, Property and Globalisation at the 'End of the Land'* (2 editions).

7 Ventsel, Aimar, 2006: *Reindeer,* Rodina *and Reciprocity. Kinship and Property Relations in a Siberian Village.*

8 Hann, Chris, Mihály Sárkány, and Peter Skalník (eds.), 2005: *Studying Peoples in the People's Democracies. Socialist Era Anthropology in East-Central Europe.*

9 Leutloff-Grandits, Caroline, 2006: *Claiming Ownership in Postwar Croatia. The Dynamics of Property Relations and Ethnic Conflict in the Knin Region.*

10 Hann, Chris, 2006: *"Not the Horse We Wanted!" Postsocialism, Neoliberalism, and Eurasia.*

11 Hann, Chris, and the "Civil Religion" Group, 2006: *The Postsocialist Religious Question. Faith and Power in Central Asia and East-Central Europe.*

12 Heintz, Monica, 2006: *"Be European, Recycle Yourself!" The Changing Work Ethic in Romania.*

HALLE STUDIES IN THE ANTHROPOLOGY OF EURASIA

13 Grant, Bruce, and Lale Yalçın-Heckmann (eds.), 2007: *Caucasus Paradigms. Anthropologies, Histories and the Making of a World Area.*

14 Buzalka, Juraj, 2007: *Nation and Religion. The Politics of Commemoration in South-East Poland.*

15 Naumescu, Vlad, 2007: *Modes of Religiosity in Eastern Christianity. Religious Processes and Social Change in Ukraine.*

16 Mahieu, Stéphanie, and Vlad Naumescu (eds.), 2008: *Churches Inbetween. Greek Catholic Churches in Postsocialist Europe.*

17 Mihăilescu, Vintilă, Ilia Iliev, and Slobodan Naumović (eds.), 2008: *Studying Peoples in the People's Democracies II. Socialist Era Anthropology in South-East Europe.*

18 Kehl-Bodrogi, Krisztina, 2008: *"Religion is not so strong here". Muslim Religious Life in Khorezm after Socialism.*

19 Light, Nathan, 2008: *Intimate Heritage. Creating Uyghur Muqam Song in Xinjiang.*

20 Schröder, Ingo W., and Asta Vonderau (eds.), 2008: *Changing Economies and Changing Identities in Postsocialist Eastern Europe.*

21 Fosztó, László, 2009: *Ritual Revitalisation after Socialism. Community, Personhood, and Conversion among Roma in a Transylvanian Village.*

22 Hilgers, Irene, 2009: *Why Do Uzbeks have to be Muslims? Exploring religiosity in the Ferghana Valley.*

23 Trevisani, Tommaso, 2010: *Land and Power in Khorezm. Farmers, Communities, and the State in Uzbekistan's Decollectivisation.*

24 Yalçın-Heckmann, Lale, 2010: *The Return of Private Property. Rural Life after the Agrarian Reform in the Republic of Azerbaijan.*

25 Mühlfried, Florian, and Sergey Sokolovskiy (eds.), 2011. *Exploring the Edge of Empire. Soviet Era Anthropology in the Caucasus and Central Asia.*

HALLE STUDIES IN THE ANTHROPOLOGY OF EURASIA

26 Cash, Jennifer R., 2011: *Villages on Stage. Folklore and Nationalism in the Republic of Moldova.*

27 Köllner, Tobias, 2012: *Practising Without Belonging? Entrepreneurship, Morality, and Religion in Contemporary Russia.*

28 Bethmann, Carla, 2013: *"Clean, Friendly, Profitable?" Tourism and the Tourism Industry in Varna, Bulgaria.*

29 Bošković, Aleksandar, and Chris Hann (eds.), 2013: *The Anthropological Field on the Margins of Europe, 1945-1991.*

30 Holzlehner, Tobias, 2014: *Shadow Networks. Border Economies, Informal Markets and Organised Crime in the Russian Far East.*

31 Bellér-Hann, Ildikó, 2015: *Negotiating Identities. Work, Religion, Gender, and the Mobilisation of Tradition among the Uyghur in the 1990s.*

32 Oelschlaegel, Anett C., 2016: *Plural World Interpretations. The Case of the South-Siberian Tyvans.*

33 Obendiek, Helena, 2016: *"Changing Fate". Education, Poverty and Family Support in Contemporary Chinese Society.*

34 Sha, Heila, 2017: *Care and Ageing in North-West China.*

35 Tocheva, Detelina, 2017: *Intimate Divisions. Street-Level Orthodoxy in Post-Soviet Russia.*

36 Sárközi, Ildikó Gyöngyvér, 2018: *From the Mists of Martyrdom. Sibe Ancestors and Heroes on the Altar of Chinese Nation Building.*

37 Cheung Ah Li, Leah, 2019: *Where the Past meets the Future. The Politics of Heritage in Xi'an.*

38 Wang, Ruijing, 2019: *Kinship, Cosmology and Support. Toward a Holistic Approach of Childcare in the Akha Community of South-Western China.*

HALLE STUDIES IN THE ANTHROPOLOGY OF EURASIA

39 Coşkun, Mustafa, 2020: *Improvising the Voice of the Ancestors. Heritage and Identity in Central Asia.*

40 Roth, Sascha, 2020: *Politics of Representation: Housing, Family, and State in Baku.*

41 Pranaitytė, Lina, 2020: *The Coffin in the Attic. Gifts, Debts and the Catholic Church in Rural Lithuania.*

42 Bellér-Hann, Ildikó, and Chris Hann, 2020: *The Great Dispossession. Uyghurs between Civilizations.*

43 Hornig, Laura, 2020: *On Money and* Mettā. *Economy and Morality in Urban Buddhist Myanmar.*

44 Berta, Anne-Erita, 2021: *Small is Good. Business and Morality among Danish Shopkeepers.*